Marketing Plans That Work

Marketing Plans That Work

Second Edition

Malcolm H. B. McDonald
Warren J. Keegan

WITHDRAWN

Boston   Oxford   Auckland   Johannesburg   Melbourne   New Delhi

Copyright © 2002 by Butterworth–Heinemann

Ⓡ A member of the Reed Elsevier group

∞ Recognizing the importance of preserving what has been written, Butterworth–Heinemann prints its books on acid-free paper whenever possible.

Library of Congress Cataloging-in-Publication Data
McDonald, Malcolm.
    Marketing plans that work / Malcolm H.B.
McDonald, Warren J. Keegan.—2nd ed.
        p. cm.
    Includes bibliographical references (p.) and index.
    ISBN 0-7506-7307-9 (pbk. : alk. paper)
    1. Marketing—Planning. I. Keegan, Warren J. II. Title.
    HF5415.13 .M3154 2002
    658.8'02—dc21

                                              2001043345

British Library Cataloguing-in-Publication Data
A catalogue record for this book is available from the British Library.

The publisher offers special discounts on bulk orders of this book. For information, please contact:

Manager of Special Sales
Butterworth–Heinemann
225 Wildwood Avenue
Woburn, MA 01801-2041
Tel: 781-904-2500
Fax: 781-904-2620

For information on all Butterworth–Heinemann publications available, contact our World Wide Web home page at: http://www.bh.com

10 9 8 7 6 5 4 3 2 1

Printed in the United States of America

Contents

Preface

The purpose of the second edition of *Marketing Plans That Work* is to explain and demonstrate, in a clear and easy-to-follow format, how to prepare and use a marketing plan. The content of the book is equally relevant for consumer, service, industrial, for-profit, and not-for-profit organizations; and for established and start-up companies. It is applicable to both traditional organizational marketing and societal marketing. The material presented here is based on the authors' research on and experience with marketing planning practices and strategic marketing issues.

Many companies that think they are planning are, in fact, only forecasting and budgeting. Other companies that have been successful in the past have merely been "moving the deck chairs on the Titanic." Instead of looking realistically at their changing competitive and market environment in the present, and incorporating that learning into future efforts, they have been attempting to extend their past success into the future by doing what they have always done. The one certain way to ensure competitive decline is to simply get up in the morning and do what you did yesterday.

Marketing planning is a simple process to outline. Any book will tell you that it consists of the following components: a situation review, key assumptions, objectives, strategies, programs, and measurement and review. What most books do not tell you is that there are a number of contextual issues that have to be considered that make marketing planning a task that baffles practitioners, teachers, and students alike.

Here are the key marketing planning issues:

1. What is strategy and what is marketing strategy?
2. Why is strategy important for successful marketing planning?
3. What are the critical measures and goals of marketing planning?
4. What is the relation between the operational and strategic marketing plan?
5. What is the relation between the marketing and the business plan?
6. When should marketing planning be done, how often, and by whom?
7. How should it be done?

8. Is marketing planning different in a large company versus a small company?
9. Is marketing planning different in a diversified company?
10. Is marketing planning different in a global as opposed to a domestic company?
11. What is the role of the CEO?
12. What is the role of the planning department?
13. Should marketing planning be top down or bottom up?

Because effective marketing planning lies at the heart of a company's revenue and profit-making activities, it is not surprising that there is great demand for a guide that strips away the confusion and mystery surrounding this subject and helps the firm to come to grips with marketing planning in a practical manner.

This book explains what marketing is, how the marketing planning process works, how to conduct a marketing audit, how to set marketing objectives and formulate marketing strategies, how to schedule and cost out what has to be done to achieve the objectives, and how to design and implement a simple marketing planning system.

In covering these areas, it serves three purposes. The first is to ensure that readers fully understand the marketing planning process and pitfalls. The second is to ensure that readers know the appropriate marketing diagnostic tools, structure, and frameworks to use at each stage of the process. And the third and most important is to give managers a practical, step-by-step guide on how to prepare a strategic marketing plan that will give their organizations a sustainable competitive advantage.

In this second edition, we have added a chapter on e-commerce and the Internet, and have updated and revised sections where appropriate, incorporating practical suggestions for readers. Readers who are familiar with both the process and the diagnostic tools of marketing planning may wish to go directly to Chapter 13, which provides a step-by-step system for preparing a marketing plan.

Warren J. Keegan
Rye, New York

Malcolm H. B. McDonald
Bedford, England

May 2001

1 What Is a Marketing Plan?

Before you start Chapter 2, Understanding the Marketing Process, it is helpful to fully understand what a strategic marketing plan is and to complete the following questionnaire, which assesses your organization's current strategic plan.

WHAT A STRATEGIC MARKETING PLAN SHOULD BE

A strategic marketing plan should be a clear and simple summary of key market trends, key target segments, the value required by each segment, and how we intend to create superior value vis-à-vis competitors. It should lay out a clear prioritization of marketing objectives and strategies, together with their financial consequences.

WHAT STRATEGIC PLANS OFTEN ARE

Based on formal critiques of the strategic plans of more than 200 multinational companies, it was found that plans often lack many of the critical components. For example, the reviewed plans were frequently:

- Diffused with confusing compilations of unconnected individual sections
- Laden with substantially more information about market overviews than is necessary, but with no hint of the implications for marketing activity

- Confusing in terms of differentiating marketing objectives from marketing strategies, which should follow logically from the portfolio summary; in addition, the resource implications of effecting the marketing plans are not always clear
- Lacking in terms of identifying key segments ("segments" are often sectors or products, rather than groups of customers with similar needs)
- Poorly analyzed and assumed no activity or reaction by competitors
- Without SWOT analyses to pin down the value that is required by consumer segments, SWOTs are rarely summarized clearly and logically in a portfolio, which provides a categorization of the relative potential of each and the organization's relative strengths in each
- Deficient in terms of isolating and building on the organization's own distinctive competencies

RATING YOUR MARKETING PLAN

Rate each question on a scale of 1 to 10, with 10 being the best. Total your score and compare it to the rankings below.

Market Structure and Segmentation

- Is there an unambiguous definition of the market segments you are interested in serving? Is it clearly described and quantified?
- Is it fully mapped out, showing product/service flows, volumes, your market share, and the critical conclusions for your organization?
- Are the real needs of these segments properly quantified, with the relative importance of these needs clearly identified?

Differentiation

- Is there a clear and quantified analysis of how well your company satisfied these needs compared to its competitors?
- Is this difference valuable to the customer?

Scope

- Are all the market segments classified according to their relative potential for growth in profits over the next three years and according to your company's relative competitive position in each segment?
- Are the objectives consistent with their position in the portfolio (volume, market share, profit)? Are the strategies—including product, price, place, and service—consistent with these objectives?
- Are the key issues requiring action for all departments plainly spelled out as needing to be addressed?

Value Capture

- Do the objectives and strategies add up to the profit goals required by your company?
- Does the budget follow logically from all of the above, or is it merely an add-on component?

The total score of the preceding test will give you an indication of how much work you have to do for strategic planning. If your score is between 80 and 100 points, your company is well on its way to having an effective plan that requires only minor modifications. If the score is between 60 and 80 points, you may want to review the entire planning process and make major modifications. If your company scores below 60 points, carefully read each chapter of this book and be prepared for some significant changes in how your company views its business.

QUESTIONS SUCCESSFUL COMPANIES ASK

1. Do you have a strategic plan?
2. What does this strategic plan consist of?
3. Is this plan effective?

2 Understanding the Marketing Process

In this chapter, we discuss the marketing concept; company capabilities; marketing environment; customer wants; marketing mix; misconceptions about what marketing is; whether industrial, consumer, and service marketing are different; and finally, whether you need a marketing department in your organization. Readers who are already familiar with the role of marketing in organizations may want to go directly to Chapter 3, which introduces the marketing planning process.

THE MARKETING CONCEPT

In 1776, when Adam Smith said that "consumption is the sole end and purpose of production," he was describing what in recent years has become known as the *marketing concept*. The central idea of marketing is to match the capabilities of a company with the needs and wants of its customers to achieve a mutually beneficial relationship.

It is important to understand the difference between the marketing concept and the marketing function, which is concerned with the management of the *marketing mix*. For the sake of simplicity, the marketing mix is often referred to as the four Ps: product, price, promotion, and place. We have added a fifth P, probe, for marketing intelligence (information gathering and research). Management of the marketing mix involves using the various tools and techniques available to managers to implement the marketing concept. However, before any meaningful discussion can take place about how the marketing function should be managed, it is vital to understand the idea of marketing itself (the marketing concept), and it is this issue that we principally address in this chapter.

COMPANY CAPABILITIES

Marketing: the match between organization capabilities and customer needs and wants to achieve mutual objectives

Marketing is a matching process, one that pairs the capabilities of a company and the wants of customers. It is important to understand what we mean by the capabilities of a company. To explain this more fully, imagine that you have been laid off from your company and have decided to set yourself up in your own business. What is the market/customer need that you will satisfy? What is the unique value that you will create? What steps will you need to take to create this unique value? What steps will you need to take to insure that you continue to have a competitive advantage?

THE ROLE OF MARKETING IN BUSINESS

What causes success in the long run—by which we mean a continuous growth in sales, earnings, and the market value of a company's shares—has been shown through research to depend on the following four elements:

1. A core product or service that customers value and the ability to adapt the product or service to changing market needs. Marketing plays a major role in the process that produces products and services that customers value.
2. Excellent, world class, state-of-the-art operations. Marketing should, of course, have an input in defining operational efficiency in customer value terms.
3. A culture that encourages employees to be creative in ways that lead to constantly increasing customer value. Bored and boring employees,

for whom subservience and compliance are the norm, give average performance at best. Only people who are engaged and excited by what they are doing are capable of creating a sustainable competitive advantage.

4. A corporate culture that is not dominated (because of its history) by production, operations, or financial orientation. Evidence shows that marketing makes an essential contribution to the achievement of corporate objectives.

The role of marketing is to ensure (1) that the company focuses on the total environment of business, markets, competition, customers, government, and trends; and (2) that it uses all knowledge and experience to develop a mutually beneficial relationship with its customers.

THE MARKETING ENVIRONMENT

The matching process, referred to earlier, takes place within the *marketing environment* (see Figure 2-1), or the milieu in which a firm is operating. The environment in which a company operates is not completely controllable. It is dynamic and must be constantly monitored. An important constituent of the marketing environment is our competitors, for what they do vitally affects our own behavior as a company. Because the actions of our competitors weigh heavily on our decisions, it is necessary to monitor them on a consistent basis, and to build this process into our company's decision making. In Chapter 13, we show how this can be done.

Other elements of our marketing environment—such as the *political, legal,* and *economic* policies of the governments of the countries where we sell our goods and services—also determine what we can do. *Technology* is constantly changing, and we can no longer assume that our current range of products will continue to be demanded by our customers. For example, the introduction of non-drip paint had a profound effect on what had been a stable market. People discovered that they could use paint without causing a mess, and eventually this product was demanded in new kinds of outlets. One can imagine what happened to paint manufacturers who continued to make only the traditional products and to distribute them solely through traditional outlets. The introduction of a new product would call for a change in pricing, promotion, and distribution policies. Failure to realize this and to act accordingly would most likely result in commercial failure.

Figure 2-1
*Marketing
Environment*

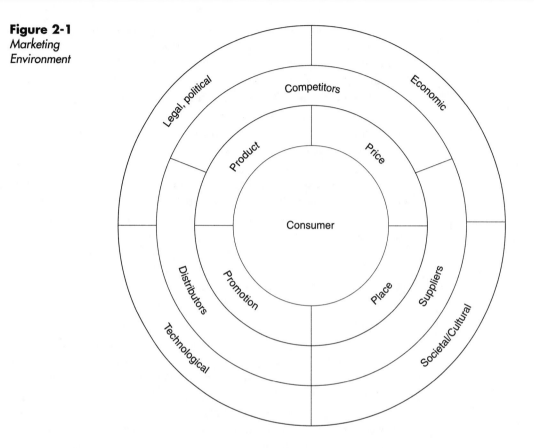

CUSTOMER WANTS

Although we deal with this subject in Chapter 6, let us briefly turn our attention to the subject of customer wants. Perhaps one of the greatest areas of misunderstanding in marketing concerns this question of customer wants. Companies are often accused of manipulating innocent consumers by making them want things they do not really need. If this were so, the new product failure rate would not be as high as it is. The fact is that people have always had needs. What changes over the course of time is the way people satisfy these needs. For example, television is a commercially viable product because people have a need for information and entertainment; television is simply a way of fulfilling that need.

Customer needs have many different ways of being satisfied, and whenever people have *choice*, they select the product that they perceive as offering the greatest benefits to them at whatever price they are prepared to pay for it. What this means, in effect, is that since all companies incur costs in bringing goods or services to market, the ultimate measure of profit, or success, is by customer satisfaction. Low cost, efficiency, quality, or any other measure is not a criterion of effectiveness. There is little point in producing anything efficiently or perfectly if people do not want it. Research has shown that there is a direct link between long-run profitability and the ability of a firm to understand its customers' needs and provide value for them. As further evidence of this, in the not-for-profit sector, customer satisfaction is a proxy for profitability.

Any organization that continues to offer goods or services for which there is a long-term fundamental decline in demand will go out of business, unless it is prepared to adapt to what the market wants. Even less sensible would be for a government, or a parent company, to subsidize such an operation. We know that to go on producing what people do not want is economically wasteful and futile, especially when people can get what they want from other companies, either domestic or foreign. Any company that lags behind its competitors in offering value to its customers will lose its share of the market and eventually go out of business.

Central to the question of customer wants is an understanding of what we mean by a *market*. To start with, customers, not markets, buy products. A market is merely an aggregation of customers who share similar needs and wants. In reality, most markets consist of a number of sub-markets, each of which has different characteristics. For example, the airline market consists of freight and passenger transport. The passenger side can be subdivided further into VFR (visiting friends and relatives), high-rated (business travel), and charter (private or group travel). The failure to understand the needs of these very different customer groups would result in failure to provide the desired services at an acceptable price. In other words, the ability to identify groups of customer wants that can be satisfied in a profitable way is central to marketing management.

THE MARKETING MIX

Managing the marketing mix involves using the tools and techniques of marketing. For the matching process to take place, we need *information*. The external and internal flow of marketing information (marketing research) and database management are discussed in greater detail in Chapter 5.

Having found out what customers want, we must develop products to satisfy those wants. This concept is known as *product management* and is discussed in Chapter 7. We must charge a price for our products, which is discussed in Chapter 11. We must also get our products into customers' hands, giving time and place utility to our product. Distribution and customer service are discussed in Chapter 12.

All that remains now is to tell our customers about our products, for without communications customers will not beat down a path to our door to buy our products and/or services. Here, we must consider all forms of communication, especially advertising, personal selling, and sales promotion. These are discussed in Chapters 9 and 10. Finally, we must consider how to tie it all together in the form of a marketing plan. This is so important that the whole of Chapter 3 is devoted to a discussion of the process of developing a marketing plan.

COMMON MISCONCEPTIONS ABOUT MARKETING

It is a sad reflection on the state of marketing that in spite of more than seventy-five years of marketing education, ignorance still abounds concerning what marketing is. The marketing process and philosophy will never be effective in an organization that historically holds a technical, production, operations, or financial orientation. Such enterprises may have adopted the vocabulary of marketing and applied a veneer of marketing terminology, but they are not customer driven.

A common misconception is to assume that marketing is all about advertising. Advertising is only one aspect of communication within marketing. Unfortunately, many firms waste their advertising expenditure because they have not properly identified their target market. Others spend more on advertising when times are good and less on advertising when times are bad. Cutting the advertising budget is often seen as an easy way to boost profits when a firm is running behind its forecast. This tendency to cut advertising is encouraged by the fact that it can be cut seemingly without any immediate adverse effect on sales.

Unfortunately, this is just another classic misunderstanding about marketing and the role of advertising. A management that cuts the advertising budget in response to poor sales acts as if advertising is caused by sales. It is naive to assume that advertising effectiveness can be measured in terms of sales when it is only a part of the total marketing process.

Consider further these additional areas of confusion about marketing:

1. *Sales.* One chief executive officer aggressively announced to everyone at the beginning of a seminar, "There is no time for marketing in this

company until sales improve!" Confusion between marketing and sales is still one of the biggest barriers to be overcome.

2. *Product Management*. A widely held belief is that all a company has to do to succeed is to produce a good product. Sony's beta videocassette recorders, Apple's Macintosh computers, the Concorde, and the many thousands of brilliant products that have seen their owners or inventors go bankrupt prove the error of this belief.

3. *Advertising*. The annals of business are replete with examples of companies throwing advertising dollars at a problem as a way of tackling deep-rooted marketing problems. For example, prior to hiring professional management, British Airways won awards for brilliant advertising campaigns while failing to deliver the goods.

4. *Customer Service*. The "have a nice day" syndrome, which was popularized by Tom Peters and Robert H. Waterman, Jr., in their book *In Search of Excellence*, is having its heyday in many countries. Many organizations now know, of course, that training everyone to be nice to customers does not help business if the basic offer is fundamentally wrong. For example, in the case of railway companies like Amtrak, although customers like to be treated nicely, they find it more important to get where they are going on time.

5. *Selling*. Selling is only one aspect of communication with customers. To say that it is the only thing that matters is to ignore the importance of the product, pricing, distribution, and other forms of communication in achieving profitable sales. Selling may be the part of the process in which the transaction is actually clinched. It can be successful only if all the other elements of the marketing mix have been properly managed. Imagine having a horse that did not have four legs; it wouldn't go far. The more attention paid to finding out what customers want, to developing products to satisfy these wants, to pricing at a level consistent with the benefits offered, to gaining distribution, and to communicating effectively with the target market, the more likely we are to be able to establish an on-going customer relationship.

WHAT DOES THE CUSTOMER WANT?

We need to be aware of the true meaning of those often-used words "finding out what the customer wants," which appear in most definitions of marketing. Customers do not really know what they want. See "Beyond Traditional Market Research" on the next page. All they really want are better ways of solving their problems. Therefore, one of the main tasks of marketing is to have an in-depth understanding of customers and their problems so that we can continuously work on ways of making life easier for them.

ARE INDUSTRIAL, CONSUMER, AND SERVICE MARKETING DIFFERENT?

The central ideas behind marketing are universal. It makes no difference whether we are marketing furnaces, insurance policies, or soft drinks.

Problems sometimes arise, however, when we try to implement marketing ideas in service companies and industrial goods companies. A service does not lend itself to being specified in the same way as a product because it does not have reproducible physical dimensions that can be measured. With the purchase of any service, there is a large element of trust on the part of the buyer, who can only be sure of the quality and performance of the service after it has been completed. The salesperson selling the service becomes part of the service, since the sales encounter is one of the principal ways in which the potential efficacy of the service can be assessed. A service cannot be made in advance and stored for selling "off the shelf" at a later date. Nonetheless, apart from differences in what elements to emphasize, the principles of marketing apply to services in essentially the same way they apply to physical products.

Industrial goods are goods sold to industrial businesses or institutional or government buyers for incorporation into their own products, to be resold or to be used by them within their own businesses. Principal types of industrial goods are raw materials, components, capital goods, and maintenance and repair equipment.

Information about industrial markets is not as readily available as information about consumer goods markets, which makes it more difficult

---

Beyond Traditional Market Research

In ten years of developing the minivan, we never once got a letter from a housewife asking us to invent one. To the skeptics, that proved there was not a market out there.

—Hal Sperlich "Father of the Chrysler Minivan"
(From Gary Hamel and C. K. Prahalad [1994], *Competing for the Future*. Boston: Harvard Business School Press, p. 101.)

to measure changes in market share. There are other difficulties aside from these that make marketing in the industrial area difficult.

All too often, many companies recruit a "marketing person" to solve the problem, and leave that person to get on with the job of marketing. Such a "solution" can never work, because for the marketing concept to work it has to be understood and practiced by all executives in a firm, not the marketing manager alone. Otherwise, all departments continue to behave as they did before, and the marketing person quickly becomes ineffective.

EVOLUTION OF THE MARKETING PHILOSOPHY

The consumer-oriented philosophy of business that emphasizes meeting consumer wants and needs is called the *marketing concept*. A good illustration of how this approach to marketing works is Honda's rise to prominence in the U.S. automobile market. Honda started in 1973 by satisfying U.S. drivers' desire for fuel-efficient cars with the economical Civic. When consumers' preferences changed to roominess, comfort, and performance, Honda brought out the Accord, which became the best-selling car in the United States in the early 1990s. When consumers began to look for luxury in their cars, Honda introduced the Acura. Every change in Honda's product line was prompted by a changing consumer need. Every success came from offering value to customers.

Marketing philosophy has changed over the years. Figure 2-2 compares the old telling-and-selling approach with the new idea (1960) of focusing on the customer and with the contemporary philosophy of marketing as a way of doing business and relationship marketing. In the early days of marketing, marketers focused exclusively on selling. That approach was succeeded by the idea of managing the marketing mix—the four Ps presented at the beginning of the chapter. With the current concept of marketing, the marketing-mix approach has expanded to include all knowledge and experience. The aim of marketing is to create a mutually beneficial relationship between companies and customers. The end result of marketing is a relationship that means long-term growth and profitability for the company and maximum satisfaction for the customer. This now or future concept of marketing is also referred to as *relationship marketing*.

Satisfying customers necessitates staying in touch with people's changing needs and ensuring the company's ability to fulfill those needs with new product lines and marketing strategies.

In cutting-edge marketing, the marketing concept has been extended to integrate concern for customer satisfaction into every corporate function.

Figure 2-2
Marketing Is Everything
Source: © Warren Keegan Associates, Inc. Reprinted by permission.

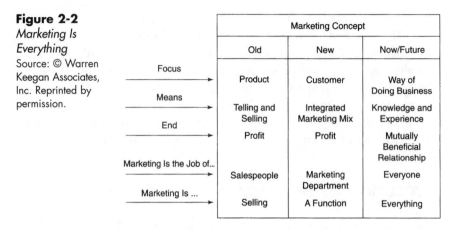

	Marketing Concept		
	Old	New	Now/Future
Focus	Product	Customer	Way of Doing Business
Means	Telling and Selling	Integrated Marketing Mix	Knowledge and Experience
End	Profit	Profit	Mutually Beneficial Relationship
Marketing Is the Job of...	Salespeople	Marketing Department	Everyone
Marketing Is ...	Selling	A Function	Everything

That is why you find discussions of relationship building in many chapters of this book. In Chapter 7, for example, we explore how the concepts of quality (excellence in products and the ways in which they are produced) and relationship building are interrelated.

QUESTIONS SUCCESSFUL COMPANIES ASK

1. What is the *deep need* that we satisfy for our customers?
2. What do our customers really want?
3. How can we implement the now concept of marketing?
4. What should be the role of our marketing department?
5. Should we set marketing objectives based on last year's performance or on an assessment of the market and competition and our value proposition?

3 The Marketing Planning Process

In Chapter 3, we discuss marketing planning, why it is essential, the difference between tactical and strategic marketing plans, the marketing planning process, marketing audits, why audits are necessary, the form of the audit, the place of a marketing audit in a management audit, when an audit is performed and who performs it, the results of audits, the relation between marketing planning and corporate planning, assumptions, marketing objectives, marketing strategies and programs, use of marketing plans, budgets, the contents of a strategic plan, and mission statements.

The purpose of this chapter is to explain as simply as possible what marketing planning is and how the process works before the more important components of marketing planning are explained in later chapters.

WHAT IS MARKETING PLANNING?

The marketing plan is an outline of a design to accomplish a specific objective: to create value for customers at a profit, or in the now concept of marketing, to create a mutually beneficial relationship. The marketing plan ties together your assessment of market needs and wants, the strengths and weaknesses of your organization and those of your existing and expected competitors, and your design for creating value to satisfy the needs or wants of targeted customers at a profit. The marketing plan includes action plans (what is to be done and when) as well as a vision, strategic intent, goals, and objectives.

This process of *marketing planning* can be defined as the application of marketing resources to achieve marketing objectives. Marketing planning, then, is simply a logical sequence of activities leading to the setting of marketing objectives and the formulation of plans for achieving them. Companies generally go through a management process in developing marketing plans. In small, undiversified companies this process is usually informal. In large, diversified organizations the process is normally systematized. Marketing planning is very simple in concept and involves the following:

- Performing a situation analysis
- Formulating basic assumptions
- Setting objectives for what is being sold and to whom
- Deciding how the objectives are to be achieved
- Scheduling and costing out the actions necessary for implementation

Each plan is unique, but in almost all cases, a plan includes detailed financial forecasts and budgets for the first year and an outline summary of these components for subsequent years. The first part of a marketing plan is the *situation analysis*. This section includes but is not limited to a strengths, weaknesses, opportunities, and threats (SWOT) analysis. The situation analysis is followed by the construction of the plan itself. Although the process of constructing a plan is simple to understand, it is the most difficult of all marketing tasks. The reason is that it involves bringing together into one coherent plan all the elements of marketing. For this to happen, at least some institutionalized practice is necessary, for example, a regular audit of customer satisfaction with company products and services. It is this institutionalization, or lack thereof, that seems to cause a great deal of difficulty for companies.

One reason companies have difficulty developing marketing plans is that management provides little guidance as to how the process should be managed: proceeding from reviews to objectives, strategies, programs, budgets, and back again until a compromise is reached between what is desirable and what is practicable, given the constraints that every company has.

Another reason companies find it difficult to develop a marketing plan is that they must be customized to your particular organization. Because of the varying size, complexity, character, and diversity of company operations, there can be no such thing as an "off the rack" system that can be implemented without fundamental adjustments to suit the situation-specific requirements of each company. The degree to which any company can develop an integrated, coordinated, and consistent plan depends on an understanding of the marketing planning process itself as a means of sharpening the focus on all levels of management within an organization.

WHY IS MARKETING PLANNING ESSENTIAL?

There can be little doubt that marketing planning is essential when we consider the increasingly hostile and complex environment in which companies operate. Hundreds of external and internal factors interact in a bafflingly complex way to affect our ability to serve customers at a profit. Consider for a moment the four typical objectives that companies set: maximizing revenue, maximizing profits, maximizing return on investment, and minimizing costs. Each one of these has its own special appeal to different managers within the company, depending on the nature of their function. In reality, the best that can ever be achieved is a kind of "optimum compromise."

Apart from the need to cope with increasing turbulence, environmental complexity, intense competitive pressures, and the sheer speed of technological change, a marketing plan is useful for the following purposes:

- To help identify sources of competitive advantage
- To force an organized approach
- To develop specificity
- To ensure consistent relationships

- To inform everyone in the organization about priorities
- To obtain resources needed to implement plans
- To engage organizational support at all levels, from the bottom to the top of the organization
- To set objectives and strategies
- To gain commitment toward goals

TACTICAL OR STRATEGIC MARKETING PLAN?

Our research has shown that in the murky depths of organizational behavior, when it comes to marketing planning, confusion reigns supreme—and, nowhere more so than over the terminology of marketing. Few practicing marketers understand the importance of a *strategic* marketing plan as opposed to a *tactical* or operational marketing plan.

The elements of strategy are:

- Stepping back from the day to day
- Ideas and thought
- Activity/Action
- Setting objectives and goals
- Important decisions and choices
- Significant commitment of resources
- Not easily reversible
- Involves choice/tradeoffs
- Differentiation
- Insight
- Vision
- Defines the business we are in and the business we are becoming
- Value
- Tradeoffs

A strategic plan is a clear and simple summary of key market trends, key target segments, the value required by each segment, how the company intends to create value vis-à-vis competitors, with a clear prioritization of marketing objectives and strategies, together with financial consequences.

- Objectives and goals
- Strategy vs. Tactics

The problem is simple. Most managers prefer to sell the products they find easiest to sell to customers who offer the least line of resistance. By developing short-term, tactical marketing plans first, and extrapolating from them, managers succeed only in extrapolating their own shortcomings.

It is a bit like steering from the wake—it's all right in calm, clear waters, but not so sensible in busy and choppy waters. Preoccupation with preparing a detailed one-year plan is typical of many companies that confuse sales forecasting and budgeting with strategic marketing planning, which we have found to be the most common mistake of all. This brings us to the starting point in marketing planning: an understanding of the difference between *strategy* and *tactics*.

Strategy describes the direction a business will pursue and guides the allocation of resources and effort. Put another way, *strategy* describes the business we are in and the business we are becoming. It also provides the logic that integrates the perspectives of functional departments and operating units, and points them all in the same direction. The strategy statement for a business unit is composed of the following three elements:

1. A business definition that specifies the area in which the business will compete.
2. A strategic thrust that describes where competitive advantage is to be gained.
3. Supportive functional strategies.

Tactics are short-term actions taken to achieve the implementation of a broader strategy. *Marketing strategy* is a statement of how a brand or product line will achieve its objectives. The strategy provides decisions and direction regarding variables such as segmentation of the market, identification of the target market, positioning, marketing mix elements, and expenditures.

Figure 3-1 shows the old style of company in which little attention is paid to strategy by any level of management. In this company, lower levels of management are not involved at all, whereas senior management and the board of directors spend most of their time on operational and tactical issues.

Conversely, Figure 3-2 is a representation of companies that recognize the importance of strategy and manage to involve all levels of management in strategy formulation.

Figure 3-1
*Tactically
Oriented
Company*

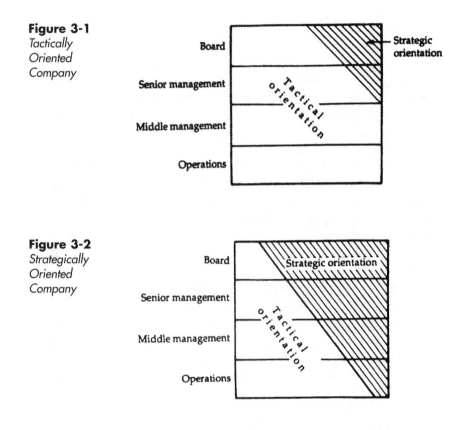

The rules for marketing planning are as follows:

- Develop the *strategic* marketing plan first. This involves placing emphasis on scanning the external environment (e.g., technological or economic trends) and identifying early on the effect this may have on the company. It also calls for development of appropriate strategic responses, involving all levels of management in the process.
- A strategic plan should cover a three-year period. Only when the plan has been developed and agreed upon should the one-year operational marketing plan be created. Never write the one-year plan first and extrapolate from it.

The emphasis throughout this book is on preparing a strategic marketing plan. The format for an operational or tactical plan is exactly the same, except for the amount of detail, which is much greater.

THE MARKETING PLANNING PROCESS

A strategic marketing plan should contain the following components:

- Executive summary
- Mission statement
- Financial summary of revenue, expenses, and earnings
- Marketing audit
- SWOT (Strengths, Weaknesses, Opportunities, and Threats) analysis
- Assumption of key determinants
- Overall marketing objectives and strategies
- Expected results
- Alternatives (contingency plan)
- Budget

Each of these components is discussed in detail later in this chapter.

Figure 3-3 illustrates the stages in the development of a marketing plan. The dotted lines in Figure 3-3 indicate the reality of the planning process, in that it is likely that each step will need to be done more than once before final programs can be written.

Although research has shown these marketing planning steps to be universally applicable, the degree to which each of the separate steps in the diagram has to be formalized depends to a large extent on the size and nature of the company. For example, an *undiversified* company generally uses less formalized procedures, because top management tends to have greater functional knowledge and expertise than subordinates and because the lack of diversity of operations enables direct control to be exercised over most of the key determinants of success. Situation reviews, setting of marketing objectives, and other tasks are not always made explicit in writing, although these steps still have to be taken.

In contrast, in a *diversified* company, it is usually not possible for top management to have greater functional knowledge and expertise than subordinate management. The whole planning process tends to be formalized to provide consistent discipline for those who have to make the decisions throughout the organization. Either way, a substantial body of evidence shows that formalized marketing planning procedures generally result in greater profitability and stability in the long term and help to reduce friction and operational difficulties within organizations.

When marketing planning has failed, it has generally been because companies have placed too much emphasis on the procedures themselves and the resulting paperwork, rather than on generating information useful

Figure 3-3
*Stages to Arrive
at a Marketing
Plan*

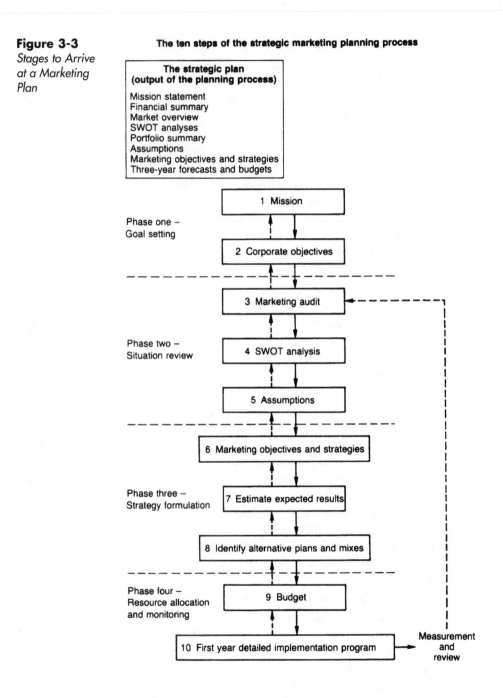

The ten steps of the strategic marketing planning process

```
┌─────────────────────────────────────┐
│     The strategic plan               │
│  (output of the planning process)    │
│                                      │
│  Mission statement                   │
│  Financial summary                   │
│  Market overview                     │
│  SWOT analyses                       │
│  Portfolio summary                   │
│  Assumptions                         │
│  Marketing objectives and strategies │
│  Three-year forecasts and budgets    │
└─────────────────────────────────────┘
```

1 Mission

Phase one –
Goal setting

2 Corporate objectives

3 Marketing audit

Phase two –
Situation review

4 SWOT analysis

5 Assumptions

6 Marketing objectives and strategies

Phase three –
Strategy formulation

7 Estimate expected results

8 Identify alternative plans and mixes

Phase four –
Resource allocation
and monitoring

9 Budget

10 First year detailed implementation program

Measurement
and
review

to and consumable by management. When companies delegate marketing planning to someone called a "planner," the plan invariably fails, because planning for line management cannot be delegated to a third party. The real role of the planner should be to help those responsible for implementation to formulate a plan. Failure to recognize this simple fact can be disastrous.

Another critical factor for success is commitment from the top. A Swedish company selling batteries internationally tried unsuccessfully three times to introduce a marketing planning system. Each effort failed because of a lack of commitment by top management to the planning process. Without the commitment of top management, those charged with introducing the planning found that there was great resistance to planning on the part of local managers. These planning efforts failed. The director of planning was replaced three times in this company. A commitment to planning by top management, training of managers, and careful thought about resource requirements would have largely overcome this company's planning problems.

THE MARKETING AUDIT

A *marketing audit* is a formal, systematic review of the executed marketing strategy and plan. It may take the form of an external audit by independent experts or an internal audit by members of the marketing organization. An audit examines external and internal information and procedures and identifies problems in the environment, within the organization, and between the organization and its suppliers. The goal is to see how well the firm is applying the marketing concepts, and in turn creating value for its customers at a profit. The marketing audit enables management to look beyond routine sales reports and market share estimates. Managers can use an audit to question the productivity of the marketing dollars.

Why Is an Audit Needed?

Often the need for an audit does not manifest itself until things start to go wrong for a company, in the form of declining sales, falling margins, lost market share, or underutilized production capacity. At times like these, management often attempts to treat the wrong symptoms. Introducing new products or dropping products, reorganizing the sales force, reducing prices, and cutting costs are just some of the actions that are taken. Such measures, however, are unlikely to be effective if more fundamental problems are not identified. Of course, if the company can survive long enough, it might eventually solve its problems through a process of elimination. Problems have to be properly defined, and the audit is a means of helping to define them.

To summarize, the audit is a structured approach to the collection and analysis of information and data in the complex business environment and an essential prerequisite to problem solving for any company.

The Form of the Audit

Any company performing an audit is faced with two kinds of variables. First are variables over which the company has no direct control. These usually take the form of what can be described as *environmental*, *market*, and *competitive variables*. Second are variables over which the company has complete control. These we can call *operational variables*. This gives us a clue as to how we can structure an audit; that is, in two parts—an external audit and an internal audit.

The *external audit* is concerned with the uncontrollable variables, and the *internal audit* is concerned with the controllable variables. The external audit starts with an examination of information on the general economy and then moves on to the outlook for the health and growth of the markets served by the company. The purpose of the internal audit is to assess the resources of the organization as they relate to the environment and the resources of competitors.

The Place of the Marketing Audit in the Management Audit

The term *management audit* merely means a company-wide audit that includes an assessment of all internal resources against the external environment. In practice, the best way to perform a management audit is to conduct a separate audit of each major management function. Thus, the marketing audit is merely part of the larger management audit in the same way that the production audit is.

Table 3-1 is a checklist of areas to be investigated as part of the marketing audit.

Each of these headings should be examined with a view toward isolating factors considered critical to the company's performance. The auditor's first task is to screen an enormous amount of information and data for validity and relevance. Some data and information will have to be reorganized into a more easily usable form. Judgment is needed to decide

TABLE 3-1 Marketing Audit Checklist

External audit	Internal audit
Business and economic environment	*Marketing operational variables*
Economic	Own company
Political/fiscal/legal	Sales (total, by geographical location, by
Social/cultural	industrial type, by customer, by product)
Technological	Market shares
	Profit margins/costs
The market	Marketing procedures
Total market, size, growth, and trends	Marketing organization
(value/volume)	Marketing information/research
Market characteristics, developments, and	Customers/consumers
trends	Marketing mix variables as follows:
Industry practices	Products
Customers/consumers	Price
Products	Distribution
Prices	Promotion
Physical distribution	
Channels	
Promotion	
Competition	
Major competitors	
Value/volume	
Market shares/coverage	
Market standing/reputation	
Marketing procedures	
Production capabilities	
Distribution policies	
Marketing mix variables	
Key strengths and weaknesses	

what additional data and information are necessary for definition of the problem.

The auditing process has the following two basic phases:

1. Identification, measurement, collection, and analysis of all facts and opinions that affect a company's problems
2. The application of judgment to uncertain areas that remain after the initial analysis

When Should a Marketing Audit Be Conducted?

A mistaken belief held by many people is that the marketing audit is a last-ditch, end-of-the-road attempt to define a company's marketing problem, or at best something done by an independent body from time to time to ensure that a company is on the right track. Because the marketing environment is constantly changing, and because marketing is such a complex function, we believe it is essential to perform a thorough situation analysis at least once a year at the beginning of the planning cycle.

Successful companies, besides using normal information and control procedures and marketing research throughout the year, start their planning cycle each year with a formal review, through an audit-type process, of all factors that have had an important influence on marketing activities.

Who Should Conduct the Marketing Audit?

A critical issue in conducting a marketing audit is who should do it. Should the audit be conducted by a company's own executives and managers or by outside consultants? We believe that periodically it is wise to engage outside consultants to perform a marketing audit. Every company is at risk of becoming blinded to reality by the influence of company culture. This is especially true for companies who have great products, or even worse, insanely great products. No amount of internal auditing will break through a company or organizational "superiority complex," which may be causing the company to miss the mark in terms of understanding what customers want and need.

Few if any outside consultants, however, have the in-depth knowledge of markets, customers, company culture, and the industry that company line managers have. This is an argument for having an audit conducted by the company's line managers in their areas of responsibility. Objections to this type of audit center around problems with lack of time and lack of objectivity.

In practice, the problems are overcome by institutionalization of procedures in as much detail as possible so that all managers have to conform to a disciplined approach and by thorough training in the use of the procedures. Rigorous discipline must be applied from the highest down to the lowest levels of management involved in the audit. Such discipline is usually successful in helping managers avoid the sort of tunnel vision that often results from lack of critical appraisal.

What Happens to the Results of the Audit?

The only remaining question is what happens to the results of the audit? Some companies consume valuable resources conducting audits that bring little by way of actionable results. Indeed, there is always the danger that at the audit stage, insufficient attention is paid to concentrating on the analysis that determines which trends and developments will actually affect the company. A checklist ensures the completeness of logic and analysis, but the people conducting the audit must discipline themselves to omit from their audits all information not central to the company's marketing problems and opportunities.

It is essential to concentrate on analysis that determines which trends and developments will actually affect the company. Because the objective of the audit is to determine the marketing objectives and strategies of a company, it follows that it would be helpful if a format could be found for organizing the findings.

One useful way of organizing findings is in the form of a SWOT analysis. This is a summary of the audit under the headings internal strengths and weaknesses as they relate to external opportunities and threats. Detailed guidance on how to complete a SWOT analysis is contained in Chapter 14.

A SWOT analysis should contain no more than four or five pages of commentary that focuses on *key factors* only. Under no circumstances should a SWOT analysis ever become a "laundry list" of all factors. The most common error in SWOT analysis is listing all factors. When this is done, the SWOT analysis is not an analysis; it is merely a useless list. It should highlight internal *differential* strengths and weaknesses in relation to competitors' *key* external opportunities and threats. A summary of reasons for good or bad performance is included. The analysis should be interesting to read, contain concise statements, include only relevant and important data, and emphasize creative analysis.

To summarize, conducting a regular and thorough marketing audit in a structured manner goes a long way toward giving a company a knowledge of the business, trends in the market, and where value is added by competitors; the audit is the basis for setting objectives and strategies.

MARKETING PLANNING AND CORPORATE PLANNING

There are five steps in corporate planning. As can be seen from Table 3-2, the starting point is usually a statement of corporate financial objectives for long-range planning, which are often expressed in terms of sales, profit before tax, and return on investment.

TABLE 3-2 Marketing Planning and Its Place in the Corporate Cycle

Step 1: Corporate Financial Objectives	Step 2: Management Audit	Step 3: Objective and Strategy Setting	Step 4: Plans	Step 5: Corporate Plans
Targeted growth in sales and earnings	Marketing audit	Marketing objectives, strategies	Marketing plan	
	Distribution audit	Distribution objectives, strategies	Distribution plan	
	Manufacturing audit	Manufacturing objectives, strategies	Manufacturing plan	Issue of corporate plan, to include corporate objectives and strategies, marketing objectives and strategies, etc.
	Financial audit	Financial objectives, strategies	Financial plan	
	Personnel audit	Personnel objectives, strategies	Human resource plan	

More often than not, this long-range planning horizon is three years away. The precise period is determined by the nature of the markets in which the company operates. For example, even five years is not long enough for a glass manufacturer, because it takes that long to commission a new furnace for production, whereas in the fashion industry where styles change with each season, the recommended three years is too long.

In order to allow for sufficient detail so that a strategic plan can be of practical use, it is advisable to keep the period down to three years if possible. Beyond this period, detail of any kind is likely to become pointless. There can certainly be scenarios of five to ten years and longer, but not a plan in the sense intended herein.

The next step (see Table 3-2) is the *management audit*, which we have already discussed. A thorough situation review, particularly in the area of marketing, enables the company to determine whether it can reach long-range financial targets with its current range of products in its current markets. Any projected gap must be filled by product development or market extension.

Undoubtedly the most important and difficult of all stages in corporate planning is the third step, *objective and strategy setting*. If this is not done properly, everything that follows is of little value.

Later, we discuss marketing objectives and strategies in detail. For now, the important point is that this is the time in the planning cycle when a compromise has to be reached between what is wanted by the several functional departments and what is practicable, given all the constraints in any company. For example, it is not good to set a marketing objective of penetrating a new market if the company does not have the production capacity to cope with the new business and if capital is not available for the investment necessary. At this stage, objectives and strategies are set for three years or for whatever the planning horizon is.

The fourth step involves producing detailed *plans* for one year that contain the responsibilities, timing and costs of achieving the first year's objectives, and broad plans for the following years. These plans can then be incorporated into the *corporate plan*, the fifth step, which contains long-range corporate objectives, strategies, plans, profit and loss accounts, and balance sheets.

One of the main purposes of a corporate plan is to provide a long-term vision of what the company is or is striving to become, taking into account shareholder expectations, environmental trends, resource market trends, consumption market trends, and the distinctive competence of the company as revealed by the management audit. What this means, in practice, is that the corporate plan usually contains at least the following three elements:

1. The desired level of profitability
2. Business boundaries
   - What kinds of products will be sold to what kinds of markets (marketing)
   - What kinds of facilities will be developed (production and distribution)
   - The size and character of the labor force (personnel)
   - Funding (finance)
   - Technologies to be developed (research and development)
3. Other corporate objectives, such as social responsibility and corporate, stock market, and employer image

Such a corporate plan, which contains projected profit and loss statements and balance sheets, is more likely to provide long-term stability for a company than plans based on an intuitive process that contain forecasts that tend to be little more than extrapolations of previous trends.

The headquarters of one major multinational company with a sophisticated budgeting system used to receive "plans" from all over the world and coordinate them in quantitative and cross-functional terms—such as number of employees, unit sales, and square feet of production area—together with the associated financial implications. The trouble was that the entire complicated edifice was built on the initial sales forecasts, which were speculative and political rather than realistic and fact based. The key strategic issues relating to products and markets were lost in all the financial activity, which eventually resulted in serious operational and profitability problems.

ASSUMPTIONS

Let us now return to the preparation of the marketing plan. All companies have key determinants of success about which assumptions have to be made before the planning process can proceed. It is a question of standardizing the planning environment. For example, it would not be helpful to receive plans from two product managers, one of whom believed the market was going to increase by 10 percent while the other believed the market was going to decline by 10 percent. Assumptions should be key, critical assumptions, and that means they are few in number. They should be consistent with relevant known facts and with defensible assumptions. This is one of the most critical steps in the preparation of a marketing plan because it is the easiest step to do carelessly. The so-called telecomm mess in 2001 was fueled by optimistic and unrealistic sales forecasts, which were based on inadequate data from buyers. This resulted in massive over capacity on the part of equipment suppliers.

The following are examples of corporate assumptions, with respect to the industrial climate of the company:

- Industrial overcapacity will increase from 105 percent to 115 percent as new plants come into operation.
- Price competition will force price levels down by 10 percent across the board.
- A new product that competes with our product x will be introduced by our major competitor before the end of the second quarter.

MARKETING OBJECTIVES AND STRATEGIES

The next step in marketing planning is the writing of marketing objectives and strategies, the key step in the entire process. An *objective* is what you want to achieve. A *strategy* is how you plan to achieve your objectives. There can be objectives and strategies at all levels in marketing. For example, there can be advertising objectives and strategies as well as pricing

TABLE 3-3 The Marketing Mix

Product	The general policies for product deletions, modifications, additions, design, packaging, etc.
Price	The general pricing policies to be followed for product groups in market segments.
Place	The general policies for channels and customer service levels.
Promotion	The general policies for communicating with customers via advertising, personal selling, sales promotion, public relations, marketing public relations, direct marketing via mail, telephone, the Internet, and exhibitions.

objectives and strategies. The important point about marketing objectives is that they are about *products* and *markets* only. Marketing objectives are about one or more of the following:

- Existing products in existing markets
- New products for existing markets
- Existing products for new markets
- New products for new markets

Marketing objectives can be measured. Directional terms such as "maximize," "minimize," "penetrate," and "increase," are acceptable only if quantitative measurement can be attached to them. Measurement is expressed in terms of some, or all, of the following: sales volume, sales value, market share, profit, percentage of penetration of outlets, awareness, and esteem.

Marketing strategies are the means by which marketing objectives are achieved and expressed in the *marketing mix* as outlined in Table 3-3.

THE MARKETING MIX

The heart of the marketing plan is expressed in the marketing mix. The mix is the set of controllable variables in the marketing plan that are usually expressed as the four Ps—product, price, place, and promotion. The challenge in marketing planning is to optimize the mix by adjusting each variable, and the budget for each variable, to maximize the value for customers and the contribution to the firm as measured in sales and profits (or other organizational goal).

For example, raising a price increases revenue per unit and either depresses or increases total revenue, depending on demand elasticity for the product. Demand elasticity depends on the quantity and quality of advertising and on other forms of communication and the features and benefits of the product itself. In 1996, Ford Motor Company appeared to have overestimated the price elasticity of demand for its cars when it added features and engineering refinements that raised Ford's prices above those of its direct competitors, who offered less engineering refinement, fewer features, and a lower price. Chevrolet engaged in direct-comparison advertising that focused on basic features and the Chevrolet price advantage, and succeeded in taking market share from Ford.

Each strategy must be costed out to determine practicability. In this exercise, assumptions concerning market response must be combined with estimates of required expenditure to arrive at feasible alternatives.

USE OF MARKETING PLANS

The marketing plan normally includes an advertising plan, a sales promotion plan, a pricing plan, a distribution plan, a product plan, and a target market plan that addresses objectives and targets by market segment. A written strategic marketing plan is the reference against which operational decisions are made on an ongoing basis. Detail is not the goal. The main function of the marketing plan is to determine where the company is now, where it wants to go, and how to get there. The marketing plan lies at the heart of a company's revenue-generating activities. From the plan flow all other corporate activities, such as timing of cash flow and size and character of the labor force. What should actually appear in a written strategic marketing plan is shown in Figure 3-3. Details and explanations of each of the components are provided later.

THE MARKETING BUDGET

The best budgeting technique is to justify all marketing expenditures from a zero base each year against the tasks that you wish to accomplish. If these procedures are followed, every item of budgeted expenditure can be related directly back to the corporate objectives. For example, if sales promotion is an important means of achieving an objective in a particular market, when sales promotional items appear in the program, each one has a specific purpose that can be related to a main objective. This method ensures that every item of expenditure is fully accounted for as part of a rational, objective, and task approach. It also ensures that when changes have to be made, they can be made in such a way that the least damage is caused to the company's long-term objectives.

WHAT IS A MISSION OR PURPOSE STATEMENT?

A mission statement is one of the most difficult aspects of marketing planning to master, largely because it is philosophical and qualitative in nature. Many organizations find different departments, and sometimes even different groups in the same department, pulling in different directions, often with disastrous results, simply because the organization has not defined the boundaries of the business and the way it wishes to do business.

The following five key points should appear in a mission or purpose statement, which should normally consist of no more than one paragraph:

1. *Role or contribution.*
    - Profit (specify)
    - Service
    - Opportunity seeker
2. *Business definition.* Define the business in terms of the *benefits* you provide or the *needs* you satisfy, rather than in terms of what you make.
3. *Core competencies.* Identify the essential skills, capabilities, and resources that are the keys to future success. Core competence is an integration of skills and technologies, not a single skill. It must be competitively unique so as to provide competitor advantage. If you can equally well put a competitor's name to competencies, they are merely baseline capabilities and are not core competencies.
4. *Company/Division positioning.* The unique and valuable position that the company has chosen to take in the marketplace.
5. *Indications for the future.*
    - What the firm *will* do
    - What the firm *might* do
    - What the firm will *never* do

Three Types of Mission Statements

Here, we can see two levels of mission. One is a corporate mission statement, the other is a lower-level or *purpose* statement. But there is yet another level, as shown in the box below.

Type 1. "Motherhood"

This type is usually found in annual reports designed to "stroke" shareholders. Otherwise, it is of no practical use for the organization.

Type 2. The Real Thing.

This type is a meaningful statement, which is unique to the organization and has an impact on the behavior of the executives at all levels.

Type 3. A "Purpose" Statement.

This type of statement is a lower-level mission statement. It is appropriate at the strategic business unit, departmental, or product group level of the organization.

The Generic Mission Statement

The following is an example of a meaningless, vapid, motherhood-type mission statement, which most companies seem to have. The statements achieve very little, and it is difficult to understand why these pointless statements are so popular. Employees mock them and they rarely say anything likely to give direction to the organization. We consider this an example of a generic mission statement, to be avoided at all costs.

The logical sequence of events, which leads to the setting of marketing objectives and the formation of plans for achieving them, is as follows: to write a mission statement, set corporate objectives, conduct the marketing audit, conduct the SWOT analysis, make assumptions, set marketing objectives and strategies, estimate expected results, identify alternative plans and mixes, set the budget, and establish the first year's implementation program. The following chapters give details on how to perform these tasks. As business becomes increasingly complex and competition increases, a marketing plan is essential.

Our organization's primary mission is to protect and increase the value of its owners' investments while efficiently and fairly serving the needs of its customers.

[... insert organization name ...] seeks to accomplish this in a manner that contributes to the development and growth of its employees, and to the goals of countries and communities in which it operates.

QUESTIONS SUCCESSFUL COMPANIES ASK

1. How do we see the logical sequence of events leading to the establishment of our marketing objectives?
2. How can we successfully achieve each of the steps in the market plan sequence?
3. What should our plan contain and how shall we use it?
4. Why should we do this? Does it create a unique value for our customers?

4 Marketing Objectives and Strategies

Chapter 4 defines marketing objectives and shows how to set them and how they relate to corporate objectives. Where and how to start the process of marketing planning by means of gap analysis is described, and new product development is discussed as a growth strategy. Finally, the definition and formulation of marketing strategies are explained.

Setting objectives and formulating strategies are the key steps in the marketing planning process. Realistic and achievable objectives must be set for a company's major products in each of its major markets. Unless this step is performed well, the entire planning process will be an exercise in futility. There is simply no way to achieve an unattainable objective, and there is no gain in formulating a brilliant plan to achieve an objective that falls far short of what is possible. Rather, it is a question of deciding on the right target. There is no gain in scoring a bull's-eye on the wrong target. Once the correct objectives are identified, strategies to achieve these objectives must be formulated.

Once again, the actual contents of a strategic marketing plan are described in Chapter 13. It is important, however, to read this chapter carefully before trying to complete the crucial step of formulating marketing objectives and strategies.

MARKETING OBJECTIVES AND CORPORATE OBJECTIVES

Setting objectives is an essential step in the planning process. A company that has set an objective knows what it expects to accomplish with its strategies and when a particular strategy has worked. Without objectives, strategy decisions and all that follows take place in a vacuum.

Most experts agree that the logical approach to the difficult task of setting marketing objectives is to proceed from the broad to the specific. The starting point is a statement of the nature of the business (the mission statement), from which flows the broad company objectives. The broad company objectives must be translated into key result areas, which are the areas in which success is vital to the firm. Market penetration and growth rate of sales are examples of key result areas. The third step is the establishment of sub-objectives necessary to accomplish the broad objectives, such as product sales volume goals, geographic expansion, product line extension, and specific objectives for each element of the marketing mix.

Advertising objectives, for example, must be wholly consistent with wider objectives. Objectives set in this way integrate the advertising effort with the other elements in the marketing mix, which ensures a consistent, logical marketing plan. For example, the buying process begins with awareness, and creating awareness is one of the functions of advertising.

An objective of attaining, for example, 50 percent unaided awareness in a specific market is an example of an advertising objective that might be part of a marketing plan. The result of this planning process is setting forth objectives that are consistent with the strategic plan, attainable within budget limitations, and compatible with the strengths, limitations, and economics of other functions within the organization.

Marketing strategies within the corporate plan become operating objectives within the marketing department, and strategies at the general level within the marketing department become operating objectives at the next level down, so that an intricate web of interrelated objectives and strategies is built up at all levels within the framework of the overall company plan.

A hierarchy of objectives and strategies can be traced back to the initial corporate objectives. Figure 4-1 illustrates this point. The most important point, however, apart from clarifying the difference between objectives and strategies, is that the farther down the hierarchical chain one goes, the less likely it is that a stated objective will make a cost-effective contribution to company profits, unless it derives logically and directly from an objective at a higher level.

CORPORATE VS. MARKETING OBJECTIVES AND STRATEGIES

A business starts with resources and wants to use those resources to achieve something. What the business wants to achieve is a *corporate objective*, which describes a desired destination or result. The way that objectives are achieved is a *strategy*. Frequently the objective is expressed in terms of profit, because profit is the means of satisfying shareholders and because it is the one universally accepted criterion by which efficiency can be evaluated. Objectives are also frequently expressed in terms of sales or revenue, since revenue is what sustains employment and jobs.

Specific targets, such as introducing a product line extension, creating a new image, and achieving a certain percentage increase in sales are corporate objectives that form the core of corporate strategy. They are the means by which a company achieves its profit objectives or its sales or revenue objectives.

For a sub-unit of a company that is responsible for, say, increasing the company's share of a specific market, increasing market share is an objective. Thus, a corporate strategy becomes a divisional objective. How the division reaches the objective of increasing market share for its products is its strategy.

To summarize, objectives are part of strategy, but we normally speak of the strategy as the means for achieving the objective. The best strategies are those that are focused on achieving demanding but achievable objectives. The worst strategies are those that either posit unachievable objectives or that posit objectives that fall far short of the organization's potential.

HOW TO SET OBJECTIVES

The Ansoff matrix, which we discuss here, is a useful tool for setting market objectives. A firm's competitive situation can be simplified to two dimensions only—products and markets. To put it even more simply,

Figure 4-1
*Hierarchy of
Objectives and
Strategies*

**Marketing planning in a
corporate framework**

Corporate mission
Define the business and its boundaries
using considerations such as:
- distinctive competence
- aspirations
- environmental trends
- resource market trends
- stakeholder expectations

Corporate objectives
e.g., ROI, ROS, image, social responsibility, etc.

Corporate strategies
e.g., involve corporate resources, and must be within corporate business boundaries

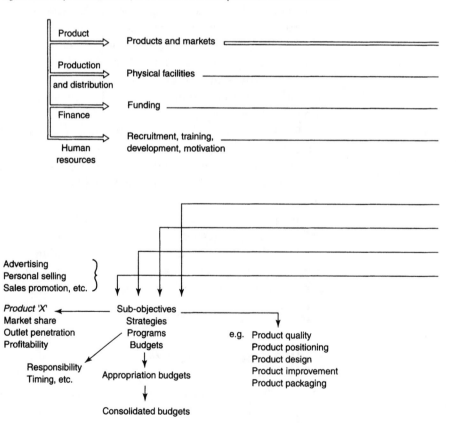

Figure 4-1
*Hierarchy of
Objectives and
Strategies
(continued)*

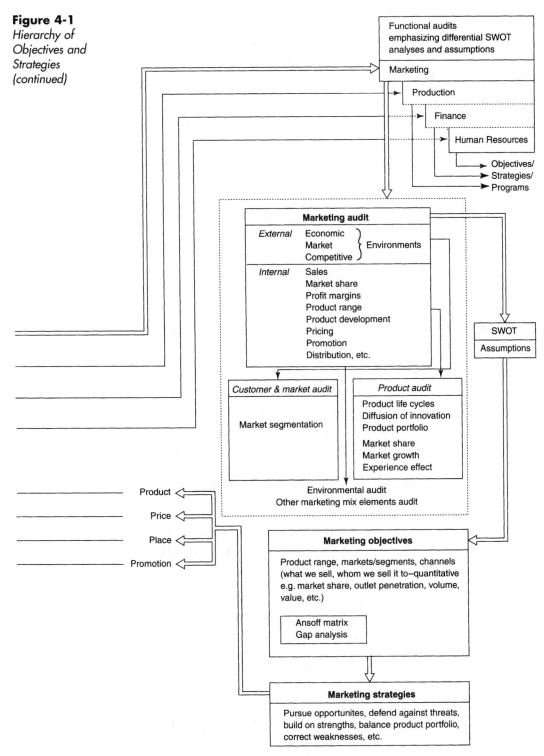

Figure 4-2
Ansoff Matrix

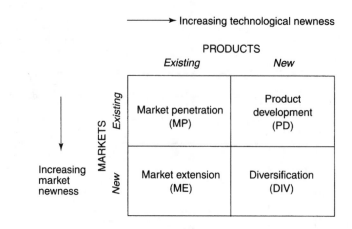

Ansoff's framework is about what is sold (the product) and to whom it is sold (the market). Within this framework, Ansoff identifies the following four possible courses of action for the firm:

1. Market penetration: Selling existing products to existing markets
2. Market extension: Extending existing products to new markets
3. Product development: Developing new products for existing markets
4. Diversification: Developing new products for new markets

The matrix in Figure 4-2 depicts these concepts.

It is clear that the range of possible marketing objectives is wide, because there are degrees of product newness and degrees of market newness. Ansoff's matrix provides a logical framework in which marketing objectives can be developed under each of the four main headings.

Market objectives are about products and markets only. Because it is only by obtaining sales that a company's financial goals can be achieved, elements such as advertising, pricing, and service levels are the means (or strategies) to do this. Market objectives are selected qualitative and quantitative commitments, usually stated either in standards of performance for a given operating period or conditions to be achieved by given dates. *Performance standards* are usually stated in terms of sales volume and various measures of profitability. *Conditions* to be attained are usually a percentage of market share and various other criteria, such as 75 percent distribution in a given category of retail outlets.

Objectives must be specific enough to guide an organization to the action required, and they must be the yardstick with which performance is measured. Objectives are the core of managerial action; they provide direction to the plans. By asking where the operation should be at some future date, a company determines objectives. Vague objectives are counterproductive to sensible planning. They are usually the result of the human propensity for wishful thinking, which often seems more like cheerleading than serious marketing leadership.

It is arguable whether directional terms such as "optimize" and "minimize" should be used as objectives. Unless there is a means of measurement, a yardstick, with which to quantify movement toward achieving an objective, setting directional objectives does not serve any useful purpose.

An objective contains the following four elements:

1. The particular attribute that is chosen as a measure of efficiency
2. The yardstick or scale with which the attribute is measured
3. The particular value on the scale that the firm seeks to attain
4. The time frame for achieving the objective

For example, if the objective is to achieve the number one share of global market position in 20XX, the share of market is the attribute, the world market is the scale, the number one rank is the value, and 20XX is the time frame.

Simply defined, product and market strategy represents a commitment by management to a company's future direction. It represents the route chosen by management to achieve company goals, through the range of products it offers and its chosen market segments. The general marketing directions that lead to the setting of objectives come out of the life cycle and portfolio analysis conducted during the audit. They revolve around the following logical options:

- *Maintain* usually refers to the "cash cow" type of product and market and reflects the desire to maintain competitive positions.
- *Improve* usually refers to the "star" type of products and markets and reflects the desire to improve the competitive position in attractive markets.
- *Harvest* usually refers to the "dog" type of product and market and reflects the desire to relinquish competitive position in favor of short-term profit and cash flow.
- *Exit* usually refers to the "dog" type of product and market and sometimes the "question mark." It reflects a desire to divest because of a weak competitive position, or because the cost of staying in the market is prohibitive and the risk associated with improving position too high.
- *Enter* usually refers to a new business area.

A further discussion of the above options takes place in Chapter 7.

Great care should be taken not to follow slavishly any set of "rules" or guidelines related to the foregoing options. The use of labels such as *dog* and *cash cow* should be avoided when referring to actual businesses or products.

A full list of marketing guidelines that can be used in establishing objectives is given in Table 4-1. Figure 4-3 includes guidelines for functions

TABLE 4-1 Strategies Suggested by Portfolio Matrix Analysis

	Business strengths		
	High		Low
High	Invest for growth Defend leadership, gain if possible Accept moderate short-term profits and negative cash flow Consider geographic expansion, product line expansion, product differentiation Upgrade production introduction effort Aggressive marketing posture, viz. selling, advertising, pricing, sales promotion service levels, as appropriate	Selective* Acknowledge low growth Do not view as a "marketing" problem Identify and exploit growth segments	Opportunistic The options are: (i) Move it to the left if resources are available to invest in it (ii) Keep a low profile until funds are available (iii) Divest to a buyer able to exploit the opportunity
Market Attractiveness	Maintain market position, manage for sustained earnings Maintain market position in most successful product lines Prune less successful product lines Differentiate products to maintain share of key segments Limit discretionary marketing expenditure Stabilize prices, except where a temporary aggressive stance is necessary to maintain market	Emphasize product quality to avoid "commodity" competition Systematically improve productivity Assign talented managers	Manage for profit Prune product line aggressively Maximize cash flow Minimize marketing expenditure Maintain or raise prices at the expense of volume
Low	share		

*Selective refers to those products or markets which fall on or near the vertical dividing line in a directional policy matrix.

Figure 4-3 *Program Guidelines Suggested for Different Positioning on the Directional Policy Matrix*

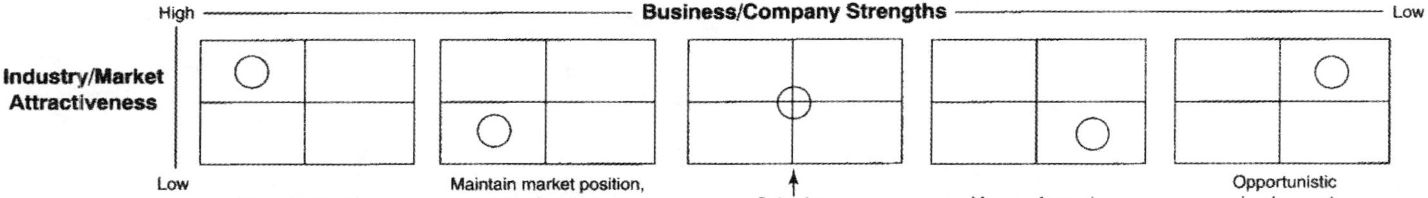

Industry/Market Attractiveness (High–Low) vs. Business/Company Strengths (High–Low)

Main thrust	Invest for growth	Maintain market position, manage for earnings	Selective	Manage for cash	Opportunistic development
Market share	Maintain or increase dominance	Maintain or slightly milk for earnings	Maintain selectively / Segment	Maintain	Increase
Products	Differentiation – line expansion	Prune less successful / Differentiate for key segments	Emphasize product quality / Differentiate	Aggressively prune	Differentiation – line expansion
Price	Lead – aggressive pricing for share	Stabilize prices/raise	Maintain or raise	Maintain	Aggressive – price for share
Promotion	Aggressive marketing	Limit	Maintain selectively	Minimize	Aggressive marketing
Distribution	Broaden distribution	Hold wide distribution pattern	Segment	Gradually withdraw distribution	Establish
Cost control	Tight control – go for scale economies	Emphasize cost reduction viz. variable costs	Tight control	Aggressively reduce both fixed and variable	Tight – but not at expense of entrepreneurship
Production	Expand, invest (organic acquisition, joint venture)	Maximize capacity utilization	Increase productivity, e.g. specialization/automation	Free up capacity	Invest
R & D	Expand – invest	Focus on specific projects	Invest selectively	None	Invest
Personnel	Upgrade management in key functional areas	Maintain, reward efficiency, tighten organization	Allocate key managers	Cut back organization	Invest
Investment	Fund growth	Limit fixed investment	Invest selectively	Minimize and divest opportunistically	Fund growth
Working capital	Reduce in process – extend credit	Tighten credit – reduce accounts receivable, increase inventory turn	Reduce	Aggressively reduce	Invest

45

other than marketing. One warning: general guidelines should not be followed blindly. They are intended to serve as checklists of questions that should be asked about each major product in each major market before marketing objectives and strategies are set.

COMPETITIVE STRATEGIES

At this stage of planning your marketing objectives and strategies, it is helpful to analyze recent developments in the strategies of your competitors. Competitive offerings will always affect how customers perceive the value of your offer. One of the principal purposes of marketing strategy is for you to be able to choose the customers, and hence the markets, whom you want to reach. In this respect, the DPM discussed in Chapter 7 is particularly useful. The main components of the strategy are the three C's:

- Company
- Customers
- Competitors

So far, we have said little about customers, although it is clear that if you are to succeed, you need to work hard at developing a sustainable competitive advantage by creating a unique value for your customers. D'Aveni, a contemporary strategy guru, has argued that there is no such thing as a sustainable advantage and that in fact all competitive advantages are temporary. In his view, the only way to succeed is to develop a series of temporary advantages (D'Aveni has a point if the definition of sustainable is forever). There is certainly no such thing as a strategy that will succeed forever; all strategies must be refreshed and renewed to respond to market and competitor changes.

To be fair to the strategic theorists that D'Aveni attacks, no one has ever suggested that a particular strategy could last forever. Fundamentally, D'Aveni's point misses the point. It is possible to formulate a strategy that is sustainable over a very long term. Intel, Microsoft, and Dell's advantage is, by almost any interpretation of the word, sustainable. Each of these companies has a strategy, and each has been able to make adjustments as needed to their strategy, as for example the about-face at Microsoft when the company acknowledged that the Internet was destined to become a major new technology.

Michael Porter identified four generic strategy alternatives (Figure 4-4) that companies may use, depending on the nature of their products and their target markets: cost leadership, outstanding success, niche/focus, and disaster.

Figure 4-4
Generic Strategy
Alternatives

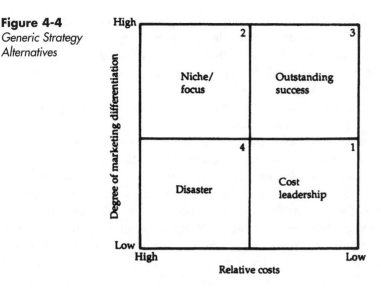

Cost Leadership

Box 1, cost leadership represents a sound strategy, particularly in commodity-type markets such as bulk chemicals, in which differentiation is difficult to achieve because the chemical composition of the products is identical. In such cases, it is wise to recognize the reality and pursue a productivity drive with the aim of becoming the lowest-cost producer. It is here that the experience effect described in Chapter 7 becomes especially important.

Niche/Focus

Box 2, high differentiation, can be successful as long as the differentiation remains strong and valuable in the customer's mind. This is the strategy for the so-called luxury brands. The key to the success of luxury brands is differentiation, and one key to differentiation is limited production and availability. The success of the Swiss with luxury watches is based on their understanding of this market segment. If there are too many Swiss luxury watches, no matter how good they are, they will lose their differentiation and therefore their value.

Seiko makes a fine watch, and has for decades gazed enviously at the luxury market. They have never even gotten close to the market in spite of their outstanding, high-tech product. They are high-tech and the luxury watch market is high fashion. They are volume producers and the luxury watch market is about limited supply. They are mass merchandisers, and luxury watches are sold in specialized outlets. They are low-priced, and luxury watches are expensive. Differentiation is something that must be achieved not only in product features and performance, but also in all of the elements that matter to customers.

Other products have differentiation in their feature set. For example, Apple Computer had ease of use. The threat to Apple has been the introduction of Microsoft Windows, which has substantially if not completely closed the ease-of-use gap and therefore Apple's differentiation.

The story of Apple Computer is an example of the disaster ahead for companies that refuse to or do not understand the discipline of market planning. The company missed its chance to leverage its ease-of-use advantage to establish the Macintosh OS as the operating system standard. By failing to recognize the opportunity, Apple handed the operating system monopoly to Microsoft without a fight. This is yet another example of the importance of goals and objectives. Apple was blind to the opportunity in software, and condemned itself to a niche by linking the Apple OS to Apple hardware.

What Apple should have recognized is that the company needed to move from box 2 to box 3 to continue to succeed. To do that, the company needed to lower the cost of Apple systems, and to do that they needed to recognize that Apple would have to aggressively license its operating system to manufacturers of personal computers. If Apple had done the obvious, it would be a major challenger or perhaps the leader in the operating system world market for personal computers. In other words, Apple would have been the Microsoft of the world, not a company on the brink of extinction.

Apple, under the leadership of Steve Jobs, has recognized that ease of use was a temporary advantage, and now positions themselves as the "Think Different" company. To date, Apple has done a brilliant job of expressing their new positioning in their overall marketing strategy. They have focused their product line, introduced products that look different (and which appeal to the eye), and focused on their traditional strengths, which include ease of use, desktop publishing, and now video editing. The success of Apple under Jobs underlines another truth about marketing strategy and planning: "It ain't over until the fat lady sings." People said Apple was finished and Jobs has proven them wrong.

Outstanding Success

Many companies, however, such as Jaguar and BMW (Box 3), cannot hope to be low-cost producers. As a consequence, their corporate philosophies are geared to differentiation and added value. This represents a sensible strategy for any company that cannot hope to be a world cost beater. Many of the world's great companies succeed by means of such a focus. Many of these companies also succeed in pushing themselves into box 3, the outstanding success box, by occupying what can be called "global fortresses." Companies like IBM, Coke, McDonald's, and General Electric typify box 3, in which low costs, differentiation, and world leadership are combined in their corporate strategies.

Procter & Gamble, the world's premier marketing organization, reduced marketing expenditures to lower prices and reduce the gap between the prices of branded (Procter & Gamble brands) and private label and store brands. P & G is clearly not asleep at the wheel; private label and store brands are increasing market share because of their price advantage. By reducing marketing expenditure, P & G will reduce its costs and be in a position to lower prices, reducing the private label competitive price advantage.

Disaster

Only box 4, disaster, remains. Box 4 shows that a combination of commodity-type markets and high relative costs will result in disaster, sooner or later. A position here is tenable only while demand exceeds supply. When these markets mature, there is little hope for companies that find themselves in this unenviable position. What Apple did was move from box 2 to box 4—from niche to disaster—when a competitor (Microsoft) took the ease-of-use advantage.

An important point to remember when thinking about differentiation as a strategy is that your plan must be cost effective. It is a myth that sloppy management and high costs are acceptable as long as the product has a good image and lots of added value. When you think about differentiation, refer to the section on benefit analysis in Chapter 6, for it is in benefit analysis that the route to differentiation is found. There is not much point in offering benefits that are expensive for you to provide but not highly regarded by customers. Consider using a matrix like the one in Figure 4-5 to classify your benefits. You will succeed by providing as many benefits as possible that fall into the top right-hand box.

When setting marketing objectives, it is essential for you to have a sound grasp of your position and your competitors' positions in your markets and to adopt appropriate postures for the several elements of your business, all of which may be different. It may be necessary, for example, to accept that part of your portfolio is in the "disaster" box (box 4). You

Figure 4-5
*Classification of
Benefits*

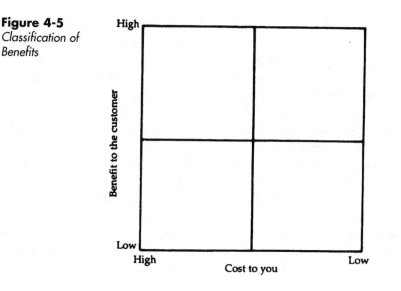

may well be forced to have some products there, for example, to complete your product range to enable you to offer your more profitable products. If this is true, you must adopt an appropriate stance toward these products and set your marketing objectives accordingly, using, when appropriate, the guidelines given in Figure 4-3.

Finally, here are some general guidelines to help you think about competitive strategies:

- Know the terrain on which you are fighting (the market).
- Know the resources and capabilities of your enemies (competitive analysis).
- Do with determination something that the enemy is not expecting.

WHERE TO START: THE GAP ANALYSIS

Figure 4-6 illustrates what is commonly known as *gap analysis*. If the corporate sales and financial objectives are greater than the current long-range sales forecasts, a gap exists that has to be filled.

The *operations gap* can be filled in two ways:

1. *Improve productivity.* For example, reduce costs, improve the sales mix, increase prices, reduce discounts, and improve the productivity of the sales force.

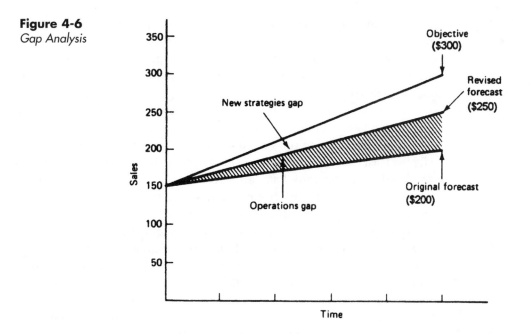

Figure 4-6
Gap Analysis

2. *Increase market penetration.* For example, increase usage and increase market share.

A *sales/profitability gap* can be filled in three ways:

1. *Market extension.* For example, find new user groups, enter new segments, and expand geographic area.
2. *Product development.* For example, new product features, improved performance, and expanded service.
3. *Diversification.* For example, new products for new markets. This is a combination of 1 and 2 above.

A fourth option is, of course, to lower the objective.

Gap analysis is best conducted in two separate steps. Step 1 is done for sales revenue only, so in the operations gap in Figure 4-6, reducing costs is not relevant. Step 2 has the same stages as step 1, however the profit and cost implications of achieving the sales growth are examined. A detailed discussion for completing both steps is given in Chapter 13.

If improved productivity is one method by which the profit gap is to be filled, care must be taken not to take measures such as reducing marketing costs by a constant, say, 20 percent overall. The portfolio analysis undertaken during the marketing audit stage almost always indicates that this amount would be totally inappropriate in some product and market areas, for which increased marketing expenditure may be needed, whereas for other areas, a 20-percent reduction in marketing costs may not be sufficient.

As for sales growth options, market penetration should always be a company's first option. It makes sense to attempt to increase profits and cash flow from existing products and markets initially, because this is usually the least expensive and the least risky method. For its present products and markets, a company has developed knowledge and skills that it can use competitively. And, marketing studies have shown that it is much less expensive to keep an existing customer than to try to find a new customer.

It makes sense in many instances to move along the horizontal axis for further growth before attempting to find new markets. The reason is that it normally takes many years for a company to get to know its customers and markets and to build a reputation. Reputation and trust, embodied in the company's name or in its brands, are rarely transferable to new markets in which other companies are already entrenched, but in some countries, like Japan, a reputation and sense of trust are necessary for the introduction of a new product.

The marketing audit should ensure that the method chosen to fill the gap is consistent with the company's capabilities and should build on its strengths. For instance, new products should be consistent with the company's known strengths and capabilities. Selling a product to existing channels by an established sales force is far less risky than introducing a new product that requires new channels and new selling skills. Gillette's acquisition of Duracell is an example of good fit. Gillette's line of personal care products moves through the same channels as batteries.

Going into new markets with new products (diversification) is the riskiest strategy of all because new resources and new management skills have to be developed. The history of business is replete with examples of companies that failed when they moved into areas in which they had little or no experience.

Exercising caution in diversification also applies to a company's production, distribution, and people. The use of existing plant capacity is generally preferable to the use of new processes. The amount of additional investment is also important. Technical personnel are highly trained and specialized, and whether their competence can be transferred to a new field must be considered carefully. A product that requires new raw materials may also require new handling and storage techniques, which may prove to be expensive.

Figure 4-7
*Ansoff Matrix:
Degrees of
Newness*

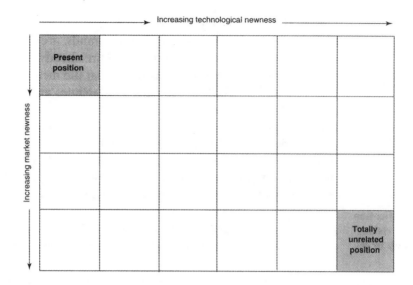

The Ansoff matrix is not a simple four-box matrix because there are degrees of technological newness as well as degrees of market newness that must be considered. Figure 4-7 illustrates this point. It also underlines why any movement should generally aim to keep a company as close as possible to its present position, rather than moving it to a totally unrelated position, except in the most unusual circumstances. Nevertheless, the product life cycle phenomenon inevitably forces companies to move along one or more of the axes of the Ansoff matrix if they are to continue to increase their sales and profits. A key concern is how this important decision is to be made, given the risks involved.

One final point to make about gap analysis based on the Ansoff matrix is that when completed, the details of exactly how to achieve the objectives still have to be worked out. This is the purpose of the tactical marketing plan.

NEW PRODUCT DEVELOPMENT, MARKET EXTENSION, AND DIVERSIFICATION

Sooner or later all organizations need to move along one or both axes of the Ansoff matrix. The objective is to maximize synergy, the $2 + 2 = 5$ effect. The starting point is the marketing audit, leading to the SWOT (strengths, weaknesses, opportunities, and threats) analysis. Development of any kind will be firmly based on the company's basic strengths and weaknesses.

(Note: There are three categories of new products: improvements to existing products, new products in the same product category, and completely new products for the company and/or the market.)

In terms of a SWOT analysis, external factors are the opportunities and threats facing the company. Once this important analytical stage is successfully completed, the more technical process of opportunity identification, screening, business analysis, and, finally, activities such as product development, testing, and entry planning can take place, depending on which option is selected. The important point is that no matter how thoroughly subsequent activities are carried out, unless the objectives of product development and market extension are based firmly on an analysis of the company's capabilities, they are unlikely to be successful in the long term. Figure 4-8 illustrates the process.

The criteria selected will be generally consistent with the criteria used for positioning products or businesses in the nine-cell portfolio matrix described in Chapter 7. The list shown in Table 4-1 (which is also consistent with the marketing audit checklist) can be used to select the criteria that are most important. A rating and weighting system can then be applied to opportunities identified to assess their suitability or lack thereof.

Figure 4-8
The Marketing Planning Process
See Figure 4-2 for the key to abbreviations.

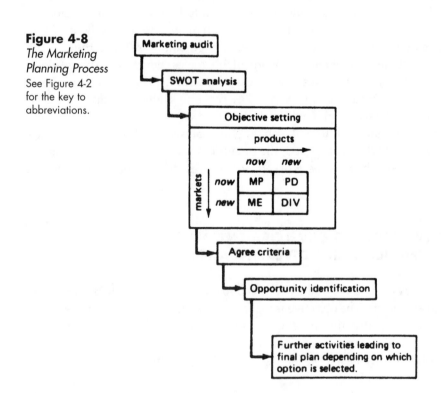

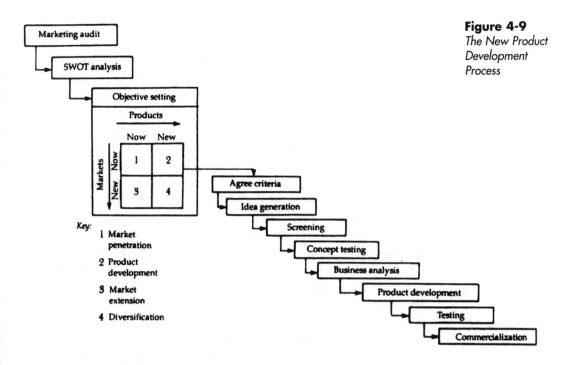

Figure 4-9
The New Product Development Process

Keep in mind that the criteria selected and the weighting system used should be consistent with the SWOT analysis.

Figure 4-9 depicts the relationship between the new product development process and the marketing audit and SWOT analysis. New product development can be seen as a process consisting of the following seven steps:

1. *Idea generation.* The search for product ideas to meet consumer needs *and* company objectives.
2. *Screening.* A quick analysis of the ideas to establish which ideas are relevant.
3. *Concept testing.* Checking with the market to see whether the new product ideas are acceptable.
4. *Business analysis.* Detailed examination of the idea in terms of its commercial fit with the business.
5. *Product development.* Making the idea into hardware.
6. *Testing.* Market tests necessary to verify early business assessments.
7. *Commercialization.* Full-scale product launch, committing the company's reputation and resources.

MARKETING STRATEGIES

What is marketing strategy? Essentially, it is a set of integrated actions in pursuit of value for customers and competitive advantage for the firm. We agree with Michael Porter that strategy is a unique and valuable position involving different and integrated activities.[1] Strategy requires decisions about which customers to target, what kind of products to offer, at what price, and where. A strategy involves significant trade-offs: decisions about what to do and what not to do. For example, Southwest Airlines, unlike its full-service competitors, does not provide first- and business-class service, meals, or baggage-transfer service. The company's unique position is its ability to provide low-cost (passed on to customers as low-priced), on-time service on short-haul domestic routes in the United States. Southwest's strategy has not been successfully copied by any challenger. The company's set of integrated activities is a major barrier to competitors who cannot easily duplicate the Southwest value system.

What a company wants to accomplish in terms of factors such as market share and volume is a marketing objective. *How* the company intends to achieve its objectives is strategy. Strategy is the overall route to the achievement of specific objectives and should describe the means by which objectives are to be reached, the timing of it, and the allocation of resources. Strategy does not spell out the detailed plans and tactics that will be required.

There is a clear distinction between strategy and detailed implementation, or tactics. As we've said, strategy is the route to achievement of specific objectives and describes how objectives are to be reached. Marketing strategy reflects the company's best opinion of how it can most profitably apply its skills and resources to the marketplace. Strategy is inevitably broad in scope. The plan that stems from a strategy spells out action and timing and contains the detailed contribution expected from each department.

There is a similarity between strategy in business and strategic military development. One looks at the enemy, the terrain, and the resources under command and decides whether to attack the whole front, to attack an area of enemy weakness, to feint in one direction while attacking in another, or to encircle the enemy's position. The policy and mix, the general direction in which to go, and the criteria for judging success all come under the heading of strategy. The action steps are tactics.

In marketing the same commitment mix—and types of resources, guidelines, and criteria that must be met—all come under the heading of

---

[1]Michael E. Porter, "What Is Strategy?" *Harvard Business Review,* November/December 1996, pp. 61–78.

strategy. For example, the decision to use distributors in all but the three largest market areas in which company salespeople will be used, is a strategic decision. The selection of particular distributors is a tactical decision.

Marketing strategies are the means by which marketing objectives are achieved and are generally concerned with the four major elements of the marketing mix. These are as follows:

1. *Product*. The general policies for product branding, positioning, deletions, modifications, additions, design, and packaging.
2. *Price*. The general pricing policies to be followed for product groups in market segments.
3. *Place*. The general policies for channels and customer service levels.
4. *Promotion*. The general policies for communicating with customers under the relevant headings, such as advertising, sales force, sales promotion, public relations, exhibitions, direct mail, and sponsorship.

General Content of Strategy Statements

The following components are generally included in strategy statements:

1. Description of the products to be offered, such as number of sbu's (strategic business units), quality, design, branding, packaging, and labeling.
2. Pricing levels to be adopted, margins, and discount policies.
3. Advertising and sales promotion, the creative approach, the type of media, types of displays, and the amount to spend.
4. The emphasis to be placed on personal selling, the sales approach, and sales training.
5. The distributive channels to be used and the relative importance of each.
6. Warehousing, transportation, inventories, and service levels in relation to distribution.

The following list of marketing strategies (in summary form) covers most of the options open under the headings of the four P's:

1. *Product*
   - Expand the line
   - Change performance, quality, or features
   - Consolidate the line
   - Standardize design

- Positioning
- Change the product mix
- Branding

2. *Price*
   - Change price, terms, or conditions
   - Skimming policies
   - Penetration policies

3. *Place*
   - Change delivery or distribution
   - Change service
   - Change channels
   - Change the degree of forward integration

4. *Promotion*
   - Change advertising or promotion
   - Change selling approach

Chapters 9 through 12 are devoted to a more detailed consideration of promotion, pricing, and distribution. Those chapters describe what should appear in the sales, pricing, place, and advertising sections of the marketing plan. This level of detail is intended for those whose principal concern is the preparation of a detailed one-year operational or tactical plan. This book contains no separate chapter on product management because all product options are covered in other chapters, particularly in Chapter 7 under the discussion of product audit. Finally, estimating in broad terms the cost of strategies and delineating alternative plans are covered in more detail in Chapter 13.

Formulating marketing strategies is one of the most critical and difficult parts of the entire marketing process. It sets the limit of success. When communicated to all management levels, marketing strategies indicate strengths to be developed and weaknesses to be remedied and in what manner. Marketing strategies are the means by which management sets operating decisions in order to bring the company into alignment with the emerging pattern of market opportunities that previous analysis has shown will offer the highest prospect of success.

This chapter confirms the need for setting clear, definitive objectives for all aspects of marketing, and shows that marketing objectives themselves have to derive logically from corporate objectives. This practice allows all concerned with marketing activities to concentrate their particular contribution on achieving the overall marketing objectives to facilitate meaningful and constructive evaluation of all marketing activity.

Once agreement has been reached on the broad marketing objectives and strategies, those responsible for programs can proceed to the detailed planning stage and develop the appropriate overall strategy statements into sub-objectives. For the practical purpose of marketing planning, overall marketing objectives have to be broken down into sub-objectives. Meeting the sub-objectives will enable the company to meet overall objectives. Breaking down the overall objectives makes the problem of strategy development manageable.

Plans constitute the vehicle for getting to the destination along the chosen route, or the detailed execution of the strategy. The term *plan* often is synonymous in marketing literature with the terms *program* and *schedule*. A plan that contains detailed lists of tasks to be completed, together with responsibilities, timing, and cost, is a detailing of the actions to be taken and of the expected financial results of taking them.

QUESTIONS SUCCESSFUL COMPANIES ASK

1. What is the principal purpose or mission of your company's existence?
2. Has there been any product and market extension during the past ten years that has not been a good fit with our integrated activities? Why? Are these factors still valid?
3. How would we conduct a gap analysis? A competitor analysis? A SWOT analysis?
4. Who should be involved in formulating the marketing strategy? How open should we be in sharing our strategic marketing plans with all levels and all divisions of the organization?

5 Marketing Research and Forecasting

Chapter 5 deals with the difference between market research and marketing research, how much to spend on it, the different forms of marketing research, marketing intelligence systems and how to organize them, and market forecasting.

Without the necessary information you will find it difficult to effectively perform many of the fairly common-sense tasks associated with marketing planning. A plan is only as good as the information on which it is based, which is why you need to make sure you know the right questions to ask, such as:

- What is the real need that we propose to satisfy?
- What benefits do our products provide to our customers?
- Who are our customers?
- Who are the competitors?

- What is our position in the market?
- What is our market share?
- What are the key trends in the market that we need to address?

Throughout this book, we have been stressing that the profitable development of a company can only come from a continual attempt to match the company's capabilities with customer needs. In order for the company to be sure that this matching process is taking place effectively, it is necessary that an information flow be instituted between the customer and the firm. This is the role of marketing research.

MARKET RESEARCH VS. MARKETING RESEARCH

Market research is concerned specifically with research about markets, whereas marketing research is concerned with research into marketing processes. We are concerned in this section with marketing research, which has been defined by the American Marketing Association as "the systematic gathering, recording and analysis of data about problems and opportunities relating to the marketing of goods and services."

The words in this definition are important. The process has to be systematic, because it is necessary to have a structured interaction between people, machines, and procedures, designed to generate an orderly flow of pertinent information collected from sources both inside and outside the company that is for use as the basis for decision-making in specified responsibility areas of marketing management.

Data alone (such as words, figures, pictures, sounds, and so on) are of little use until they are analyzed, assembled, and transformed into information. But without some purpose in mind, some marketing problem to solve or some marketing opportunity to discover, information is not of much use either. Indeed, research has shown that one of the biggest problems facing management today is a *surplus* of data and information, rather than too little of it. This brings us to our definition of *intelligence*, which is "information consumable and usable by management in converting uncertainty into calculated risk."

Uncertainty, of course, is when any outcome is considered to be equally possible. When a probability can be assigned to certain outcomes, however, we are talking about *risk*, which is just quantified uncertainty. Based on marketing intelligence, a marketing manager might feel, for example, that a new product has a 90 percent chance of achieving 30 percent market share in its first year, and therefore she plans distribution and advertising accordingly. Clearly, our ability to make successful decisions is enhanced if we are operating under conditions of known risk rather than uncertainty.

Conversion of uncertainty into risk with the minimization of risk is one of marketing management's most important tasks, and in this process the role of marketing research is of paramount importance.

HOW MUCH TO SPEND ON MARKETING RESEARCH

Before looking at the different kinds of research available to the marketing manager, any book written about marketing planning should address the issue of the marketing research budget.

Marketing information has to be produced, stored, and distributed, but it has a limited life—it is perishable. Like other resources, information has a value in use; the less the manager knows about a marketing problem and the greater the risk attached to a wrong decision, the more valuable the information becomes. This implies the need for a cost/benefit appraisal of all sources of marketing information, since there is little point in investing more in such information than the return on it would justify.

Although costs are easy to identify, the benefits are more difficult to pin down. They can best be expressed in terms of the additional profits that might be achieved through identifying marketing opportunities and through the avoidance of marketing failures that could result without the use of such information. However, there is no guarantee that findings are foolproof!

The decision about how much to spend on marketing information is not an easy one. On the one hand, it would, generally speaking, be foolhardy to proceed without any information at all; while, on the other hand, the cost of perfect information would be prohibitive. One way of estimating how much to spend is based on the theory of probability and expected value. For example, if by launching a product you had to incur development costs of $1 million and you believed there was a 10 percent chance that the product would fail, the maximum *loss expectation* would be $100,000 ($1 million × 0.1).

Obviously, then, it is worth spending up to $100,000 to acquire information that would help avoid such a loss. However, because perfect information is seldom available, it makes sense to budget a sum for marketing research that effectively discounts the inaccuracy of information. Such an approach can be a valuable means of quantifying the value of marketing research in a managerial context.

FORMS OF MARKETING RESEARCH

The increasing sophistication of the techniques available to the researcher, particularly in the handling and analysis of multivariate data, has made marketing research into a specialized function within the field of marketing management. Nevertheless, any company, irrespective of whether or not it has a marketing department, should be aware of tools that are available and where these may be used.

Marketing research can be classified either as *external* or *internal*. External marketing information gathering should always be seen as a complement to internal marketing analysis. External research activity is conducted within the competitive environment outside the firm, whereas much valuable intelligence can be gained from internal marketing analysis in the form of sales trends, changes in the marketing mix such as price, advertising levels, and so on.

There is another basic split between *primary* and *secondary* research. Primary data is obtained from original research in order to answer a specific research question. Secondary data is "off the shelf" information gathered at some earlier time for another purpose by an outside organization, but that can shed light on a current problem.

Primary Research

The most widely used method of primary marketing research involves the asking of questions by means of a *questionnaire* survey, a highly flexible instrument. The survey can be administered by an interviewer, either in person or by telephone, or it can be sent by mail, the Internet, and so on. All of these different methods have their advantages and disadvantages, and all have different cost consequences. For example, the greatest degree of control over the quality of the responses is obtained by getting an interviewer to administer each questionnaire personally, but this is very expensive and time-consuming. Telephone interviews are quick and relatively inexpensive, but there is a severe limit to the amount of technical information that can be obtained by this means. Increasingly, consumers resent being interrupted during mealtime (prime time for market researchers) and refuse to participate in interviews. The mail questionnaire is a much-favored method, but here great care is necessary to avoid sample bias. For example, is there something special (and possibly therefore unrepresentative of the population) about those who reply to a mail questionnaire? The same thing is true of any survey that is completed by a non-probability sample of respondents. Indeed, any survey method that is not based on a known probability sample is subject to sample bias.

The biggest potential pitfalls with the questionnaire lie in its design. Everyone knows about the "loaded" question or the dangers of ambiguity, yet these are not always easily detectable. The order in which questions are asked can also bias answers (the so-called sequence bias). For example, a sample of owners of Nokia telephones were shown packages containing a cell phone leather case. One package was identified with a well-known brand name and the other with no brand name. If the Nokia phone owners are asked, "Who made or sponsored this product?," the sequence of the questions will affect answers. If respondents see the package with the well-known brand first and then the package with no source identification, the number of people who say that the package with no source identification is made or sponsored by Nokia will be higher than if the respondent is shown the package with no source identification first. In other words, the sequence of the questions clearly biases the answer in this example. Such pitfalls can be reduced by *pilot testing* a questionnaire; in other words, by giving it a trial run on a sub-group of the intended sample to isolate any problems or biases that may arise.

Sometimes, it may be more appropriate to gather information not by large surveys, but by smaller-scale, more detailed studies intended to provide qualitative insights rather than quantitative conclusions. Focus groups can provide such insights. These are loosely structured discussions between ten to twelve people who broadly represent the population in which the researcher is interested. The moderator attempts to draw from the group their feelings about the subject under discussion.

Experimentation is another type of primary marketing research that can provide a valuable source of information about the likely market performance of new products, or about the likely effects of variations in the marketing mix. Thus, different product formulations, different levels of promotional effort, and so on can be tested in the market place to gauge their different effects.

Sometimes, market experimentation can take place in laboratory conditions, particularly in the case of advertising. Samples of the target audience will be exposed to the advertisement and their reactions obtained. Eye cameras, polygraphs, and tachistoscopes are just some of the devices that can be used to record physical reactions to marketing stimuli.

Secondary Research

In contrast to primary research, which relies on data derived directly from respondents, is information classified as *secondary* research. The best-known types of secondary research are *retail audits* and *consumer panels*, both widely used by consumer companies. Retail audits use UPC/scanning data to measure actual consumer purchase. Retail audits may also involve the regular monitoring of a representative sample of store warehouses. At regular periods, researchers visit the warehouse and record the current level of stocks of the product group being audited and the delivery notes for any such goods delivered since their last visit. With the information on inventory levels from their last visit, it is now a simple matter to determine sales of the audited items (i.e., opening inventory *plus* deliveries between visits *minus* closing inventory *equals* product movement during the period).

The consumer panel is simply a sample group of consumers who records in a diary their purchases and consumption over a period of time. Or, they may have their purchases recorded over a period of time at a store with UPC scanning capabilities. This technique has been used in industrial as well as consumer markets and can provide continuous data on usage patterns as well as much other useful data.

Another important and valuable marketing research tool is the review of published material or *desk research*, which should always be the starting point of any marketing research program. A wealth of information can be obtained from published information such as government statistics, OECD, EU, the United Nations, newspapers, technical journals, trade association publications, published market surveys, and so on. There are, for example, eleven pages of marketing statistical data listed at cyberatlas.imnternet.com. Two or three days spent on desk research nearly always provides pleasant surprises for the company that believes it lacks information about its markets. When combined with internal sales information, this can be the most powerful research method open to a company.

ORGANIZING INFORMATION TO DEVELOP SOUND PLANS

The practice of marketing planning is intrinsically a difficult one. The main concern of marketing planning is to choose markets to go after and to work out strategies to win them. The methods in this book can be applied to make up a plan that describes the marketing objectives and the winning strategies. The trouble is that such a plan could in theory be written without a scrap of supporting evidence; and, in practice, many plans are created upon the flimsiest of evidence.

Two challenges involving evidence and information face executive management. The first challenge, faced by companies of any substantial size and diversity, is how to manage the complexity of the planning data. The question arises: how can the planners know very much about what is happening throughout the geographical regions with all of its products and in all the market segments? Auditing the market requires its subdivision into many component parts: by geography, by product, by segment, etc. Then, portfolio analysis requires the reassembly of these components into a coherent structure.

The second challenge is how to assess whether a plan is based upon a combination of good evidence and reasonable assumptions or on flawed evidence and fallacious assumptions. In the process (Figure 5-2), planners need to match external facts about the market to internal facts and figures to create a clear and harmonious picture. However, it is rare for the same categories to apply internally and externally, which makes the job of the planner especially difficult.

Figure 5-1
One Hundred Levels of Market Subdivision and Summarization

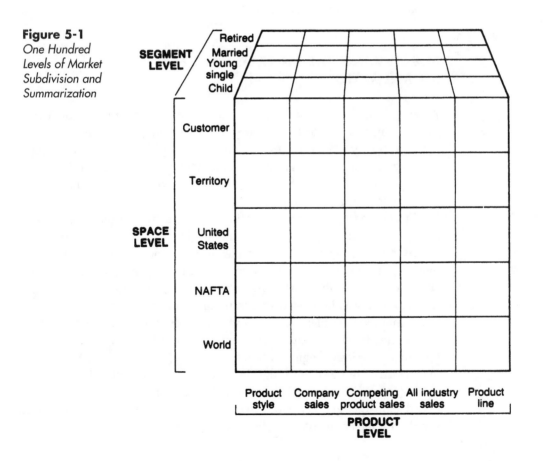

Figure 5-2
Planners Must Match the Internal Categories and Facts and Figures to the External Ones

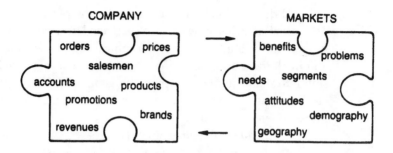

Fortunately, some large companies have found a way to address both of these problems, thanks to increased availability of information on computer databases, and the power of computer software to make complexity more manageable. Planners must, however, understand the limitations and weaknesses of the databases and master the software tools if they are to make the planning decisions sound as well as easy.

SUBDIVIDING THE MARKET: DATA FOR SEGMENTATION

As we will see in Chapter 6, market segmentation is a process of subdividing a market into distinct groups of buyers who might separate products and/or marketing mixes. For each segment, a profile is developed, and, very often, a meaningful and memorable name. Segmentation is only effective when it results in realistic commercial opportunities that can be targeted and measured in practice.

Market segments change over time as the buyers' needs evolve and as new product offerings become available. The planner must constantly review new combinations of variables to see which ones reveal the best new opportunities. Segments are identified by applying successive variables to subdivide the market. As an illustration, a global telecommunications company is interested in stimulating line usage among low users (segmentation variable: *product usage*). Low users consist of those who fear technology, those who are indifferent to it, and those who are positive toward technology (segmentation variable: *attitude*). Among those who feel positive are those with high incomes who can afford to increase line usage (segmentation variable: *income*). The telecommunications company may decide to target high-income people who have a positive attitude, but simply use the competitors' networks.

The following is a review of the steps involved in market segmentation:

Segmentation objectives. The researcher requires a clear, brief setting out of the business objectives. Different segmentation schemes may result from different objectives. If the objective is market extension, then the key segmentation variable may be income. If the objective is communication, then the key segmentation variable may be attitude.

Desk research and market hypothesis. The researcher collects readily available data and lays it out into a hypothetical map of the marketplace. This map contains many gaps, and relies on various assumptions. It suggests areas where more, or better, information needs to be collected.

Data collection and survey. The researcher collects information from and about potential buyers, including:

- Buying and/or usage behavior
- Buyer attitudes to the product category
- Buyer characteristics, such as geographics, demographics, psychographics

As we have seen, this can be obtained from:

- Public databases
- Proprietary databases (owned by research agencies)

- Questionnaires sent by mail
- Telephone research
- Face-to-face research
- Internet research

Note that internal customer data cannot be used in this context because it is not representative of the whole market, unless the company's customers are representative of all areas of the entire market. Large data samples often need to be collected to cover all combinations of variables. For example, in a survey where the variables are sex, age (split into five categories), geography (ten regions), and products (five categories), with a minimum sample per combination of ten people, the survey would need to cover at least 5,000 individuals to cover all combinations of segmentation variables.

Data analysis. A wide range of statistical techniques can be used to identify market segments. These include factor analysis, cluster analysis, and multiple regression. More recent techniques that go beyond the traditional limits of statistics include neural networks and pattern-finding algorithms.

Profile definition. Each segment is defined in terms of the key variables. Often the segments are named on the basis of a dominant characteristic.

Flexibility in Revising Analyses

The market is changing too rapidly for the traditionally slow process of data collection, data analysis, and data presentation. Much data remains unanalyzed. Cost and time limit analysis to the simplest levels—often only to the use of cross tabulations. There is little opportunity to explore interesting features that emerge from this first stage. As targeted marketing moves closer and closer toward the ultimate market of one person, the facts produced by the old research techniques are being replaced by newer models and information on demand.

More than one segmentation approach is needed to fit the strategic objectives at all levels: this covers the advertising and sales promotion plan, the sales plan, the pricing plan, and the distribution plan. Cutting the data in many different ways, to explore all the variables, can be prohibitively expensive if done by an external research agency but may be beneficial in evaluating the synergistic effects of various marketing strategies and programs. Table 5-1, "Examples of Business Objectives and Segmentation Methods," provides a good example.

British Telecom utilizes multiple segmentation strategies in the small business market in the UK. For advertising and sales promotion, they recognize:

- *Enthusiasts.* These people treat telecommunications almost as a hobby and love to be kept up-to-date with the latest functions and features. All communications with them need to reflect these attitudes.
- *Luddites.* They hate everything modern and technical. However, give them a few practical examples, and you might get them interested.
- *Corporate executives.* Managers and directors who respond best to arguments about benefits and competitive advantage.
- *Shopkeepers.* Shopkeepers have very little use for the telephone, so there is little justification for communicating with them.
- *Traditionalists.* These people are interested in ease-of-use and easy maintenance.

For sales planning, their targeting is based on the size of revenue opportunity, which is based on a model that combines:

- *Sales.* Larger companies tend to spend more on communications.
- *Standard Industry Code (SIC).* Certain industries are bigger communications users than others.

TABLE 5-1 Examples of Business Objectives and Segmentation Methods

Business Objective	Segmentation Method	Information Source
Market extension		
New locations	Geodemographics	Consumer research
New channels	Prospect profiles	Business research
New segments	Survey analysis	Market studies
Market development	Customer profiling	Sales ledger and added profile data
	Behavioral scoring	Models from internal data source
Product development	Factor analysis	Surveys
	Qualitative methods	Panels/discussion groups

Competitive Advantage and Segmentation

Standard segmentation strategies bought from external agencies generally do not provide significant competitive advantage. They are too generic. Even if you gain advantage from them today, your competitor can buy them tomorrow and rapidly catch up with you. Unique segmentation strategies are the best solutions to unique problems.

Take the automobile industry for example. Henry Ford assumed that price was the dominant segmentation variable, then General Motors recognized different income and preference groups in the market. Much later, the Japanese recognized the importance of car size and fuel economy, and more recently manufacturers have identified the vehicle type market, as a segmentation tool [for example, Multipurpose Vehicle (MVP) market]. The success of new entrants into any market often results from discovering new segmentation possibilities in the market.

THE MARKETING AUDIT

Two major challenges in conducting a marketing audit are:

1. Getting sound data from external and internal sources.
2. Matching external and internal categories.

External Data Sources

One of the primary tasks in the external audit is to estimate the market size and its breakdown by geography, product, and segment. This should be straightforward, given the vast quantities of market data that do exist. However, knowing where to begin to collect, store, and analyze data presents a real challenge. It helps to differentiate clearly between research on new markets and existing markets. Each presents a very different set of problems in terms of data:

- For *new markets*, data is comparatively scarce, and extrapolation from surveys is often the main source. Carefully designed analysis methods are necessary to resolve uncertainties introduced by small sample sizes. Models based on limited data and plausible assumptions have to be used to infer market size, structure, and dynamics.
- For *existing markets*, public and agency-owned data sources can provide a rich and detailed picture. Behavioral data is often widely available on

buying patterns; often quite detailed information is available on buyer attitudes and characteristics. Sophisticated statistical techniques that rely on large sample sizes can then be used to infer market size, structure, and dynamics.

WHAT INFORMATION IS NEEDED TO SUPPORT A MARKETING STRATEGY?

The answer to this question is something of a conundrum, since the information needed depends upon the marketing objectives that form the strategy. If you change the strategic marketing objectives, then you may need different kinds of information to support your strategy. Table 5-1 (earlier in this chapter) illustrates how different objectives require different supporting information. Figure 5-3 describes the path that information takes.

The critical issue when building such a system is that it is not self-contained within the marketing department. It requires interface programs that will allow the systems to be used by finance, sales, and other internal departments, as well as data-feeds from external sources.

The secrets of success in developing marketing research systems are:

- Understanding what marketing needs and particularly how the internal and external views will be reconciled.

Figure 5-3
Information Flows in a Marketing System

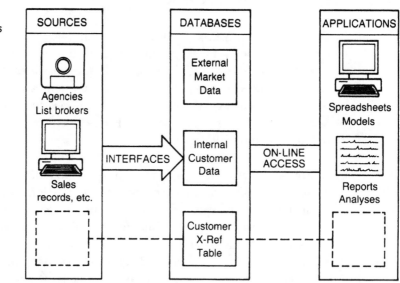

The main components of the marketing research system are as follows:

- *External market data* that are purchased from external agencies. These include governmental agencies, market research firms, list brokers, etc.
- *Internal customer data* that are collected from sales records and other internal sources such as customer service, field sales, and telemarketing. It is coded and segmented in such a way that market share figures can be created by comparison with external data.
- *Customer reference table* that is needed to make the system work effectively. It identifies customers (as defined by marketing) and provides a cross-reference to sales record accounts. Whenever a new sales account is created, the cross-reference table is used to determine the customer associated with that account. This avoids the need for costly manual matching after the account is created. It is also used by marketing applications as a standard reference table for customers.
- *Database* refers to all three of the above data types. It needs to be structured using a technique known as *data modeling* that organizes the data into the component types that

marketing wants, and not the structure that finance or anyone else provides. Usually, the data is held using *relational database* software, since this provides for maximum flexibility and choice of analysis tools.

- *Interfaces* refers to the computer programs that grab the data from the source systems and restructure it into the components to go onto the marketing database. These programs have to be written by the in-house IT (Information Technology) staff, since they obtain and restructure data from the in-house sales records, and other in-house systems.
- *Applications* are the software programs that the planners use to analyze the data and develop their plans. They include data-grabbing tools that grab the items of data from their storage locations; reporting tools that summarize the data according to categories that marketing defines; and spreadsheets that carry out calculations and what-if analyses on the reported summary data. Applications may also include specific marketing planning software decision support tools for strategic marketing planning. For further information on planning support software, see the authors' note at the end of the book.

- Developing a strong cost-benefit case for information systems, given that other systems, including financial ones, will have to be altered to accommodate the needs of marketing departments.
- Working continuously with internal IT staff until the system is built. They are under pressure from other sources, especially finance, and unless marketing maintains momentum and direction, then other priorities will inevitably win.

Marketing planners need to become far less insular and parochial if they are to obtain the information they require to plan effectively. Cross-functional understanding and cooperation must be secured by marketing departments if they are to develop the systems they need.

FORECASTING

There are two major types of forecasting, which can be loosely described as *macro-forecasting* and *micro-forecasting*. Selection of the appropriate technique is dependent on four main factors, the first of which is the degree of accuracy required. Second is the availability of data and information. Third is the time horizon. For example, are we forecasting next period's sales, in which case quantitative extrapolative approaches may be appropriate, or are we forecasting what will happen to our principal market over the next three years, in which case qualitative approaches may be appropriate? Lastly, the position of the product in its life cycle will also be a key determinant of the forecasting method. For example, at the introductory stage of a product's life cycle, less data and information will be available than at the maturity stage when time series can be a useful forecasting method.

There is an important distinction between macro- and micro-forecasting. Macro-forecasting is the markets in total, whereas micro-forecasting is a detailed product unit forecast. Macro-forecasting has to precede the setting of marketing objectives and strategies, while detailed unit forecasts, or micro-forecasts, should come after the company has decided which specific market opportunities it wants to take advantage of and how best this can be done.

There are two major techniques for forecasting, which can be described as *qualitative* and *quantitative*. It would be unusual if either of these methods were used entirely on its own, mainly because of the inherent dangers in each. Forecasters should combine an intuitive approach with the purely mathematical approach. For example, it is comparatively easy to develop an equation that will extrapolate statistically the world population up to, say, the year 2010. The problem with such an approach, however, is that it does not take account of likely changes in past trends. It would be easy to list a whole series of possible events that could affect world population, and then assign probabilities to the likelihood of those events happening.

The task of management is to take whatever relevant data is available to help predict the future, to use on it whatever quantitative techniques are appropriate, but then to use qualitative methods such as expert opinions, market research, analogy, and so on to predict what will be the likely *discontinuities* in the time series. It is only through the sensible use of the available tools that management will begin to understand what has to be done to match its own capabilities with carefully selected market needs. Without such an understanding, any form of forecasting is likely to be a sterile exercise.

QUESTIONS SUCCESSFUL COMPANIES ASK

1. Over what period of time do you forecast in your organization? Is it the right period?
2. Do all relevant managers have an opportunity to make a contribution? If not, say how they could become involved.
3. Is there ever a significant variance between forecasts and sales? If so, how do you explain it?
4. What additional information would you like to help you make more accurate forecasts? How could you obtain such information? Why have you not obtained it in the past?
5. If you were to establish a new marketing information system for your company, what would it contain? In what ways is it different from your current one and how could such a system be organized and made to work?

6 The Marketing Audit: Customers and Markets

The next two chapters are designed to help perform a meaningful marketing audit. We have already discussed the issues to be considered; now you need the tools to undertake such an analysis. The contents of the marketing plan, outlined in Chapter 3, represent the conclusions from the marketing audit and are only as good as the audit allows. The marketing audit is a separate step in the process, and under no circumstances do voluminous data and analysis appear in the strategic plan. They may, however, be necessary in the tactical plan to get a full and accurate picture of the product. The marketing audit is a crucial stage in the marketing planning process. Do not confuse it with the marketing plan itself, the actual contents of which are set out in detail in Chapter 4.

This chapter focuses specifically on to whom one sells, and Chapter 7 focuses on what one sells to them. We begin by defining the difference between customers and consumers, the meaning of market share, and the meaning of Pareto analysis. We then describe market segmentation and the several methods of segmenting markets, including customer behavior, benefit analysis, and customer attitudes. Examples of market segmentation and image mapping are provided. The chapter closes by emphasizing why market segmentation is vital to marketing planning.

When you understand the process of marketing planning, you can begin to look in more detail at its principal components. You have, as it were, seen the picture on the jigsaw puzzle; now you can examine the individual pieces with a better understanding of where they fit.

THE DIFFERENCE BETWEEN CUSTOMERS AND CONSUMERS

One of the key determinants of successful marketing planning is *market segmentation*. This is fundamental to the matching process described in Chapter 1. To understand market segmentation, it is first necessary to appreciate the difference between *customers* and *consumers*, the meaning of *market share*, and the phenomenon known as the *Pareto effect*.

Start with the difference between customers and consumers. The final consumer is not necessarily the customer. Take the example of a mother buying breakfast cereals. The chances are she is an intermediate *customer*, acting as agent on behalf of the *consumers* (her family). To market cereals

A fertilizer company with a product advantage prospered during the 1970s and 1980s, using distributors to reach its farmer consumers. However, as other companies copied the company's technology, distributors began to carry competitive products and drove prices and margins down. Had it paid more attention to the needs of its different farmer groups, and developed products especially for them on the basis of farmer segmentation, the company would have continued to create demand through differentiation. As it was, the company's products became commodities, and the power shifted almost entirely to the distributors. This company is no longer in business. There are countless other examples of companies that did not pay sufficient attention to the needs of users farther down the value chain. They eventually ceased to provide any real value to their direct customers and went out of business.

effectively, it is necessary to understand what the end-consumer wants as well as what the "agents" want.

When you appreciate the distinction between customers and consumers and the need to be constantly alert to any changes in the ultimate consumption patterns of products, the next question is: Who are our customers? Direct customers are people or organizations who buy *directly* from you. They could, therefore, be distributors, retailers, and the like. There is a tendency for marketers to confine their marketing efforts only to the final consumer of consumer goods, or only to those who actually place the order for industrial or business products. This can be a major mistake as seen in the example of the fertilizer company mentioned above.

MARKET SHARE

Closely related to this question of the difference between customers and consumers is the question of what constitutes market share. Most business people already understand that there is a direct relation between a relatively high share of any market and high returns on investment, as shown in Figure 6-1. It is important to be most careful about how *market* is defined. For example, SMH, a Swiss company, sells many different brands of watches, including Omega and Swatch. Although both Omega and Swatch are watches, they do not compete in the same market. Omega is in the luxury jewelry market, and Swatch is in the fashion accessory market. Correct market definition is crucial for measurement of market share and market growth, specification of target customers, reconfirmation of

Figure 6-1
The Relationship Between Market Share and Return on Investment
Source: IE–PIMS Database, Profit Impact of Marketing Study

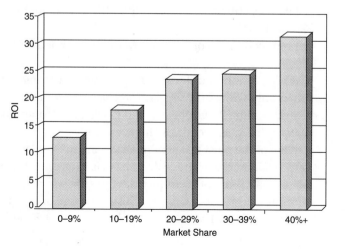

relevant competitors, and, most important of all, formulation of a marketing strategy that delivers differential advantage.

A market is the aggregation of all the products that appear to satisfy the same need and all of the actual or potential customers who have the same need. A metamarket is a broadly defined need. For example, the golf market is limited to existing and potential golf players and fans. It is part of a sports metamarket.

For example, the in-house caterer is regarded as only one option when it comes to satisfying lunchtime hunger. This particular need also can be satisfied at restaurants, fast food outlets, and delicatessens. The emphasis in the definition, therefore, is clearly on the word *need*.

It is important to arrive at a meaningful balance between a broad market definition and a manageable market definition. Too narrow a definition has the pitfall of restricting the range of new opportunities and segments that can open up for your business. On the other hand, too broad a definition may make marketing planning meaningless. For example, the television broadcasting companies are in the *entertainment* market, which also consists of theaters, cinemas, and theme parks, to name but a few. This is a fairly broad definition. Therefore, it may be more manageable for television broadcasters, when looking at segmenting their market, to define their market as being the *home information and entertainment* market. This could be further refined into the *preschool, child, teenager, family,* or *adult home information and entertainment* market.

To help with calculating market share, the following definitions are useful:

- **Product class.** For example, cigarettes, computers, fuel, and earth-moving equipment.
- **Product subclass.** For example, filter, personal computers, gasoline, and crawler tractors.
- **Product brand.** For example, Marlboro, Compaq, Mobil, and Caterpillar.

Coke, as a brand, for the purpose of measuring market share, is concerned only with *the aggregate of all other brands that satisfy the same group of customer wants.* Nevertheless, the Coca-Cola Company also needs to be aware of the sales trends of all beverages.

One of the most frequent mistakes made by people who do not understand what market share really means is to assume that their company has only a small share of a product class or subclass market. If the company is successful, it probably has a much larger share of a segment of one of these broader markets. For example, Psion, a United Kingdom company with sales of less than $300 million, has a trivial share of the world computer market. For handheld computers weighing less than two pounds, Psion had an impressive 34 percent share of the world market in 1996, which made the company number one in the world in this segment. The company's strength is its tight focus, which insures that it offers a product with functionality, features, and fashion that appeals to its market. Although it is tempting to believe that the foregoing examples amount to "rigging" the definition of market and that there is a danger of fooling ourselves, never lose sight of the purpose of market segmentation, which is to provide one's company with a competitive advantage by providing greater value to customers. A New York orchestra may define its market as the audiences served by aggregation of all New York classical orchestras rather than as all entertainment. The key is that a market definition enables it to outperform its competitors and grow profitably. The definition must be continuously reviewed and revised.

To summarize, correct market definition is crucial for the following purposes:

- Share measurement
- Growth measurement
- Specification of target customers
- Recognition of relevant competitors
- Formulation of marketing objectives and strategies
- Formulation of communication objectives and strategies

PARETO EFFECT

An interesting and very important market fact is known as the Pareto effect. The *Pareto effect* is a phenomenon commonly observed by companies that a small proportion of their customers account for a large proportion of their business. This is also referred to as the 80/20 rule, because generally 20 percent of customers account for 80 percent or more of a company's sales.

A graph of the proportion of customers who account for a certain proportion of sales may provide the relation similar to that in Figure 6-2. Here, customers have been categorized simply as A, B, or C, according to the proportion of sales for which they account. The A customers, perhaps 20 percent of the total, account for about 80 percent of sales; B customers, about 60 percent of the total, account for 15 percent of total sales; and C customers, 20 percent of the total, account for the remaining 5 percent of sales.

Figure 6-2
*Pareto Effect:
Log Normal
Distribution*

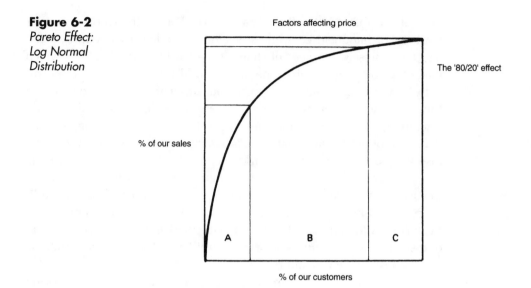

The Pareto effect is found in all markets, from capital industrial goods to financial services to consumer goods. The implication of this fact about markets is clear: marketers need to focus efforts and programs on high-volume customers, also known as heavy users. One of the most important tasks in marketing planning is being able to choose the best 20 percent of your market and focus on that. A method for doing this is provided in Chapter 6.

MARKET SEGMENTATION

We can now begin to concentrate on a method for making market segmentation a reality. Failure to understand the importance of market segmentation is a principal reason for failure to compete effectively in world markets.

A market segment consists of a group of customers or consumers with the same or similar need. These segments form separate markets in themselves and can often be of considerable size. Taken to its extreme, each individual consumer is a unique market segment, for all people are different in their requirements. However, it is clearly uneconomical to make unique products for the needs of individuals. Products are made to appeal to groups of customers who share approximately the same needs.

For example the market for skis is vast. It includes people of all ages, from five-year-old beginners to active ninety-year-old recreational skiers.

It includes downhill, cross country, and telemark skiers. The downhill segment is itself segmented by price, performance, features, and style. Any success in this market must begin with focus on segments, targeting, and the creation of a unique value for the target segment.

Unless you succeed in identifying a viable market segment for your product, you will not achieve a differential advantage and will become just another company selling "me too" products or, even worse, products that are irrelevant or of inferior value. There are basically three steps to market segmentation. The first is measuring customer behavior and answering the question *who* is buying *what*? The second answers the question *why* are they buying what they buy? The third step involves searching and identifying market segments.

Market segments have the following characteristics:

- Segments should be of an adequate size to provide the company with the desired return for its effort.
- Members of each segment should have a high degree of similarity, yet be distinct from the rest of the market.
- Criteria for describing segments must be relevant to the purchase situation.
- Segments must be reachable, that is, they must respond to a distinctive marketing mix.

MARKET MAPPING

A useful way of tackling the complex issue of market segmentation is to start by drawing a *market map* as a precursor to a more detailed examination of who buys what. A market map defines the value chain between the manufacturer and the final user, which takes into account the various buying mechanisms found in a market, including the part played by *influencers*. In general, if an organization's products or services go through the same channels to similar end users, one composite market map can be drawn. If, however, some products or services go through totally different channels or to totally different markets, more than one market map is needed.

Business units normally are mapped individually in that such structures usually exist because the volume or value of business justifies a specific focus. For example, in the case of a farming cooperative that supplies seeds, fertilizer, crop protection insurance, and banking to farmers, it would be sensible to start by drawing a separate market map for each of these product groups, even though they all appear to go through similar

Figure 6-3
A Simple Market Map

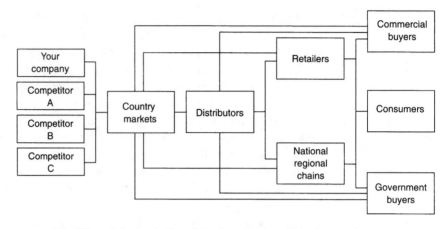

Note: This market map combines domestic and business-to-business end users. Some of the distribution channels are common to both of them.

channels to the same end users. In other words, start the mapping (and subsequent segmentation) process at the lowest level of disaggregation within the current structure of the organization.

An example of a very basic market map is shown in Figure 6-3. It is very important that your market map tracks your products and services along with those of your competitors all the way through to the final users, even though you may not actually sell directly to them.

In some markets, the direct customer-purchaser will not always be the final user. For example, a company (or household) may commission a third-party contractor to provide some redecoration, or an advertising agency to develop and conduct a promotional campaign, or a bank, accountant, or financial adviser to produce and implement a financial program. The physician you visit when seeking treatment is, in many respects, a contractor when it comes to prescribing medicine. Although the contractor specifies the product (the drug prescription), he or she is not the final user. The distinction is important; to win the assignment the contractor has to understand the requirements of the customer. To leave the final user out of the market map therefore ignores an array of different needs of which the supplier must be aware (and include in the product offer) if the supplier is to ensure the company name appears on the contractor's *preferred supplier list*. The inclusion of a contractor on a market map is illustrated in Figure 6-4.

So far we have mapped out the different transactions that take place in a market all the way through to the final user and have shown how the transactions relate to each other. By quantifying the various routes and

Figure 6-4
*Market Map with
Contractor*

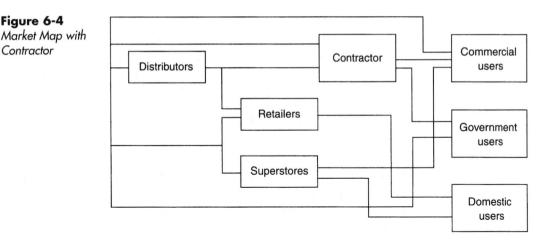

determining your company's share along them, you identify the most important routes and your company's position along each of them.

By looking at when decisions are made between the products or services of competing suppliers, you identify a number of stages (junctions) at which segmentation can occur. For most companies, we recommend that segmentation first take place at the junction farthest away from the supplier and manufacturer; it is at this junction that decisions are made.

WHO BUYS

A useful method for dealing with this stage of market segmentation is to refer to the market map, and at each point at which there is a critical purchase influence, attempt to describe the characteristics of the customers who belong to the segment. The descriptions can consist of a single characteristic or a combination of characteristics, whichever is appropriate to the market being analyzed.

Analysis of customer attributes is important in helping to design a communication program. It is used to find a way to describe the customer groups identified in the previous analysis for the purpose of communicating with them. However clever you may be in isolating segments, unless you can find a way to describe the segments in order to address them through a communication program, the efforts are to no avail. Demographic descriptors are the most useful method for this purpose. For consumer markets, these descriptors are income, age, sex, education, stage in the family life cycle, nationality, and socioeconomic group.

WHAT IS BOUGHT

When you look at what is bought, the value of the market map becomes apparent. We are really talking about the actual structure of markets in the form of volume, value, the physical characteristics of products, place of purchase, frequency of purchase, price paid, and so on. This tells you, if there are any groups of products (or outlets, or price categories) that are growing, remaining static, or declining, this is where the opportunities are and where the problems are. Analysis of product and purchase characteristics tells how the market works and helps one understand the market structure.

For example, a pharmaceutical company whose sales were declining found during analysis that although the market in total was rising, the particular outlets to which they had traditionally sold were accounting for a declining proportion of total market sales largely due to the increase of purchases on the Internet, a market they had not sold to. Furthermore, demand for higher-priced products was falling as the health care plans exercised more control over medication purchases. All this added up to a decline in sales and profitability and led the company to re-target its efforts on the growing sectors of the market.

This is market segmentation at its most elementary level, yet it is surprising to find even today how many companies run apparently sophisticated budgeting systems based on little more than crude extrapolations of past sales trends and that leave the marketing strategies implicit. Such systems are usually the ones that cause serious problems when market structures change.

The next task is to list *all* relevant competitive products and services, whether or not you manufacture them. Make sure that you unbundle all the components of a purchase so that you arrive at a comprehensive list of *what is bought*. Also, draw up a list that covers the different frequencies of purchase experienced for your own, and your competitors' products and services. Features to take into account when drawing up your list include:

- Type of product
- Specifications
- Color
- Size of package
- Level/intensity of use
- Type of service
- End-use applications

- Brand
- Country of origin
- Independent influencers
- Type of delivery
- Value of purchase

Next, draw up a separate list covering the different methods of purchase and, if applicable, the different purchasing organizations and procedures observed in your market. For example:

Methods of payment. Credit cards, direct debit, cash, or check.

Type of purchase. Switch, re-buy, or new purchase.

Purchasing organization. Centralized, decentralized, buying influencers, or decision makers.

Next, attempt to identify for each segment the unique combinations of *what is bought* as observed in buying activity. The resulting cascade produces a large number of micro-segments, each of which has a volume or value figure attached. These can be reduced in number by determining the important from the unimportant and by removing anything that is obviously superfluous.

Some preliminary screening at this stage is vital to cut this long list down to manageable proportions. This also acts as a preliminary form of market segmentation.

WHY CUSTOMERS BUY

The second part of analyzing customer behavior is trying to understand why customers behave the way they do. If we can explain the behavior of our customers, we are in a better position to sell to them.

The most useful and practical way of explaining customer behavior is benefit segmentation, that is, the benefits sought by customers when they buy a product. For example, some customers buy products for functional characteristics (product), for economy (price), for convenience and availability (place), for emotional reasons (promotion), or for a combination of these reasons (a tradeoff). Understanding the benefits sought by customers helps organize the marketing mix in the way most likely to appeal to the target market. The importance of product benefits is clarified in Chapter 7 in the discussion of product management.

Customers don't buy products; they seek to acquire benefits. Behind this statement lies a basic principle of successful marketing. When people purchase products, they are not motivated in the first instance by physical features or objective attributes of the product but by the benefit that those attributes bring with them. To take an example from industrial marketing, a purchaser of industrial cutting oil is not buying the particular blend of chemicals sold by leading manufacturers of industrial lubricants; he is buying a bundle of benefits that includes the solution to a specific lubrication problem.

The difference between benefits and products is not simply a question of semantics. It is crucial to the company seeking success. Every product has its features, such as size, shape, performance, weight, and the material from which it is made. Many companies fall into the trap of talking to customers about these features rather than about what the features mean to the customer. This is not surprising. For example, if a salesperson being asked a question about a product cannot provide an accurate answer, the customer might lose confidence and, doubting the salesperson, soon doubt the product. Most salespeople, therefore, are very knowledgeable about the technical features of the products they sell. They have to have these details at their fingertips when they talk to buyers, designers, and technical experts.

Being expert in technical detail, however, is not enough. The customer may not be able to see the benefits that particular features bring. It is therefore up to the salesperson to explain the benefits that accrue from every feature mentioned. A simple formula to ensure that this customer-oriented approach is adopted is always to use the phrase "which means that" to link a feature to the benefit it brings, as follows:

Maintenance time has been reduced from four to three hours, *which means that* most costs are reduced by . . .

The new special bearing has self-aligning symmetric rollers, *which means that* the rollers find their own equilibrium with the load always symmetrically distributed along the length of the roller, *which means* an extended life capacity of one year on average.

BENEFITS ANALYSIS

A company must undertake a detailed analysis to determine the full range of benefits it has to offer its customers. This can be done by listing the features of major products with what they mean to the customer. The analysis produces various classes of benefits.

Standard Benefits

Standard benefits are the basic benefits that arise from the features of the company and its products. Every benefit must be listed. Care is needed to produce a comprehensive list. Because company staff are familiar with the company and its products, they may take some features for granted. Take care not to fall into this trap when providing a benefit analysis.

Double Benefits

A company often can identify double benefits. For example, it may be selling a product that benefits the customer and, by means of improvement in the customer's product, the end user. For example, a combination fax, copier, printer, scanner model performs four different tasks, *which means that*:

- The product will appeal to a wide variety of customers.
- Users save space and money.
- It offers a unique value for the small business customer.

In the example, the first benefit applies to the customer because it widens the customer's potential market, and the additional benefits apply to the potential end user.

Company Benefits

Customers rarely simply buy products; they buy a relationship with the supplier. Factors such as delivery, credit, after-sales service, location of depots and offices, and reputation are relevant to the customer. The benefit analysis therefore examines the company and the back-up services it offers. Typical company benefits are as follows:

We offer a twenty-four hour service because we have a national network of deliverers, *which means that* you will never lose production because of down time.

We are a large international corporation, *which means that* you can rely on comprehensive service throughout the world.

We are a small family business *which means that* you can be sure of individual attention from us.

Differential Benefits

Although it is important for the salesperson to conduct the benefit analysis most thoroughly, it is vital in the analysis that differential benefits compared with those of chief competitors be identified. If a company cannot identify any differential benefits, it means that either what they are offering is identical to its competitors' offerings (which is unlikely) or the company has not conducted the benefit analysis properly. It is in differential benefits or USPs (unique selling propositions) that the greatest chance of success lies.

Perception Mapping

From all the benefits and experiences that a consumer has with a product, they develop a perception of the product in their mind, a mental space, which is positioned vis-à-vis other competing products in terms of their most important decision making criteria. The result is a "perceptual map," which can be diagrammed. Figure 6-5 shows a map of automobile makes and models in terms of four product attributes: upscale/luxury, sporty/youthful, practical/economy, and family/conservative.

Figure 6-5
A Perceptual Map for Automobile Makes and Models

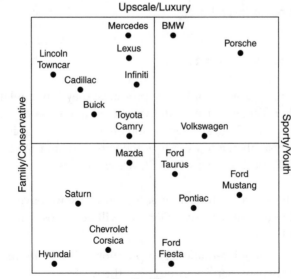

BRINGING IT ALL TOGETHER

The segmentation is almost complete. The second step involves taking each cluster identified earlier (who buys and what they buy) and listing *why* they buy. In other words, what benefits are customers seeking by buying what they buy?

The third and final step is to look for *clusters* of segments that share similar needs and to apply to the resulting clusters the organization's minimum volume and value criteria to determine viability. This final step can be difficult and time-consuming, but care lavished on this part of the market segmentation process pays handsome dividends at later stages of the marketing planning process, such as in developing advertising copy.

Summary of Bases for Market Segmentation

What is bought	Price
	Outlets
	Physical characteristics
	Geography
Who buys	Demographic
	Socioeconomic
	Brand loyalty
	Heavy or light user
	Personality traits, lifestyle
Why	Benefits
	Attitudes
	Perceptions
	Preferences

WHY MARKET SEGMENTATION IS VITAL IN MARKETING PLANNING

In today's highly competitive world, few companies can afford to compete only on price. The product has not yet been sold that someone, somewhere, cannot sell less expensively. In many markets it is rarely the least expensive product that succeeds anyway. This issue is discussed in Chapter 11, "The Pricing Plan." You have to find a way to differentiate yourself from the competition; the answer is market segmentation.

The truth is that few companies can afford to be all things to all people. The main aim of market segmentation as part of planning is to enable a firm to target its efforts at the most promising opportunities. But what is an opportunity for firm A is not necessarily an opportunity for firm B. So, a firm needs to develop a *typology* of the customer or segment it prefers; this can be an instrument of great productivity in the marketplace. The typology of the customer or the segment can be based on a myriad of criteria, such as the following:

- Size of the firm
- Consumption level of the firm or usage rate of consumer
- Nature of the firm's products, production, or processes or consumer behavior (e.g., recreational skier vs. racer)
- Motivation of the decision-makers (e.g., desire to deal with large firms)
- Geographic location

The point of segmentation is that a company must do one of the following:

1. Define its markets broadly enough to ensure that the costs for key activities are competitive.
2. Define its markets in such a way that it can offer unique value to customers.

Both tasks have to be related to a firm's *distinctive competence* and to that of its competitors.

All this comes to the fore as a result of the marketing audit and is summarized in SWOT (strengths, weaknesses, opportunities, and threats) analysis. In particular, the differential benefits of a firm's product or service should be beyond doubt to all key members of the company. Even more important than this, however, is the issue of marketing planning and all that follows in this book. It is worth repeating why market segmentation is so important. Correct market definition is crucial for the following:

- Share measurement
- Growth measurement
- Specification of target customers
- Recognition of relevant competitors
- Formulation of marketing objectives and strategies

TABLE 6-1 GM's Sad Decline

1921 Brands positioned along different price points		1996 No focus or position—all brands in the center of the market	
Chevrolet	$450 to $600	Saturn	$9,995 to $12,895
Pontiac	$600 to $900	Chevrolet	$7,295 to $67,543
Oldsmobile	$900 to $1,200	Pontiac	$9,904 to $26,479
Buick	$1,200 to $1,700	Oldsmobile	$13,510 to $31,370
Cadillac	$1,700 to $2,500	Buick	$13,734 to $31,864
		Cadillac	$32,990 to $45,330

Source: Trout, Jack, with Steve Rivkin, *The New Positioning: The Latest on the World's #1 Business Strategy.* New York: McGraw-Hill, 1996, p. 52.

Segmentation is not something a company can do once and forget. Because markets and customers are constantly changing, segments constantly change. Table 6-1 shows what happens to a company that treats segments as fixed points rather than as constantly evolving targets. In 1921, General Motors brands were differentiated and focused on distinctive target markets. By 1996, these same brands had lost their distinctive price positioning in the marketplace. The market had shifted from segmentation based on price and size to one based on multiple factors, including lifestyle and vehicle category. Price was still a factor but one of many factors. General Motors' powerful 1921 price and size brand segmentation is more of a drag than a lift in the markets of today.

To summarize, the objectives of market segmentation are as follows:

- To help determine how best to focus the firm's resources and efforts to create differential advantage and customer value.
- To help determine realistic and achievable marketing and sales objectives.
- To improve decision making by forcing managers to consider in depth the options ahead.

QUESTIONS SUCCESSFUL COMPANIES ASK

1. Are we serving customers or consumers? Look at one of your company's products. Identify its feature. Identify the consumer benefits of each feature.
2. How do we define our market?

3. What is our market share?
4. Who are our most important competitors and what features do their products have?
5. Why do our customers buy what they buy and why do they buy from us?
6. How is our market changing? What are the new segments we need to address?

7 The Marketing Audit: Products

Chapter 7 defines what we mean by *product* as well as defining product life cycle analysis and the Boston Consulting Group (BCG) matrix. It outlines certain weaknesses in the BCG matrix approach and introduces the directional policy matrix as a tool of analysis. The chapter outlines the types of information needed about products as part of the marketing audit and presents a number of fundamental diagnostic marketing tools.

WHAT IS A PRODUCT?

A product (or service) is the total experience of the customer or consumer when dealing with an organization. The central role of the product in marketing management makes it such an important subject that mismanagement in this area is unlikely to be compensated by good management in other areas.

The vital aspects of product management discussed in this chapter are the nature of products, product life cycles, the concept of the product portfolio, and new product development. The purpose of this discussion is to help in the performance of a product audit in order to set meaningful marketing objectives. Before a discussion of product management can take place, it is necessary to understand what a product is, because this is the root of misunderstanding about product management.

A product is a problem solver in the sense that it solves the customer's problems. It is also the means by which the company achieves its objectives. The clue to what constitutes a product can be found in an examination of what it is that customers appear to buy. For example, Theodore Levitt, the legendary marketing guru, points out that what customers *want* when they buy one-quarter inch drills is one-quarter inch holes. In other words, the drill itself is only a means to an end. The lesson here for the drill manufacturer is that if the company really believes its business is the manufacture of drills, rather than the manufacture of the means of making holes in materials, it is in grave danger of going out of business as soon as a better means of making holes is invented, such as, for example, a pocket laser.

A company that fails to think of its business in terms of customer benefits rather than in terms of physical products or services is in danger of losing its competitive position in the market. This is why so much attention is paid to the subject of benefit analysis.

So far, we have not said much about service products, such as consulting, banking, and insurance. The reason for this is simply that, as stated in Chapter 2, the marketing of services is not very different from the marketing of goods. The greatest difference is that a service product has benefits that cannot be stored. An airline seat, for example, if not used at the time of the flight, is gone forever, whereas a physical product may be stored and used at a later date.

In practice, this disadvantage makes little difference in marketing terms. The problem seems to lie in the difficulty many service product companies have in perceiving and presenting their offerings as *products*. Consider the example of the consultant. The world is full of a constantly changing army of people who set themselves up as consultants, and it is not unusual to see people presenting themselves, for example, as general marketing consultants. It would be difficult for any prospective client to glean from such a description exactly what benefits this person is offering. Yet the market for consulting is no different from any other market. It is a simple matter to segment the market and develop products that deliver the particular package of benefits desired.

When customers buy products, even as an industrial buyer purchasing a piece of equipment for a company, they are still buying a particular bundle of benefits that they perceive to satisfy their own particular needs and wants. This is illustrated in Figure 7-1.

There is a great danger in leaving product decisions to engineers and scientists. If these people are not market driven, they focus on the formal product and ignore the core benefit or service and the augmented product. In Figure 7-1, the three shaded outer circles are depicted as "product surround." The product surround can account for as much as 80 percent of the added value and impact of a product. Often, these only account for 20 percent of the costs, whereas the reverse is often true of the core product.

IMPORTANCE OF THE BRAND

It will be clear that here we are talking about not just a physical product, which is an object or service, but about the customer's belief and experience with the company's products. A company's most important asset is its brand. The brand is not just the physical product or service. It exists solely in the minds of the customer. The brand may be a company brand, sometimes referred to as an umbrella brand, or it may be a product brand, or it may be a combination of both. Procter & Gamble and Philip Morris are examples of companies who rely upon product brands like Tide, Cascade, and Crest (for P & G), and Marlboro, Kraft foods, Jell-O, and Cool Whip (for Philip Morris). IBM, BMW, and Harley-Davidson are excellent examples of company brand names. For these companies, the products and the company name get the same name. Ford is an example of a combination

Figure 7-1
*What Is a
Product?*

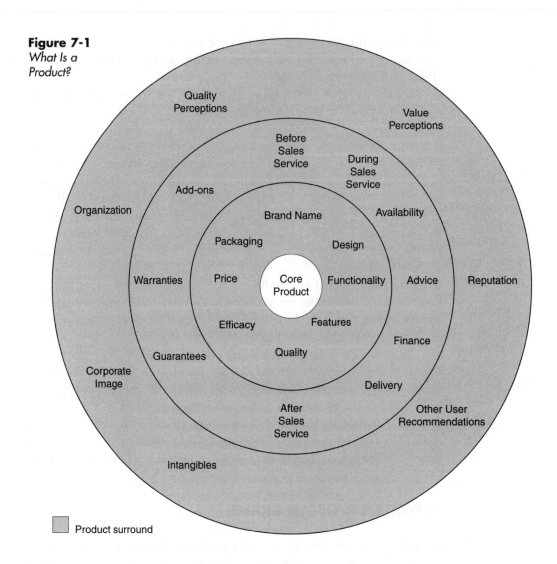

approach: Ford for the regular line of cars and trucks, and Lincoln, Jaguar, Volvo, and Land Rover for the luxury priced line.

Most people are aware of the Coca-Cola/Pepsi-Cola blind taste tests, where Pepsi was preferred to Coke. On revealing the labels, however, 65 percent of consumers claimed to prefer Coca-Cola. This is one of the best indications of the value of what we have referred to as the "product surround"—that it is a major determinant of commercial success there can be little doubt. When one company buys another, as in the case of Nestlé and Rowntree, it is abundantly clear that the purpose of the acquisition is not to buy the tangible assets that appear on the balance sheet, such as factories, plant, vehicles, and so on, but the brand names owned by the company to be acquired. This is because it is not factories that make profits, but rather relationships with customers, and it is company and brand names that secure these relationships. The difference between a brand and a commodity can be summed up in the term "added value," which are the additional attributes, or intangibles, that the consumer perceives as being embodied in the product. Thus, a product with a strong brand name is more than just the sum of its component parts. The Coca-Cola example is only one of thousands of examples of the phenomenon.

It is also a fact that, whenever brand names are neglected, what is known as "the commodity slide" begins. This is because the physical characteristics of products are becoming increasingly difficult to differentiate and easy to emulate. In situations like these, one finds that purchasing decisions tend to be made on the basis of price or availability in the absence of strong brands.

Business history is replete with examples of strong brand names that have been allowed to decay through lack of attention, often because of a lack of both promotion and continuous product improvement programs. Figure 7-2 depicts the process of decay from brand to commodity as the distinctive values of the brand are eroded over time, with a consequent reduction in the ability to command a premium price.

Research has shown that perceived product quality, as explained above, is a major determinant of profitability. This issue was discussed in Chapter 4 under the heading "Competitive Strategies."

Successful vs. Unsuccessful Brands

Successful brand building helps profitability by adding value that entices customers to buy. It also provides a firm base for expansion into product

Figure 7-2
Brand Decay

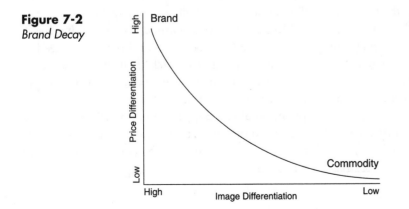

improvements, variants, added services, new countries, and so on. Successful brands also protect companies against the growing power of intermediaries. And last, but not least, brands help transform organizations from being faceless bureaucracies to ones that are attractive to work for and deal with.

We must not, however, make the mistake of confusing successful and unsuccessful "brands." The world is full of products and services that have brand names, but which are not successful brands. They fall down on other important criteria:

- A successful brand has a name, symbol, or design (or some combination) that identifies the "product" of an organization and is a fundamental basis for a sustainable competitive advantage. For example, Coca-Cola, IBM, BMW, Harley-Davidson.
- A successful brand contributes to superior profit and market performance.
- Brands are only assets if they have sustainable competitive advantage.
- Like other assets, brands depreciate without further investment, for example, Hoover, Singer, MG, and so on.

Seen in this light, pseudo brands can never be mistaken for the real thing, because the genuine brand provides added brand value. Customers believe that the product:

- Will be reliable
- Is the best
- Is something that will suit them better than product X
- Is designed with them in mind

These beliefs are based not only on perceptions of the brand in relation to other brands, but also on customers' perceptions of the company behind the brand and beliefs about its reputation and integrity.

The title "successful brand" has to be earned. The company has to invest in everything it does so that the product meets the physical needs of customers, as well as having an image to match their emotional needs. Thus it must provide concrete and rational benefits that are sustained by a marketing mix that is compatible, believable, and relevant.

AT&T is an example of what can happen to a brand if it is not sustained by a consistent ability to deliver superior value to customers. The value of the AT&T brand is in decline because the competitive performance of AT&T has been in decline.

The Components of a Brand

There are three principal components of a brand: brand strategy, brand positioning, and brand personality.

The first of these, brand strategy, stems from the position of the brand in the portfolio of the organization that owns the brand. Later in this chapter we will see that some poor brands are competing in high-growth markets, while others are competing in mature or declining markets. Thus the objectives for the brand could well call for different levels and types of investment (invest or harvest), innovation (relaunch, augment, cut costs), sales and distribution patterns (extension, reduction, broad, narrow), market share, usage aims (new, existing behavior), and so on.

The second component, brand positioning, is concerned with what the brand actually does and with what it competes. In other words, brand positioning starts with the physical, or functional, aspects of the brand (the center circle in Figure 7-1). For instance, Canada Dry is positioned in the UK as a mixer for brandies and whiskies, rather than as a soft drink competing with Coca-Cola, Pepsi-Cola and 7-Up. Tide is a tough, general-purpose detergent, rather than a product for delicate fabrics. Singapore Airlines is positioned as the businessperson's airline but it also competes successfully for budget/economy travelers by offering competitive prices.

There are usually several main motivators in any market, only one or two of which are of real importance. These dimensions are best seen as bipolar scales along which brands can be positioned. For example:

- Expensive/inexpensive
- Strong/mild
- Big/small
- Hot/cold
- Fast/slow
- Male/female

Because they are so obvious, they are easy to research in order to establish which are those that people regard as the most fundamental basis for buying. It will be obvious that not all consumers look for the same functional performance, so market segmentation becomes important at this stage. A useful starting point in this kind of primary market interpretation is to draw a bipolar map, as shown in Figure 7-3. Getting more specific, Figure 7-4 shows a bipolar map for detergents.

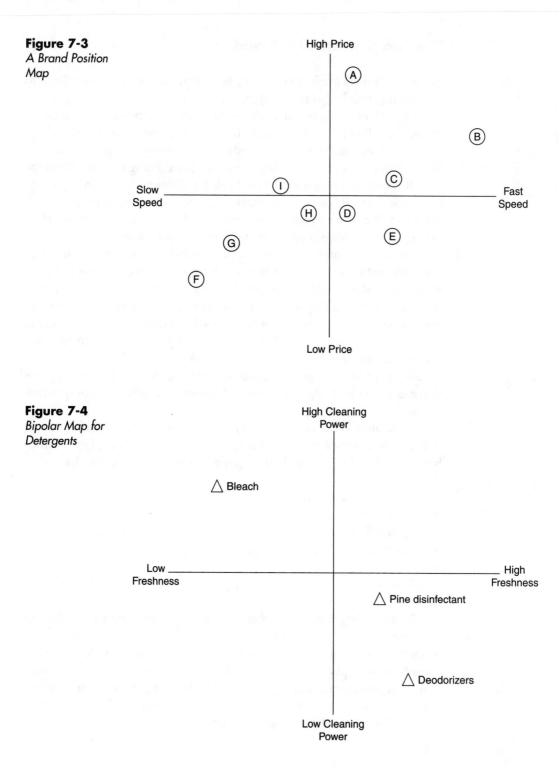

Figure 7-3
A Brand Position Map

Figure 7-4
Bipolar Map for Detergents

Clearly the physical dimensions of any market will change over time, so this kind of basic research should be conducted on a regular basis to establish, firstly, what the main dimensions are and, secondly, whether the position of any competing product has changed.

In highly mature markets, brands are likely to be positioned close to one another, thus indicating that the basic functional or physical characteristics are less likely to be the sole basis on which a product or service is selected.

Brand personality, the third component of a brand, is a useful descriptor for the total impression that consumers have of brands. In many ways brands are like people, with their own physical, emotional, and personality characteristics. Thus two brands can be very similar in terms of their functions, but have very different personalities.

Sensual appeal, that is, how the product or service looks, feels, sounds, and so on, can have an important influence on buying behavior. It is easy to imagine how this appeal can differ in the case of, say, cigarettes or cars. *Rational* appeal, that is, how the product or service performs, what they contain, and so on, can also have an important influence on buying behavior. *Emotional* appeal, however, is perhaps the most important and has a lot to do with the psychological rewards the products or services offer, the moods they conjure up, the associations they evoke, and so on. It is easy to imagine the overt appeal of certain products as being particularly masculine, or feminine, or chic, or workmanlike, or flashy.

The point is that, for any brand to be successful, all these elements have to be consistent, as they will all affect the brand's personality, and it is this personality, above all else, that represents the brand's totality and makes one brand more desirable, or appealing, than another.

Put at its simplest, it is a brand's personality that converts a commodity into something unique and enables a higher price to be charged for it.

Figure 7-5 combines brand functionality and personality in a matrix.

The vertical axis refers to a brand's ability to satisfy utilitarian needs, such as quality, reliability, effectiveness, and so on, where the consumer's need for such benefits is high. The horizontal axis represents the brand's ability to help consumers express something about themselves, be it, for example, their mood, their membership of a particular social group, their status, and so on. Brands are chosen on this dimension because they have values that exist over and above their physical values. We call this dimension "representationality." For example, products such as Yves St Laurent neckties are effective brands for expressing particular personality types and roles, with functional attributes being secondary.

It is possible, by means of market research, to identify the degree to which consumers perceive a brand as reflecting functionality and representationality.

Figure 7-5
Brand Function-
ality and
Personality

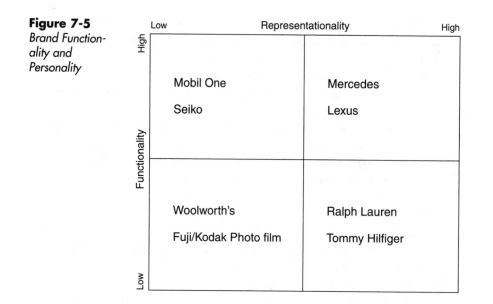

Having done this, it is then possible for the marketer to consider how best to use the available resources to support the brand.

For products and services in the top right-hand box (that is, ones that both provide functional excellence and are good vehicles for non-verbal communication about themselves), a creative strategy that reinforces consumers' lifestyle requirements should be adopted, and communicated through appropriate media channels. Additionally, the quality of the brand needs to be maintained through high standards of quality control and continuous product development. Also, strict control over channels of distribution should be exercised.

For products and services in the top left-hand box (that is, ones bought by consumers because of a high utilitarian need rather than because of a need to say something about themselves), product superiority needs to be continuously maintained, as "me-tooism" is a continuous threat to such brands. Also, heavy promotional support is important in communicating the functional benefits of the brand.

For products and services in the bottom right-hand box (that is, ones that are less important for their functional attributes, but which are high as symbolic devices), it is clearly important to reinforce continuously the cultural and lifestyle aspects of the brand and a heavy advertising presence is almost certainly more important than product-development issues.

For products and services in the bottom left-hand box (that is, those that are bought by consumers who are not particularly concerned about either functional differences or self image), successful branding is more difficult, because it is likely that they must have wide distribution and be very price competitive. Cost leadership, then, becomes important to the brand owner, which entails being an efficient producer. Brands in this sector are obviously vulnerable, and to succeed an attractive price proposition is usually necessary.

The Company as a Brand

It will, by now, be obvious that it is frequently the case that a company's name is the brand used on different products or services, as opposed to an individual brand name for each product, as in the case of, say, Marlboro.

To present themselves in the most favorable way, firms develop a corporate identity program, ensuring that all forms of external communication are coordinated and presented in the same way. Corporate identity can be a valuable asset, which if effectively managed, can make a major contribution to brand success.

Classic examples of this include IBM, ICI, Mercedes, Sony, Yamaha, JCB, and countless others. It works well as a policy, given the prohibitive costs of building individual brands *ab inititio*, providing the product or service in question is consistent with the corporate image. While there is a "halo" effect of using a famous corporate name on a new product or service, there are also risks to the total portfolio, should any one new product prove to be disastrous. For example, Levi-Strauss was known and respected for jeans. Their extension into Levi tailored classic suits failed. Adding the name Pierre Cardin to bathroom tiles in Spain did little for the value of this core brand!

Peter Doyle developed a useful matrix for considering what an appropriate strategy might be toward corporate, as opposed to individual, product branding. This is given in Figure 7-6.

Global vs. Local Brands

So, if we can now distinguish between a brand and a pseudo brand, what is a global brand? Here is a definition: a global brand is a product that bears the same name and logo and presents the same or similar message all over the world. Usually, the product is aimed at the same target market and is promoted and presented in much the same way.

A survey that encompassed 10,000 people in the United States, Japan, and Europe discovered that the following were the ten most widely

Figure 7-6
Corporate Branding Positions

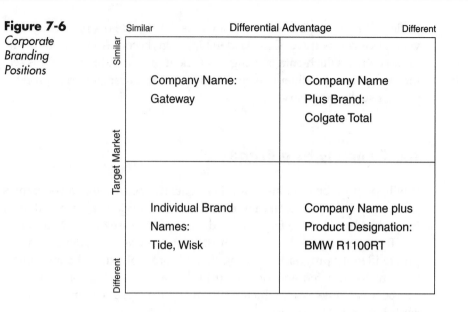

recognized brand names. At the top was Coca-Cola, followed by Sony, Mercedes-Benz, Kodak, Disney, Nestlé, Toyota, McDonald's, IBM, and Pepsi. Probably there are a few surprises here, but what are the alternative options to having a global brand?

There are only two broad options:

1. Develop a global brand.
2. Have a local or regional brand in each country or region of operation.

What fuels the decision making regarding which choice? Clearly, it depends mainly upon the types of customer. However, there are some other practical considerations to take into account, such as the cost of production, the distribution costs, promotion, competitive market structure, channels, legal constraints, and operational structures.

Procter & Gamble experienced major problems trying to get their detergents established under one brand name across Europe. For one thing, they had to try to accommodate different types of washing machines, different types of water, different washing habits, and different cultures. Then there was the business of coming to grips with market structures and competition, and, last but not least (because it can be the greatest barrier of all), getting its own operating structure right.

Clearly, then, the benefits to be derived from economies of scale have to be weighed very carefully against the difficulty of setting up a global brand, as the following matrix, Figure 7-7, shows.

Figure 7-7
*Global versus
Local Brands*

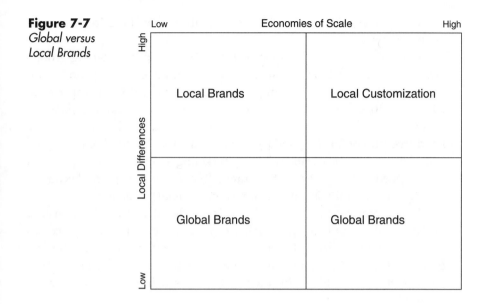

Although three of the boxes reduce to fairly obvious choices, the top right-hand box is still something of a poser. Our own inclination is that, when faced with high difficulty but with high economies of scale, we would endeavor to establish global brands.

Of course, while the matrix only represents a concept, it is possible to develop concrete data for it in much the same way as the directional policy matrix, which is described later in this chapter. For example, all the savings attributable to economies of scale could be calculated, for example, manufacturing, research and development, purchasing, logistics, better management control, and so on. Equally, local differences could be assessed, taking into account the infrastructure of markets, demand homogeneity, culture, political/legal framework, market structure, competition, and the like.

By looking at international markets in this way, the odds come out very much higher in favor of global brands as against local ones. Predictions about future trends only serve to reinforce this hypothesis. For example, in the EU (European Union) it has been predicted that:

- Prices will tend to harmonize toward the lowest levels.
- Purchasers will tend to buy on a Pan-European basis to gain maximum price advantage.
- Major distributors (especially importers) will operate transnationally and take advantage of remaining price differentials and low-cost suppliers.

There is already much evidence to confirm that these trends are already happening.

The portents are clear. Already, large Pan-European retailing groups are appearing and if an organization does not have a European brand, especially if it is in fast-moving consumer goods, it does not appear to have very good prospects. It is brand names that win customers, make a profit, and create customer loyalty. As stated earlier, Nestlé wanted to buy Rowntree purely for its brands, not for its factories. A good brand, at the end of the day, is the company's best marketing asset. For that reason, it is shortsighted not to invest in the brand. To allow it to slip and become a "me-too" commodity is tantamount to commercial vandalism.

To summarize, a successful brand is an identifiable product, service, person, or place augmented in such a way that the buyer or user perceives relevant, unique added values that match their needs most closely. Its success results from being able to sustain these added values against competitors. Being able to do this on a global basis will bring great rewards, but it will not be easy.

PRODUCT LIFE CYCLE

Product life cycle is the postulate that if a new product is successful at the introductory stage (and many fail at this point), then repeat purchases gradually grow and spread, and the rate of sales growth increases. At this stage, competitors often enter the market, and their additional promotional expenditures further expand the market. But no market is infinitely expandable, and eventually the *rate* of growth slows as the product moves into its maturity stage. The point eventually is reached at which there are too many firms in the market, price wars break out, some firms drop out of the market, and finally the market itself falls into decline. Figure 7-8 illustrates this apparently universal phenomenon, which is critical in successful strategic planning.

Although the product life cycle may well be a useful practical generalization for a product category, specific product brand life cycles are determined more by the activities of the company than by any underlying marketing principle. For example, Marlboro cigarettes, although exhibiting all the characteristics of the classic product life cycle, recorded new sales heights after the decision in the 1950s to reposition the brand from a women's cigarette to a cigarette for anyone who identified with the archetype of freedom. Had this repositioning not been made, the brand would probably have gone into decline.

Figure 7-8
*Product Life
Cycle*

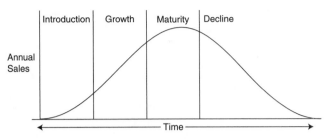

Motorcycles were a product category in a declining life cycle until companies like Honda, Harley-Davidson, and others revitalized the entire category with new models, new target markets, new brand images and positions, and owner groups like HOG (Harley Owners Group, which now has more than 500,000 dues-paying members around the world). Harley, for example, extended its market beyond the traditional Harley market of "cops and robbers" (i.e., the police and the Hell's Angels) to the Rubbie (rich urban bikers) market and to women (now over 10 percent of the market for Harley motorcycles).

From a management point of view, the product life cycle concept is useful in that it focuses attention on the future sales pattern that is likely if no corrective action is taken. Several courses of action are open to maintain the profitable sales of a product over its life cycle.

The implications of the product life cycle concept are important in every element of the marketing mix. Figure 7-9 shows the degree of profitability, while Figure 7-10 gives a guide to how the marketing mix has to change over its life cycle. In addition to this, however, every other element also has to change. For example, if a company rigidly adheres to a premium pricing policy at the mature stage of the product life cycle, when markets are often overcrowded and price wars begin, it loses market share unless it repositions itself as a luxury or premium-priced product.

The same applies to promotion. During the early phase of product introduction, the task of advertising is to create awareness. During the growth phase, the task may be to change to creation of a favorable attitude toward the product. The policy toward channels should not be fixed. At first, one is concerned with distribution of the product in the most important channels. During the growth phase, one has to consider ways of reaching the new channels that want the product.

Drawing a product life cycle can be extremely difficult, even with time series analysis. This is connected with the complex question of measurement of market share. A firm needs to be concerned with its share (or its proportion of volume or value) of an *actual* market, rather than with a

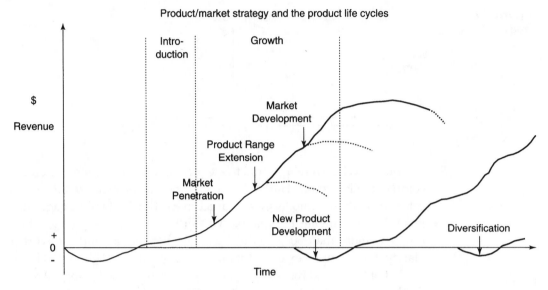

Figure 7-9
Profitability during Product Life Cycle

potential market. One of the most frequent mistakes made by companies that do not understand what market share really means is to assume that their company has only a small share of the market. In short, if a company is successful, it probably has a large share of a small market segment. Table 7-1 shows a checklist used by one large company to help it determine the location of its markets in the life cycle.

DIFFUSION OF INNOVATIONS

For completely new product categories, an interesting and useful extension of the product life cycle is what is known as *diffusion of innovation. Diffusion* is the adoption of new products or services over time by customers within social systems as encouraged by marketing.

Figure 7-10
Product Life Cycle Characteristics

Characteristic	Introduction	Growth	Maturity	Decline
Competitors	None/few	Several	Maximum	Fewer
Promotion	Concept	Features	Price	None
Place	Limited	Multi-channel	Mass	Mass
Profit	Investment spending	High	Declining	Milking—Cash Cow
Price	Skimming	High to premium	Competitive	Cutthroat
Product	Innovation	Added benefits	Brand extension	Line extension

TABLE 7-1 Guide to Market Maturity

Maturity Stage Factor	Introduction	Growth	Mature	Declining
1 Growth rate	Much greater than GNP (on small base).	Sustained growth above GNP. New customers. New suppliers. Rate decelerates toward end of stage.	Approximately equals GNP.	Declining demand. Market shrinks as users' needs change.
2 Predictability of growth potential	Hard to define accurately. Small portion of demand being satisfied. Market forecasts differ widely.	Greater percentage of demand is met and upper limits of demand becoming clearer. Discontinuities, such as price reductions based on economies of scale, may occur.	Potential well defined. Competition specialized to satisfy needs of specific segments.	Known and limited.
3 Product line proliferation	Specialized lines to meet needs of early customers.	Rapid expansion.	Proliferation slows or ceases.	Lines narrow as unprofitable products dropped.
4 Number of competitors	Few	Reaches maximum. New entrants attracted by growth and high margins. Some consolidation begins toward end of stage.	Entrenched positions established. Further shakeout of marginal competitors.	New entrants unlikely. Competitors continue to decline.
5 Market share distribution	Unstable. Shares react unpredictably to entrepreneurial insights and timing.	Increasing stability. Typically, a few competitors emerging as strong.	Stable with a few companies often controlling much of industry.	Highly concentrated or fragmented as industry segments and/or is localized.
6 Customer stability	Trial usage with little customer loyalty.	Some loyalty. Repeat usage with many seeking alternative suppliers.	Well-developed buying patterns with customer loyalty. Competitors understand purchase dynamics and it is difficult for a new supplier to win over accounts.	Extremely stable. Suppliers dwindle and customers less motivated to seek alternatives.
7 Ease of entry	Normally easy. No one dominates. Customers' expectations uncertain. If barriers exist, they are usually technology, capital, or fear of the unknown.	More difficult. Market franchises and/or economies of scale may exist, yet new business is still available without directly confronting competition.	Difficult. Market leaders established. New business must be "won" from others.	Little or no incentive to enter.
8 Technology	Plays an important role in matching product characteristics to market needs. Frequent product changes.	Product technology vital early, while process technology more important later in this stage.	Process and material substitution focus. Product requirements well known and relatively undemanding. May be a thrust to renew the industry via new technology.	Technological content is known, stable, and accessible.

Diffusion refers to the cumulative percentage of adopters of a new product or service over time. Everett Rogers examined some of the social forces that explain the product life cycle. The body of knowledge, often referred to as *reference theory* (which incorporates work on group norms, group pressures, and other dynamics), helps explain the snowball effect of diffusion. Rogers found that the actual rate of diffusion is a function of the following aspects of a product:

- Relative advantage (over existing products)
- Compatibility (with factors such as lifestyles and values)
- Communicability (is it easy to communicate?)
- Complexity (is it complicated?)
- Divisibility (can it be tried out on a small scale before commitment?)

Diffusion is also a function of the newness of the product itself, which can be classified broadly in three headings, as follows:

1. Continuous innovation (e.g., the new miracle ingredient)
2. Dynamically continuous innovation (e.g., disposable lighter)
3. Discontinuous (e.g., microwave oven)

However, Rogers found that for all new products, not everyone adopts new products at the same time and that a universal pattern emerges, as shown in Figure 7-11.

In general, innovators think for themselves and try new things (when relevant). Early adopters, who have status in society, are opinion leaders, and they adopt successful products, making them acceptable and respectable. The early majority, who are more conservative and who have slightly above-average status, are more deliberate and only adopt products that have social approbation. The late majority, who have below-

Figure 7-11
Adopter Categories

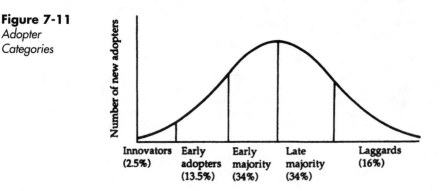

average status and are skeptical, adopt products much later than the first three categories. The laggards, with lower status and income and less education than the earlier adopters, see life through the rearview mirror and are the last to adopt products.

This particular piece of research can be very useful, particularly for advertising and personal selling. For example, if you can develop a typology for opinion leaders, you can target your early advertising and sales effort specifically at them. Once the first 7 to 8 percent of opinion leaders have adopted your product, there is a good chance that the early majority will try it. Once 10 to 12 percent is reached, the champagne can be opened, because there is a good chance that the rest will adopt your product.

The general characteristics of opinion leaders are that they are venturesome, socially integrated, cosmopolitan, socially mobile, and privileged. So you need to ask about the specific characteristics of these customers in your particular industry. You can then tailor your advertising and selling message specifically to these customers.

Diffusion of innovation analysis can, however, be both a practical diagnostic and a forecasting tool. Table 7-2 illustrates how forecasts, and eventually strategic marketing plans, were developed from the use of the diffusion of innovation curve for computerized business systems for the construction industry in one market. In the example, three independent estimates are made of market size to establish the current position on the diffusion of innovation curve.

TABLE 7-2 Using Diffusion Theory to Create Sales Objectives

1	Number of contracting firms	160,596	
2	Number of firms employing 4–79 direct employees	43,400	
3	Exclude painters, plasterers, etc.	6,100	
4	Conservative estimate of main target area	37,300 or 23% of total	(1)
5	Using the Pareto (80/20 rule) likelihood that 20 percent will be main target area, i.e., 160,596 x 20%	32,000	(2)
6	Total number of firms in construction industry	217,785	
7	Number of firms classified by sales from $200,000 to $2,000,000		
	$100–499	26,698	
	$500–999	10,651	
	$1,000–5,000	5,872	
		43,221	(3)

Figure 7-12
Diffusion of
Innovation
Curves

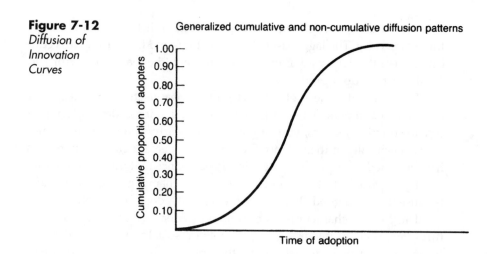

The diffusion of innovation curve, in conjunction with the product life cycle, helps to explain the dynamics of markets. Figure 7-12 illustrates this relation. It shows that when all potential users of a product are using it, the market is a replacement market.

PRODUCT PORTFOLIO THEORY

We might well imagine that at any point in time, a review of a company's different products would reveal different stages of growth, maturity, and decline. In Figure 7-13, the dotted line represents the time of analysis. This shows product A in severe decline, product B in its maturity stage, and product C in its introductory stage. If the objective is to grow in profitability over a long period of time, analysis of the product portfolio should reveal a situation like the one in Figure 7-14, in which new product introductions are timed to ensure continuous sales growth.

Figure 7-13
Stages of
Product Life
Cycle over
Time

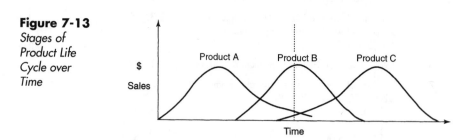

Figure 7-14
*Product Portfolio:
Growth Plan*

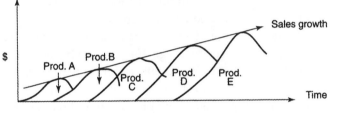

The idea of a portfolio is for a company to meet its objectives by balancing sales growth, cash flow, and risk. As individual products progress or decline and as markets grow or shrink, the overall nature of the company's product portfolio changes. It is therefore essential that the entire portfolio be reviewed regularly and that an active policy toward new product development and divestment of old products be pursued. In this respect, the work of the Boston Consulting Group (BCG), begun in the early 1960s, has had a profound effect on the way managers think about this subject and about their product and market strategy.

UNIT COSTS AND MARKET SHARE

There are two parts to the thinking behind the work of the BCG. One is concerned with *market share*, the other with *market growth*. One becomes better at doing things the more one does them. This phenomenon is known as the *learning curve*. It manifests itself especially with items such as labor efficiency, work specialization, and methods improvement.

Benefits such as process innovations, productivity from plant and equipment, and product design improvements are a part of the *experience effect*. In addition to the experience effect, and not necessarily mutually exclusive, are *economies of scale* that come with growth. For example, capital costs do not increase in direct proportion to capacity, which results in lower depreciation charges per unit of output, lower operating costs in the form of the number of operatives, lower marketing, sales, administration, and research and development costs, and lower raw materials and shipping costs. It is generally recognized, however, that cost decline applies more to the value-added elements of cost than to bought-in supplies. The BCG discovered that costs decline by as much as 30 percent for every doubling of cumulative output and that costs decline forever—that is, every time cumulative output doubles, costs decline by a percentage, the so-called *experience curve* percentage.

The implications of this phenomenon for marketing strategy are quite profound. If this reduction in costs is obtained, the firm with the greater volume is going to have a cost advantage over the firm with smaller volume. With a cost advantage, the firm can be more competitive (with more margin to spend on any or all elements of the marketing mix). Irrespective of what happens to the price of your product, providing you have the greatest volume (and therefore the highest market share), you will always be more profitable and more competitive than your competitors.

This is not to say that there is a casual relation between market share and profitability. The experience effect is not automatic. Simple increases in production or output without working smarter do not lead to declining costs. The experience effect is a reflection of companies in industries that constantly continue to innovate in design, process, and materials to increase their productivity and lower their costs. Integrated circuits and computer memory are two spectacular examples of the experience effect in action.

Research has confirmed that market share and profitability are related. However, as previously discussed, you have to be certain that you have carefully defined your market or segment. This explains why it is apparently possible for many small firms to be profitable in large markets.[1] The reason is that they have a large share of a smaller market segment. This is another reason why understanding market segmentation is the key to successful marketing. Nevertheless, the evidence provided by the BCG shows overwhelmingly that these laws apply universally for consumer, industrial, and service markets.

As for *market growth*, in markets that are growing at a very low rate per annum, it is extremely difficult and expensive to increase market share. This is usually because the market is in the steady state (possibly in the maturity phase of the product life cycle) and is dominated by a few large firms that have probably reached a state of equilibrium that is difficult to upset.

In markets that are experiencing a period of high growth, the most attractive policy is to gain market share by taking a larger proportion of the market growth than your competitors. However, such a policy is expensive in promotional terms. Many companies prefer to sit tight and enjoy rates of growth lower than the market rate. The problem with this approach is that these companies are losing market share, which gives cost advantages (hence margin advantages) to competitors.

---

[1] See Simon, Hermann (1996). *Hidden Champions*. Boston, Mass.: Harvard Business School Press, for an excellent description of small companies with dominant world market positions.

Because experience with product life cycles shows that the market growth rate will fall when the maturity stage is reached and the market inevitably becomes price sensitive, unless expenses are cut, profitability declines. The challenge to marketers is to extend the product life cycle by innovating in product features, finding new target markets, repositioning the product, and so on. When this is done, the "inevitable" demise of a product can be avoided and the product can be pushed into an earlier and more profitable stage of the life cycle.[2]

THE BOSTON CONSULTING GROUP MATRIX

The BCG combined the foregoing ideas in the form of a simple matrix, which has profound implications for the firm, especially with regard to *cash flow*. Profits are not always an appropriate indicator of portfolio performance, because they often do not reflect changes in the liquid assets of a company, such as inventories, capital equipment, or receivables, and thus do not indicate the true scope for future development. Cash flow, on the other hand, is a key determinant of a company's ability to develop its product portfolio.

The BCG matrix classifies a firm's products according to cash flow and cash generation along the two dimensions: relative market share and market growth rate. Market share is used because it is an indicator of the ability of a product to generate cash. Market growth is used because it is an indicator of the product's cash requirements. The measurement of market share used is the product's share *relative* to the firm's largest competitor. This is important because it reflects the degree of dominance enjoyed by the product in the market. For example, if company A has a 20 percent market share and its largest competitor also has a 20 percent market share, this position is usually less favorable than if company A had a 20 percent market share and its largest competitor had only a 10 percent market share. The relative ratios would be 1:1 compared with 2:1. This ratio, or measure of market dominance, is measured along a horizontal axis (Figure 7-15).

The definition of high relative market share is taken to be a ratio of one or greater than one. The cut-off point for high, as opposed to low, market growth is defined according to the prevailing circumstances in the industry, but this is often taken as 10 percent. There is, however, no reason why the

---

[2]Theodore Levitt, "Exploit the Product Life Cycle," *Harvard Business Review,* November-December 1965, pp. 81-94.

Figure 7-15
*The Boston
Consulting
Group Product
Portfolio Matrix*

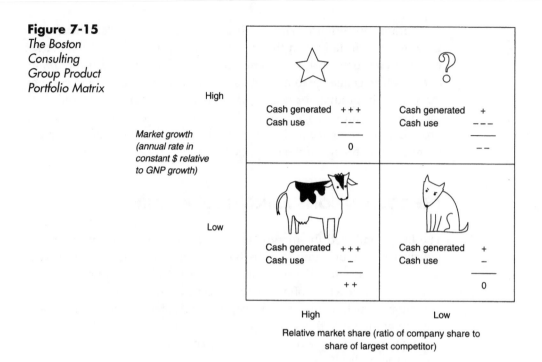

dividing line on the vertical axis cannot be zero, or even a negative number. It depends entirely on industry (or segment) growth or decline. Sometimes, in very general markets, gross national product (GNP) can be used.

The somewhat picturesque labels attached to each of the four categories of products give some indication of the prospects for products in each quadrant. The *question mark* is a new product that has not yet achieved a dominant market position and a high cash flow, or perhaps it once had such a position but has slipped back. Question mark products are high users of cash because they are in a growth market. The *star* is a relatively new and successful product that has achieved a high market share and may be self-financing in cash terms. *Cash cows* are leaders in mature markets in which there is little additional growth, but a great deal of stability. These are excellent generators of cash and tend to use little because of the state of the market. *Dogs* may generate a moderate amount of cash but often have little future. They may be candidates for divestment and thus a source of cash, although often such products fall into a category aptly described by Peter Drucker as "investments in managerial ego."

Given this analysis, the task of product portfolio management becomes a lot clearer. What you are seeking to do is to use the surplus cash generated by the cash cows to invest in stars and to invest in a selected number of question marks (Figure 7-16).

Figure 7-16
*Product Portfolio
Management*

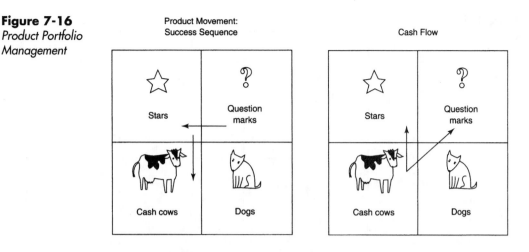

The BCG matrix can be used to forecast the market position of your products, say, three to five years from now, if you continue to pursue your current policies. Such a framework also shows the flow of marketing objectives, such as "to achieve 10 percent growth and 20 percent return on investment." Such an objective may be self-defeating. For example, to accept a 10 percent growth rate in a market that is growing at, for example, 15 percent per annum, is likely to prove disastrous in the long run. Likewise, to try to achieve a much higher than market growth rate in a low-growth market is certain to lead to unnecessary price wars and market disruption.

Unfortunately, many companies started using the BCG matrix indiscriminately during the 1970s. As a result, it gradually lost its universal appeal. The reason had more to do with lack of real understanding on the part of management than with defects in the method. Nonetheless, there are circumstances in which great caution is required in the use of the BCG matrix. Imagine a company with 80 percent of its products in low-growth markets and only 20 percent of its products as market leaders. The matrix would look like the one in Figure 7-17. Almost 65 percent of the company's products are "dogs." To divest these may be tantamount to throwing the baby out with the bath water.

Consider industries in which market share for any single product in the range has little to do with its profitability. Often a low-market-share product enjoys the same production, distribution, and marketing economies of scale as other products in the portfolio, as, for example, in the case of beer and chemical products. For example, a product manufactured with basically the same components as other large-market-share products is manufactured in the same plant as part of a similar process and is distributed on the same vehicles and through the same outlets. It is

Figure 7-17
*A Doggy Product
Portfolio*

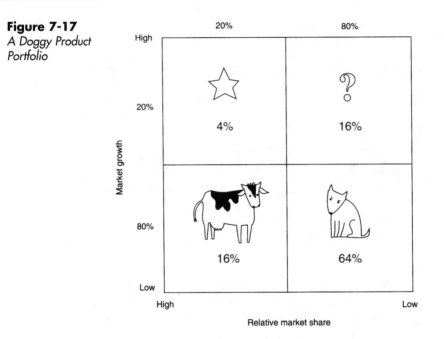

easy to see how this low-market-share product can indeed be extremely profitable.

None of this, however, invalidates the work of the BCG, the principles of which can be applied to companies, divisions, subsidiaries, strategic business units, product groups, and products. If great care is taken with the market share axis, the BCG matrix is an extremely valuable planning tool.

THE DPM MATRIX

Complications such as those outlined earlier make the BCG matrix irrelevant in certain situations and thus lead us to develop the Directional Policy Matrix (DPM) discussed below. Although it is impossible to give absolute rules about what these situations are, businesses should adhere to the following two principles: (1) A business should define its markets in such a way that it can ensure that its costs for key activities are competitive and (2) in such a way that it can develop specialized skills in servicing those markets and overcome a relative cost disadvantage. Both ways of defining itself have to be related to a company's *distinctive competence.*

The BCG approach is fairly criticized as relying on two single factors, that is, relative market share and market growth. To overcome this limitation, and to provide a more flexible approach, General Electric and McKinsey jointly developed a multifactor approach using the same fundamental ideas as the BCG. They used *industry attractiveness* and *business strengths* as the two main axes and built on these dimensions from a number of variables. With these variables and a scheme for weighting them according to their importance, products (or businesses) are classified into one of nine cells in a three-by-three matrix. The same purpose is served as in the BCG matrix (i.e., comparing investment opportunities among products or businesses) but with the difference that multiple criteria are used. These criteria vary according to circumstances but often include those shown in Figure 7-18.

It is not necessary to use a nine-box matrix, and many managers prefer to use a four-box matrix similar to the BCG box. This is our preferred method, because it seems to be more easily understood by and useful to managers.

The four-box Directional Policy Matrix is shown in Figure 7-19. The circles represent sales into an industry, market, or segment. In the same way as in the BCG matrix, each is proportional to that contribution of the segment to sales.

Figure 7-18
The General Electric McKinsey Matrix

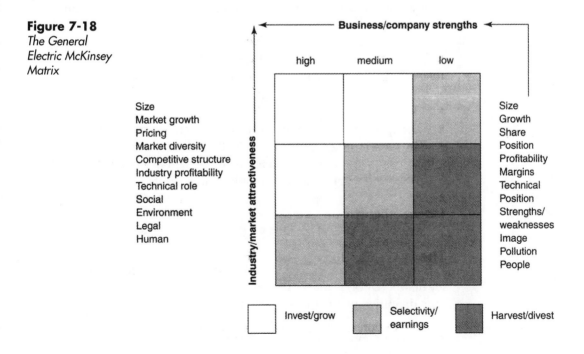

Size
Market growth
Pricing
Market diversity
Competitive structure
Industry profitability
Technical role
Social
Environment
Legal
Human

Business/company strengths

high   medium   low

Industry/market attractiveness

Size
Growth
Share
Position
Profitability
Margins
Technical
Position
Strengths/
weaknesses
Image
Pollution
People

Invest/grow   Selectivity/earnings   Harvest/divest

Figure 7-19
*Directional Policy
Matrix*

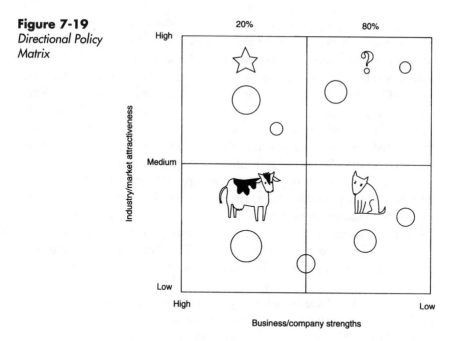

Rather than only two variables, the criteria used for each axis are totally relevant and specific to the company using the matrix. It shows the following:

- Markets categorized on a scale of attractiveness to the firm
- The relative strengths of the firm in each of these markets
- The relative importance of each market

The specific criteria for determining attractiveness are decided by key executives using the matrix. Table 7-3 lists factors contributing to market attractiveness. It is advisable to use no more than five or six factors; otherwise, the exercise becomes too complex and loses its focus.

THE STRATEGIC BUSINESS UNIT

The level at which a firm can be analyzed with use of the directional policy matrix (DPM) is that of the *strategic business unit* (SBU). The most common definition of an SBU is as follows:

- It has common segments and competitors for most of its products.
- It is a competitor in an external market.

TABLE 7-3 Classification of Market Attractiveness Factors

Factors	Example Weight
Growth rate	40
Accessible market size	20
Profit potential	40
Total	100

Note: Because profit equals market size multiplied by margin multiplied by growth, it would be reasonable to expect the *weighting* against each of these to be at *least* as shown, although an even higher weight on *growth* would be understandable in some circumstances (in which case, the corresponding weight for the others is reduced).

- It is a discrete, separate, and identifiable entity.
- Its management has control over activities and resources that are critical to success.

Let us take a hypothetical two-dimensional market into which a number of products (A, B, C, D, and E) are sold (Figure 7-20). Each square might be considered a segment, and various combinations can be considered to be the market, as follows:

a. The actual product-customer cells served
b. The intersection of product function A, B, C and customer groups 2, 3, 4
c. Product functions A, B, C for *all* customer groups
d. Customer groups 2, 3, 4 for *all* product functions
e. The entire matrix

Figure 7-20
Factors that Contribute to Market Attractiveness

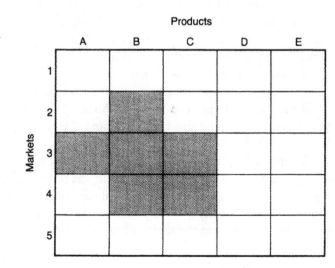

Preparation

Before analysis is begun, the following preparation is recommended:

- Ensure that product profiles are available for all products or services to be scored.
- Define the markets in which the products or services compete.
- Define the time period being scored. Three years is recommended.

- Define the competitors against which the products or services are to be scored.
- Ensure sufficient data are available to score the factors (when no data are available, this is not a problem as long as a sensible approximation can be made for the factors).
- Ensure up-to-date sales forecasts are available for all products or services, including any new products or services.

The DPM is useful when there is more than one (at least three and a maximum of ten are suggested) market or segment between which the planner wishes to distinguish. These can be either existing or potential markets, in which a market is defined using the following steps.

> An identifiable group of customers with requirements in common are, or may become, *significant* in determining a separate strategy.

A market in this sense is clearly a matter of management judgment. At the beginning of any exercise using the DPM, the priority must be to define correctly the unit of analysis in terms of the combinations of product and markets. For example, it is clearly possible to put twenty-five circles (or crosses, where there are no sales) on a portfolio matrix with markets 1 through 5 on the vertical axis and each of products A through E on the horizontal axis (i.e., choice e, listed earlier), but that would result in a confusing array of circles and crosses.

It would also be possible to put six circles on a matrix. That is, the actual product-customer cells served (choice a), with markets 2, 3, and 4 on the vertical axis and products A, B, and C as appropriate for each of these served markets on the horizontal axis.

An alternative to individual plotting of products A, B, and C is to plot an aggregate value or volume for all products in any served market. Any of the combinations listed in the example above also could be used. The user has to decide early exactly what will be the unit of analysis for the purpose of determining the size of each circle that appears in the matrix.

To summarize, the principal unit of analysis for the purpose of entering data is the user's definition of *product market*.

Analysis Team

To improve the quality of scoring, it is recommended that a group of people from a number of different functions score. This encourages the challenging of traditional views by means of discussion. We recommend that no more than six people be involved in the analysis.

MARKET ATTRACTIVENESS AND BUSINESS STRENGTH

Market attractiveness is a measure of the *potential* of the marketplace to yield growth in sales and profits. It is important to emphasize that assessment of market attractiveness is an objective process, made with data *external* to the organization. The criteria themselves are determined by the organization performing the exercise and are relevant to the objectives the organization is trying to achieve, but are independent of the position of the organization in its markets. It is an objective assessment of an organization's ability to satisfy market needs relative to competitors' ability to satisfy needs. *Business strength and position* is a measure of an organization's *actual* strengths in the marketplace (i.e., the degree to which it can take advantage of a market opportunity).

There are ten steps in completing a directional policy matrix.

Step 1: List the Population of Products or Services for Markets That You Intend to Include in the Matrix.

The list can consist of countries, companies, subsidiaries, regions, products, markets, segments, customers, distributors, or any other unit of analysis that is important. The DPM can be used at any level in an organization and for any kind of SBU.

Step 2: Define Market Attractiveness Factors.

In this step, list the factors you want to consider in comparing the attractiveness of your markets. It is important to list the markets in which you intend to apply the criteria before deciding on the criteria themselves, since the purpose of the vertical axis is to discriminate between more and less attractive markets. The criteria themselves must be specific to the population and must not be changed for different markets in the same population. This is a combination of a number of factors. These factors, however, can usually be summarized under the following three headings (Table 7-3):

- *Growth rate.* Average annual growth rate of revenue spent by that segment for the last three years (percentage growth 1997 over 1998, *plus* percentage growth 1998 over 1999, *plus* percentage growth 2000 over 2001, divided by 3). If preferred, compound average growth rate can be used.
- *Accessible Market Size.* An attractive market not only is large but also can be accessed. One way of calculating ability to access a market is to estimate the *total* revenue of the segment in $t + 3$, *less* revenue impossible to access, regardless of investment made. Another method is to use total market size. This method does not involve any managerial judgment, which can distort the truth. *The second is the preferred and more frequently used method.* A market size factor score is simply the score multiplied by the weight (20 in the example). Note: Because profit equals market size multiplied by margin multiplied by growth, it would be reasonable to expect the *weighting* against each of these to be at *least* as shown, although an even higher weight on *growth* would be understandable in some circumstances (in which case, the corresponding weights for the others are reduced).
- *Profit Potential.* This is much more difficult to deal with and varies considerably from industry to industry. For example, Michael Porter's Five Forces model can be used to estimate the profit potential of a segment, as in the example in Table 7-4. In this example, the total score is 845.

TABLE 7-4 Profit Potential Estimate: Porter's Five Forces

Subfactor	10 = Low 1 = High	x Weight	Weighted Factor Score
1 Intensity of competition	10	50	500
2 Threat of substitute	8	5	40
3 Threat of new entrants	7	5	35
4 Power of suppliers	9	10	90
5 Power of customer	6	30	180
Profit potential factor score	40	100	845

TABLE 7-5 Profit Potential Estimate: Industry-Specific Factors

Subfactor	High	Medium	Low	x Weight	Weighted Factor Score
1 Unmet medical needs (efficacy)				30	
2 Unmet medical needs (safety)				25	
3 Unmet medical needs (convenience)				15	
4 Price potential				10	
5 Competitive intensity				10	
6 Cost of market entry				10	
Profit potential factor score					

If each of the forces is scored at 10, which is low, the total score is 1,000 in contrast to a score of 100 if each force is scored at the high level of 1. In other words, low competitive intensity, a low threat of substitutes and new entrants, and low power of suppliers and customers produce the highest score for profit potential.

An alternative is to use a combination of these and industry-specific factors. In the case of the pharmaceutical industry, the factors may be as in Table 7-5.

These are clearly a proxy for profit potential. Each is weighted according to its importance. The weights add to 100 to give a *profit potential factor score*, as in the Porter's Five Forces example cited earlier. After this calculation, the profit potential factor score is simply multiplied by the weight (40 in the example).

Variations

Naturally, growth, size, and profit do not encapsulate the requirements of all organizations. For example, in the case of an orchestra, artistic satisfaction may be an important consideration. In another case, social considerations may be important. In yet another, cyclicity may be a factor. It is possible, then, to add another heading, such as *Risk* or *Other* to the three factors listed at the beginning of Step 2. In general, however, it is possible to reduce the list to the three main headings with subfactors incorporated into them.

Step 3: Score the Relevant Products or Services for Markets.

In this step, you should score the products or services for markets against the factors defined in Step 1. One question that frequently arises is, can market attractiveness factors change while the DPM is being constructed?

The answer to this is *no*. Once agreed upon, under no circumstances should market attractiveness factors be changed; otherwise, the attractiveness of the markets is not being evaluated against common criteria, and the matrix becomes meaningless. Scores, however, are specific to each market.

Another question is, can the circles move vertically? *No* is the obvious answer, although *yes* is possible if the matrix shows the current level of attractiveness at the present time. This implies performing one set of calculations for the present according to market attractiveness factors to locate markets on the vertical axis, then performing another set of calculations for a future period (for example, three years' time) on the basis of forecasts made with the same factors. In practice, it is easier to carry out only the latter calculation, in which case the circles can move only horizontally.

Step 4: Define Business Strengths and Position Analysis Organization Level.

This is a measure of the *actual* strengths of an organization in the marketplace and differs according to market or segment opportunity. The factors that determine the strengths of an organization usually are a combination of an organization's relative strengths in relation to competitors' strengths in connection with *customer-facing needs*, that is, things required by the customer. These can often be summarized as follows:

- Product requirements
- Price requirements
- Place requirements
- Promotion requirements
- Service requirements

The weight given to each requirement should be specific to each market or segment. In the same way that *profit* on the market attractiveness axis can be broken down into subheadings, each type of requirement can be broken down and analyzed. This process is strongly recommended. These subfactors should be dealt with in the same way as the subfactors described for market attractiveness. For example, in the case of pharmaceuticals, product strengths can be represented as follows:

- Relative product strength
- Relative product safety
- Relative product convenience
- Relative cost effectiveness

Broadening the Analysis

An organization's relative strengths in meeting customer-facing needs is a function of its *capabilities* in connection with *industry-wide success factors*. For example, if a warehouse is necessary in each large town or city for any organization to succeed in an industry, and the organization performing the analysis does not have a depot, it is likely that this deficiency accounts for poor performance in the category of customer service, which is a customer requirement. If it is necessary to have low raw material costs for any organization to succeed in an industry, and the organization conducting the analysis does not have this criterion, it is likely that this deficiency accounts for poor performance in the category of price, which is a customer requirement.

In the same way that subfactors should be estimated to arrive at market attractiveness factors, an assessment of the capabilities of an organization with respect to *industry-wide success factors* can be made to understand what needs to be done in the organization to satisfy customer needs. This assessment is separate from quantification of the business strengths and position axis. The purpose is to translate the analysis into actionable propositions for other functions within the organization, such as purchasing, production, and distribution.

In the case of pharmaceuticals, for example, factors such as patent life are simply an indication of the capability of an organization to provide product differentiation. They are irrelevant to the physician but have to be taken into account by the organization conducting the analysis.

How to Deal with Business Strengths and Position

The first concern is quantification of business strengths within a market. The only way a company can do this is to understand the real needs and wants of the target customer group, find out by means of market research how well these needs are being met by existing products in the market, and seek to satisfy these needs better than their competitors.

The following is a typical calculation to assess the strength of a company in a market. The information was gathered by means of a self-assessment questionnaire. The following three questions were used to plot the firm's or SBU's position on the horizontal axis (competitive position and business strengths):

What are the key things that any competitor has to do right to succeed (i.e., what are the critical success factors in this industry sector)?

How important is each of these critical success factors (measured comparatively on a scale of 1 to 100)?

TABLE 7-6 Competitive Strength: Overall Estimate

Critical Success Factors (What Are the Key things That a Company Must Do Right to Succeed?)	Weighting (How Important Is Each of These CSFs? Score out of 100.)		Strengths/Weaknesses Analysis (Score Yourself and Each of Your Main Competitors out of 10 on Each of the CSFs, Then Multiply the Score by the Weight.)		
			Competition		
			You	Comp A	Comp B	Comp C
1 Product	20		9 = 1.8	6 = 1.2	5 = 1.0	4 = 0.8
2 Price	10		8 = 0.8	5 = 0.5	6 = 0.6	10 = 0.1
3 Service	50		5 = 2.5	9 = 4.5	7 = 3.5	6 = 3.0
4 Image	20		8 = 1.6	8 = 1.6	5 = 1.0	3 = 0.6
These should normally be viewed from the customer's point of view.	**Total 100**	**Total score x weight**	**6.7**	**7.8**	**6.1**	**5.4**

How do you and each of your competitors score (out of 10) on each of the critical success factors?

These questions yield the information necessary to make an overall assessment of the competitive strengths of an SBU (Table 7-6).

The analysis shows (1) this organization is not the market leader and (2) all competitors score more than 5.0.

The problem with this and many similar calculations is that rarely does this method allow one to discriminate sufficiently well to indicate the relative strengths of a number of products in a particular company's product or market portfolio. Many of the SBU's products would appear on the left of the matrix.

A method is needed to prevent all products from appearing on the left of the matrix. This can be achieved by use of a ratio, as in the BCG matrix. This indicates a company's position relative to the best in the market.

In the example provided, competitor A has the most strengths in the market, so your organization needs to market some improvements. To reflect this, your weighted score should be compared with that of competitor A (the highest weighted score). Thus 6.7: 7.8 = 0.86:1.

If we were to plot this on a logarithmic scale on the horizontal axis, this would place our organization to the right of the dividing line as follows:

3× | 0.3

A scale of 3× to 0.3 was chosen because such a band is likely to encapsulate most extremes of competitive advantage. If it does not, simply change it to suit your own circumstances.

Step 5: Producing the Directional Policy Matrix.

Circles are drawn on a four-box matrix. Market size (as defined in Step 2) is used to determine the area of the circle. An organization's market share can be put in as a wedge in each circle. An organization's own sales in each market also can be used. It is advisable to use both variables and compare them to see how closely actual sales match the opportunities.

Step 6: Analysis and Generation of Marketing Objectives and Strategies.

The objective of producing a DPM is to see the portfolio of products or services for markets relative to each other in the context of the criteria used. This analysis indicates whether the portfolio is well balanced and should give a clear indication of any problems. As an option, it is sometimes advisable to move to Step 7 at this point.

Step 7: Forecasting (Optional).

The forecast position of the circles is made by means of re-scoring the products or services for markets in three years' time, if the organization does not change its strategies (see Step 3). This forecast indicates whether the position is becoming worse or better. It is not absolutely necessary to change the scores on the vertical axis (see Step 3).

Step 8: Setting Marketing Objectives.

Setting marketing objectives involves changing the volumes and values or market share (marketing objectives) and the scores on the horizontal axis (relative strength in market) to achieve the desired volumes and values. Conceptually, one is picking up the circle and moving and revising it without specifying how this is to be achieved. Strategies are then defined, which involve words and changes to individual critical success factor scores (see Step 9).

Step 9: Detail Strategies.

Detailing of strategies involves making specific statements about the marketing strategies to be used to achieve the desired volumes and values.

Step 10: Sales and Profit Forecasts.

Sales and profit forecasts are made as follows (Figure 7-21):

1. Plot average percentage growth in sales revenue by segment ($t - 3$ to $t0$).
   Plot average percentage return on sales (ROS) by segment ($t - 3$ to $t0$).
2. Plot *forecast* average percentage growth in sales revenue by segment ($t0$ to $t + 3$).
   Plot *forecast* average percentage ROS by segment ($t0$ to $t + 3$).

Using the DPM

A large chemical company used the DPM to select fifty distributors from the 450 with whom they were dealing. They needed to do this because the market was in decline and the distributors had begun *buying* for customers rather than *selling* for the supplier. This led to a dramatic fall in prices. The only way the chemical company could begin to tackle the problem was by appointing a number of exclusive distributorships. The issue of which distributorships to choose was tackled by use of the DPM, be-

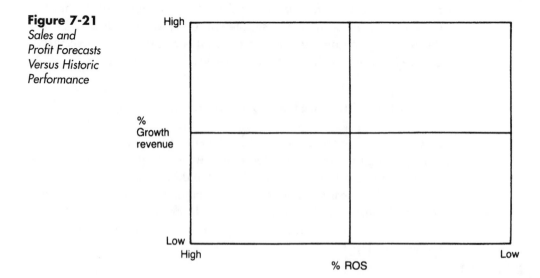

Figure 7-21
*Sales and
Profit Forecasts
Versus Historic
Performance*

cause some distributorships clearly were more attractive than others, and the company had varying strengths in its dealings with each distributor.

PRODUCT LIFE CYCLES AND PORTFOLIO MANAGEMENT

Figure 7-22 illustrates the consequences of failing to appreciate the implications of the product life cycle concept and the combination of market share and market growth.

Companies A and B both start out with question marks (wildcats) in years five and six in a growing market. Company A invests in building market share and quickly turns into a star. Company B, meanwhile, manages its products for profit over a four-year period so that while still growing it steadily loses market share (i.e., it remains a question mark or wildcat). In year ten, when the market becomes saturated (when typically competitive pressures intensify), company B with its low market share (hence typically higher costs and lower margins) cannot compete and quickly drops out of the market. Company A, on the other hand, aggressively defends its market share and goes on to enjoy a period of approximately ten years with a product that has become a cash cow. Company B, by pursuing a policy of short-term profit maximization, loses at least ten years of profit potential.

The analyses described in this chapter should be an integral part of the marketing audit. The audit should contain a product life cycle for each major product, and an attempt should be made (using other audit information) to predict the future shape of the life cycle. It should also contain a product portfolio matrix that shows the present position of the products.

Figure 7-22
Short-term Profit Maximization Versus Market Share and Long-term Profit Maximization

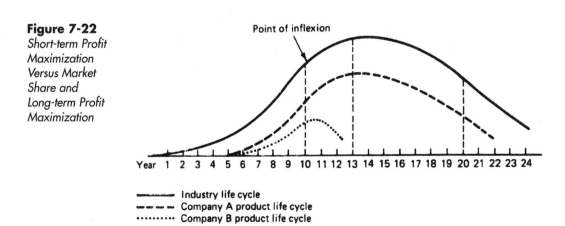

133

QUESTIONS SUCCESSFUL COMPANIES ASK

1. Do we need to strengthen our brand name?
2. What is our market share? Are we holding, gaining, or losing share?
3. What unique value do we create for our customers?
4. Should we get rid of our "dogs"? (This decision is always a matter of timing. It is possible sometimes to squeeze extra earnings from a "dog." Sometimes a "dog" is supportive of another product. Sometimes a "dog" can be profitable because it shares in the economies of scale of another product in the range.)

8 E-commerce and Internet Marketing

Technology and technological change have always been important issues. In a few years, the world, as we know it, will have ceased to exist. Networked computers are changing our environment. And again, the changes are not evolving in comfortable incremental steps, but are turbulent, erratic, and often quite unsettling. To illustrate the dramatic and paradigmatic nature of the changes brought about by information and communication technology (ICT), researchers resort to metaphors: parallels are drawn with the invention of electricity, the invention of the steam engine, or even the invention of the wheel. And as to strategic market planning, ICT is turning out to be the driving force for accelerating changes in a more competitive, global environment.

This chapter summarizes how the Internet affects strategic planning and provides a new value chain necessary to compete in this environment.

CONCEPTS AND DEFINITIONS

E-commerce: Trading goods and services over the Internet, both business-to-consumer and business-to-business. The latter is sometimes also referred to as e-business, or B to B.

Internet: The largest computer network in the world, which links people worldwide in a network that is open to all users.

Intranet: A computer network with access restricted to a single organization or company.

Extranet: A computer network with access limited to defined users. In contrast to the Internet, an extranet is not open to the general public and, in contrast to the intranet, is not entirely private.

Portals: Content suppliers that attract millions of Web users with a wide swath of information, search services, e-mail, and chat-rooms. Among the most important context providers are internet online services like America Online, Web-browsers like Netscape Communicator, and search engines such as Yahoo.

Web Browser: Software used to navigate the hyperlinks that make up the World Wide Web.

World Wide Web: Makes the Internet more accessible and easier to use by non-experts. Technically a system of hypermedia linking text, graphics, sounds, and video on computers spread across the globe.

Virtual Reality: Imaginary "worlds" created by cutting edge computer technology. For example, wearing special headsets, consumers might get the impression of walking through a house and visualizing and experiencing the rooms before the house is actually built.

TECHNOLOGICAL CONVERGENCE AND UBIQUITY OF TECHNOLOGY

In information and communication technology, it is not only the improved speed and reliability of devices that have brought about the rapid technological change, but also the convergence between the transmission of information and the processing of information. Moreover, some experts believe that there will be a convergence of different information and communication technologies into a common Internet standard.

A second development has been labeled technological ubiquity. Andersen Consulting described it as follows: "A world in which information technology is an integral part of everything we see and do in the workplace and at home."[1] In addition to its functions as a business, communications, and distribution tool, every kitchen device, car, or exercise machine is or will be packed with easy-to-use electronics that will add value to the product, be it by tailoring it to personal preferences, enabling remote communication, or what have you.

---

[1]"Technology Visioning Workshop." (Andersen Consulting, Sophia Antipolis, July 1999.)

Explosive Growth of the Internet

Arguably, the Internet represents one of the most important drivers of the technological revolution, in that it led to the development of an entirely new form of doing business, so called e-commerce or e-business (see Concepts and Definitions, above). Today, the World Wide Web is often used synonymously for the entire Internet, although the latter also hosts traditional Internet services like Telnet, Gopher, and FTP. Figure 8-1 depicts the geographic distribution of users.

Technological change as such, of course, is nothing new. What is remarkable today is the speed of change. While it took, for example, some thirty-eight and twenty-five years, respectively, for the radio and telephone to reach fifty million U.S. consumers, television only needed thirteen years and cable ten years to reach the same threshold. The Internet, with the World Wide Web, achieved the same penetration level in less than 5 years (Figure 8-2). On a worldwide basis, the Internet is doubling in size every

Figure 8-1
Geographic Distribution of Internet Users

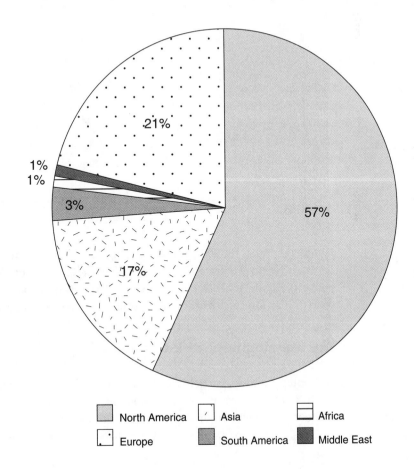

	North America	Asia	Africa
	Europe	South America	Middle East

Figure 8-2
Adoption of Consumer Technologies

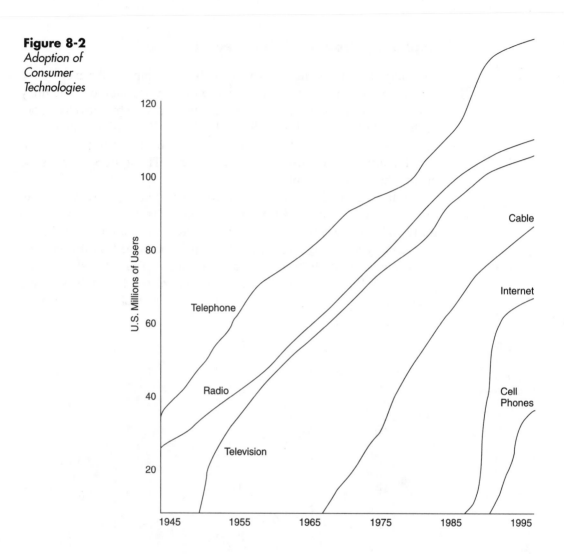

6 to ten months. By 2003, there are projected to be 350 million users, split between North America (35 percent), Europe (30 percent), Asia Pacific (21 percent), South America (9 percent), and the rest of the world (about 5 percent). Other forecasts expect the Internet to exceed 1 billion users by 2008.

The Development of E-Commerce

Technology, and in particular information and communication technology (ICT), is more than merely an "enabler." It has become the basis for an entirely new business model, starting with electronic data exchange (EDI) (i.e., the transfer of standardized data between corporations). The Internet has undergone a metamorphosis from a medium primarily used to advertise a product or service to an e-commerce platform, combining information, transactions, dialogue, and exchange. In short, the Internet has given birth to an entirely new business model and opened completely novel opportunities for marketing that is not limited by international boundaries.

The scope for new developments arising from the new technologies is considerable. Consider the example of Amazon.com. Using a virtual network, which connects suppliers and customers, the firm has changed the way in which books are sold. Over 30,000 "associated Web sites" are recommending the company for a commission and provide links to the Amazon site. Of course, Amazon does not only offer books but also informs customers about new publications and encourages readers to post reviews of books they have read. Virtual chat-rooms and meetings with authors also foster the formation of an Amazon community. Already, more than half the business Amazon conducts is with loyal customers.

Further examples of companies that developed their business around the possibilities offered through e-commerce are Dell Computers, a major supplier of PCs; E*Trade, an online brokerage; and eBay, an online auction "house." At eBay, customers provide the entire content, starting from the goods for sale up to the chat-rooms in which they exchange background information on these goods.

But while most media attention has focused on consumer marketing on the Internet, the large majority of Internet activities are generated in the business-to-business field. The relationship between business-to-business and business-to-consumer e-commerce is approximately five to one.

For a strategic marketer, rapid technological advances, in general, and the unprecedented speed of change in ICT, in particular, have resulted in numerous new challenges: virtual organizations, symbiotic relationships, electronic markets, new forms of co-option, blurring corporate boundaries, and flatter organizational hierarchies, among the most important. While these challenges open entirely new business opportunities, they also represent fundamental threats to established organizations. Companies have to learn how to live with a high degree of volatility. Companies that were success stories only a few years ago are now fighting to survive; Westinghouse or DEC spring to mind. On the other hand, there are companies that have appeared virtually overnight. In this context, one expert coined the phrase "mushroom companies."[2] A well-known characteristic of mush-

---

[2]Bodo B. Schlegelmilch, and R. Sinkovics, "Marketing in the Information Age—Can We Plan for an Unpredictable Future?," *International Marketing Review* 14, no. 3 (1998): 162–170.

rooms is, of course, that they grow virtually overnight but then often disappear rather quickly as well.

Given these dramatic business histories, it is not surprising that Microsoft's CEO Bill Gates reportedly said: "We are always two years away from failure," and Intel's CEO Andy Grove titled his recent book, "Only the Paranoid Survive."

NEW TECHNOLOGIES CHANGE THE RULES OF COMPETITION?

In addition to increasing volatility, the move from an industrial to a post-industrial e-economy also presents the strategic marketer with a new set of proposed business rules. Some experts believe that long established principles, such as the emphasis of retailers on "location, location, location" are passé. Why should a busy executive spend her valuable time and fight traffic to buy some books or videos for her children in town? She can do the same in much greater comfort from home via the Web. Changing business principles forced by the new e-economy are summarized in Table 8-1.

In a similar vein, the new economy will encourage companies to review their strategies. Companies have been urged to:

- Secure a dominant market position as quickly as possible
- Form alliances that maximize market access and synergies
- Anticipate very high start-up investments
- Defend positions through an ongoing process of innovations

Below, we will look at some of these issues in more depth.

Importance of Dominant Market Positions

In the industrial environment, scale advantages have their limits. This is referred to as decreasing returns to scale. While a large factory might be more cost efficient than a small one, there is a point where adding capac-

TABLE 8-1 Evolution of Business Context and Strategy

From:	To:
• Market Share	• Dominant Market Position
• Scale Advantages	• Optimal Efficiency
• Corporate Boundaries	• Alliances
• Improvement	• Innovation

ity at the same location will be uneconomical. The cost of adding labor and material will exceed the added returns. This effect permits smaller competitors to compete against those with larger market shares, providing they can achieve production sizes that yield optimal efficiency. Under the new technological regime, the rule of decreasing returns to scale does not universally hold any more.

In many cases, the optimal output is not determined by the factory size but based on the point where the market is saturated. This can be observed in markets where fixed costs are much higher than variable costs. Examples of this are computer software or pharmaceutical products, which demand a high degree of intellectual factor input. The same holds for products or services that become more valuable when used by more people (i.e., products that develop into a de facto standard and profit from the frequently mentioned *network effect*). Microsoft Office is an example that shows how useful it is to use the same product as many other people. In all these cases, the returns achieved through increasing market shares are not diminishing over time, but grow!—a reversal of the "law" of decreasing returns. Figures 8-3 and 8-4 illustrate the argument.

Being placed in such a technological environment, it is important for companies to gain market share quickly and to achieve market dominance. This explains why America Online (AOL) distributes its disks through all sorts of available media, for example glued into journals and handed out at supermarkets. New subscribers are lured with irresistible trial offers. Netscape pursued a different strategy. It gave its product away in the hope of earning money with follow-up deals. The new technological environment

Figure 8-3
*Decreasing
Return to Scale*

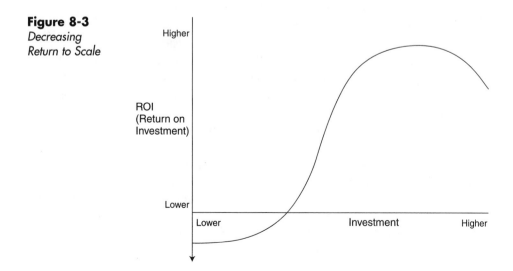

Figure 8-4
Increasing Return to Scale

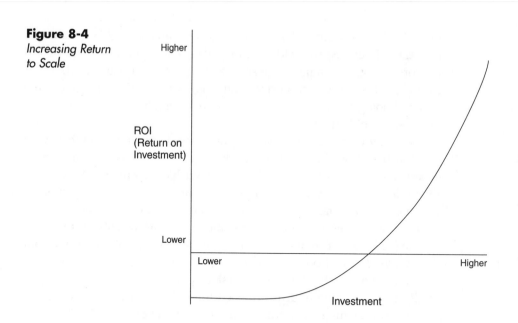

has increased the importance of achieving market share. Conversely, the strategic marketer can no longer afford to tolerate even small attacks from competitors, but has to be prepared for a vigorous defense.

Importance of Strategic Alliances

This post-industrial economy is more and more characterized by a dilution of traditional corporate structures and boundaries in favor of a move toward symbiotic alliances with external partners. Companies involve legally and economically independent firms to fulfill various tasks. Technology is important in this context, since the use of ICT leads to a reduction of transaction costs and thus promotes the market—and alliances—orientation of companies. Video-conferencing, electronic data exchange (EDS), extranets, and so on offer companies involved in symbiotic alliances cost-efficient means of communication.

Three types of alliances can be distinguished:

1. *Vertical* co-operations describe partnerships between companies active in different stages of the value-chain, such as a collaboration between a manufacturer and a retailer in the marketing of an innovative product.
2. *Horizontal* co-operations comprise companies in the same industry, such as research and development co-operations of two or more microelectronic companies.

3. *Diagonal* co-operations refer to situations in which companies from different industries collaborate.

While co-operations and alliances as such are not a new phenomenon, the changes in the technological environment have not only made cross-country alliances easier to manage, but have also influenced the motivation behind the alliances. Besides the desire to increase efficiency, it is now primarily the desire to gain market access and market share that drives co-operations. The desire to utilize network effects and to achieve synergies in products and services, for example, is behind the co-operation between various airlines. E-commerce permits airlines to utilize their brand names in online reservations through so called "code-sharing." This, in turn, eventually results in higher market shares for the globally networked partner airlines.

Importance of Ongoing Innovations

In the traditional technical environment, innovations were primarily a means to gain a few points of market share. It was a rare event that consumers changed allegiances in droves. Information about goods and services diffused relatively slowly, and there were significant gaps between lead and lag countries in the up-take of technology.

In today's technological environment, the situation is drastically different. Not only has the diffusion speed increased significantly but the penalties for falling behind the latest world-class technological and marketing standard are also quick and sharp. Consider WordPerfect, which was the leading word-processing package in the world. Its fall was drastic, when Microsoft offered the suite of programs known as Microsoft Office, which included the spreadsheet Excel, the presentation application Power-Point, and the word processor Word. At the time of the Microsoft entry, their applications were probably inferior in usability and functionality to the competition in each of the categories, but the suite offer, the attractive pricing, sales to computer manufacturers who offered the suite with their computers, and Microsoft's success at constantly improving its products and fixing "bugs" simply swept all contenders out of the field. Today, WordPerfect's share of market is in the 1 percent range.

WordPerfect was simply outclassed in both marketing and product innovation. Microsoft innovated in marketing and in functionality and ease of use; they fixed "bugs" and they shipped product. Their competition could not keep up with them. This was true in both applications software and in operating systems, where Apple, the company with the "better" operating system (OS) was simply outclassed in every way by Microsoft. Apple did not fix "bugs," they did not ship product, and worst of all, they could not understand that their refusal to license their OS to other equipment manufacturers left them at an enormous disadvantage vis-à-vis the open system world of Microsoft's MS-DOS. The very simple fact was that Apple was taking hostages and Microsoft was in business. Anybody who elected to adopt the Apple OS had one supplier of equipment: Apple. They were at the tender mercies of a monopolist. It was Apple against the world. Most customers, and almost all business customers, decided to go for choice and competition instead of the Apple monopoly.

Increasing use of ICT is leading to greater efficiencies in all stages of the new product development process. Many companies are encouraging their employees, customers, and suppliers to submit ideas for new products or improvements through interactive Web sites or e-mail. After new ideas are generated, expert systems can be used in the evaluation of these ideas. At the design stage, computer-aided design (CAD) and design teams that work in parallel in different time zones substantially speed up this stage. ICT applications, such as virtual reality, further aid the development process. To achieve a better fit between the product features and the customer needs, customers are increasingly involved in the design of the product. Smartcar, for example, permits customers to design their own version of the car on the Web (Figure 8-5).

Business and marketing analyses, running concurrently with the technical development of new product ideas, may use ICT in the form of data mining to identify whether there is a likely demand for the new product from existing customers. Finally, simulated test markets again speed up the new product development process. Such approaches use mathematical modeling of marketing mix data to gauge the likelihood of the new product's success and may render real-life test marketing superfluous.

Figure 8-5
Customers Design Their Own Products

Configure the smart menu

| Version | Optional extras | Exterior color | Interior color | Accessories |
| Financing | Insurance | Assistance | Mobility products | Order smart |

Choose the model

Figure 8-6
*A Global Value
Chain*

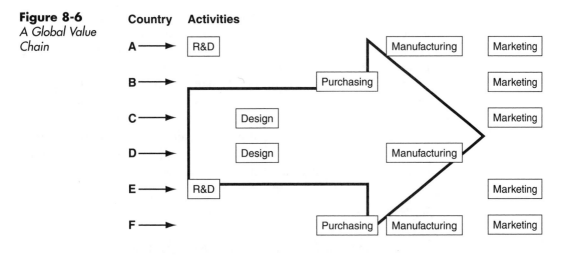

COMPONENTS OF THE ELECTRONIC VALUE CHAIN

For strategic marketers, one of the most dramatic and relevant effects of the technological changes has been the "death of distance." As Frances Cairncross[3] of the *Economist* put it: "The death of distance as a determinant of the cost of communications will probably be the single most important economic force shaping society in the first half of the 21st century. It will alter, in ways that are only dimly imaginable, decisions about where people live and work, concepts of national borders, patterns of international trade. Its effects will be as pervasive as those of the discovery of electricity." Some effects are already emerging in the shape of a re-configuration of the value chain.[4] Figure 8-6 illustrates that ICT permits an organizational structure where not all parts of the value chain need to be *physically* present in each country, although they may be viewed as *virtually* present from the perspective of suppliers and customers.

A major part of the attractiveness and dynamics of the new technological environment stems from the ability to "modularize," "segment," or "fragment" the value chain into small and distinct customer-oriented processes. ICT facilitates the co-ordination between these modules in largely

---

[3]Frances Cairncross, "The Death of Distance," *Economist: Special Report on Telecommuniations,* 30 September 1995, p. SS5.

[4]J. Griese. "Auswirkungen globaler Informations und Kommuniktionssysteme auf die Organisation weltweit tätiger Unternehmen." In *Managementforschung* 2, edited by W.H. V. Staehle and P. Conrad,. Berlin: de Gruyter, 1992, p. 163–175.

non-hierarchical systems and increases the scope for outsourcing specific modules. Closely related to the modularization within companies is the transformation of linear value chains into multidimensional networks. For the customer, it is often not apparent what part of a transaction is carried out by which particular member of the network. For example, the customer usually does not know which reservation system a travel agency uses to book a flight. Indeed, most often he does not care as long as the required goods or services are delivered as requested. What appears to emerge under the new technological regime is a network of specialists, which permits participants to focus on their respective core values.

Portals

Portals are an entrance or doorway to Internet content. Their key functions are to offer access to content and reduce the complexity of the electronic environment. Among the most important portals are Internet online services like America Online, which combine ISP (Internet Service Provider) dial-up access to the Web with the portal function, and services like Yahoo, which provide access to content such as financial information and weather and services like e-mail addresses and mail boxes, search engines, and so on.

Sales Agents

These companies support suppliers primarily through offering high-quality address banks of potential customers. Metromail provides an example. It offers suppliers carefully sifted address banks of potential customers that typically contain a wealth of information about customers' preferences, demographics, and the like.

Purchase Agents

On the customers' side, electronic purchase agents help the Internet shopper find the desired goods or services. Auto-By-Tel, for example, is a service that helps customers find the right car for the right price. Similarly, search robots like PriceSCAN permit consumers to find the best price on thousands of computer hardware and software products. Such programs automatically travel the Web and gather data from magazine ads and vendor catalogues, for instance. Web robots are also sometimes referred to as Web crawlers, or spiders.

Market Makers

Market makers are mediators that bring together buyers and sellers and increase market efficiency. Typical examples are the numerous auction sites that have sprung up on the Web. And the need to innovate can also be felt in this part of the supply chain. In a quest to offer value to consumers, eBay,[5] the world's leading person-to-person online trading community, added the availability of pagers featuring "eBay a-go-go," a service that allows users to receive updates on their eBay auctions via pagers. Plastic-Net.com for plastics, Metals.com for steel, and various other sites bring together buyers and sellers in business-to-business markets.

Payment and Logistic Specialists

Currently, one of the main stumbling blocks for the use of electronic markets is still the payment through the Internet. However, the development of efficient electronic payment systems is advancing rapidly. In the meantime, traditional credit and charge card companies are managing the transfer of payments and the associated risks, and new companies have emerged to provide insurance against fraud.

Physical distribution via the Internet is only possible for software products or information services (e.g., investor, stock market, database information). All other products have to be shipped via traditional channels. Nevertheless, the Internet and the World Wide Web offer a complete new view for the traditional distribution function. While physical distribution was one of the core functions for the traditional retail/commerce systems, this aspect can be unbundled and outsourced using international distribution experts (e.g., UPS). Moreover, the logistic functions of warehouses get outsourced to logistic experts and software companies.

SUMMARY

The rapid advances in information technology are profoundly affecting the way marketing is conducted. The global, instant reach of customers has not only opened up additional distribution and communication channels and enabled precise targeting (segment of one), customization, and

---

[5]http://www.ebay.com/index.html (cited 30 August 1999).

interaction, but has also given rise to fundamentally new business models. Technological changes have also empowered customers by providing more transparency, allowing them to propose their own prices, and offering a platform for dealing directly with each other at auction sites. This chapter documented some of the strategic changes in the technological environment and discussed the impact of these changes on established rules of competition. The need to reach a dominant market position in a very short time, the shift from firm focused strategies to strategic alliances and networks, high start-up investment requirements, and the heightened importance of ongoing innovations are among the issues raised in this context. Finally, we have taken a closer look at the components of the electronic value chain to demonstrate the different roles strategic marketers can play in e-commerce. The Internet cannot be ignored and must be considered in all facets of strategic market planning.

QUESTIONS SUCCESSFUL COMPANIES ASK

1. Who are the key players in an electronic value chain and which functions do they serve?
2. How does the consumer buying process on the Internet differ from that in physical stores?
3. How can information and communication technology contribute to shorter new product development cycles?
4. What are the implications of the described technological changes on (1) the organizational structure of corporate activities across countries and (2) the importance of organizational boundaries?
5. Some experts believe that the Internet requires a complete revision of business models and business strategy. Do you agree? Please provide reasons why you do or do not support this proposition.

9 The Communication Plan: Advertising and Sales Promotion

This chapter explains the difference between personal and impersonal communications and provides a method for deciding on the communications mix. It shows how to prepare the advertising plan, and discusses in some detail what advertising objectives are, and how to set them. The sales promotion plan is then introduced. There is a section on how it can be used, what different types there are, and its strategic role is discussed. Finally, there is a section on how to prepare a sales promotion plan.

DIFFERENT FORMS OF COMMUNICATION

Now that we have explored the important area of marketing objectives and strategies, let us turn our attention to the question of how we communicate with customers, both current and potential.

Organizations communicate with their customers in a wide variety of ways. The two main categories of communications are:

1. *Impersonal Communications.* For example, advertising, point-of-sale displays, promotions, public relations, direct mail, and the Internet.

2. *Personal* (or direct person-to-person) *communications*. For example, the face-to-face meeting between a salesperson and the customer.

Companies have at their disposal a variety of communication techniques, which may be used either singly or in a combination (the "communication mix") as the situation demands, to achieve maximum effect within budget constraints. Companies who successfully communicate with customers continually experiment with the mix of communicating techniques they employ in an attempt to become more cost-effective in this important, sometimes expensive, part of their business.

Deciding on the Communications Mix

Advertising is impersonal communication using such media as newspapers, magazines, television, radio, billboard posters, and so on. However, there are a number of problems that need to be carefully considered before any decision can be made about whether to spend any money on advertising at all, let alone *how* to spend it. The first question that has to be grappled with is the question of how to determine the communications mix.

Figure 9-1 provides a logical approach to analyzing an organization. As can be seen, it can be used equally effectively in either a product or service company. Having done this analysis for major customers/potential customers, it should be comparatively easy to group them in some way (i.e., segmentation) and to determine the most cost-effective way of communicating these benefits to each group.

Only then can some qualitative judgments be made about the relative cost-effectiveness of, for example, advertising versus personal selling, neither of which, incidentally, will be mutually exclusive in anything but unusual circumstances. Table 9-1 lists some consumer communication objectives.

Integrated Marketing Communications

Until the late 1980s, most organizations thought "functionally" about their communications mix. They assumed they were doing a good job if they had memorable advertising, effective public relations, good sales promotions, and salespeople who met their sales objectives. Because each of these different functions requires special skills, each was handled separately. Consequently, the functional approach created industries of communication specialists—advertising agencies, direct-response specialists, and the like—who largely worked independently of each other.

Customer analysis form

Salesperson _____

Products _____

_____

Date of analysis _____

Date of reviews _____

Customer _____

Address _____

_____ Telephone number _____

Buy class: New buy   Straight re-buy   Modified re-buy

_____   _____   _____   _____

Member of decision-making-unit (DMU)		Production	Sales and marketing	Research and development	Finance and accounts	Purchasing	Data processing	Other
Buy phase	Name							
1. Recognizes need or problem and works out general solution								
2. Works out characteristics and quantity of what is needed								
3. Prepares detailed specification								
4. Searches for and locates potential sources of supply								
5. Analyzes and evaluates bids, plans, products								
6. Selects supplier								
7. Places order								
8. Checks and tests product								

Factors for consideration	1. Price	4. Back-up service	7. Guarantees and warranties
	2. Performance	5. Reliability of supplier	8. Payment terms, credit, or discount
	3. Availability	6. Other users' experience	9. Other, e.g., past purchases, prestige, image

Figure 9-1

Customer Analysis Form

(Adapted from P. Robinson, C. W. Farris, and G. Wind, *Industrial Buying and Creative Marketing*, Allyn & Bacon, 1967.)

TABLE 9-1   Some Consumer Communication Objectives

Objective	To
Education and information	Create awareness Inform Get inquiries
Branding and image building	Get company name in mind Create company image Reach personnel
Affecting attitudes	Ease the selling task Overcome prejudice Influence end-users
Loyalty and reminding	Reduce selling costs Achieve sales

Today, more and more firms recognize the need to coordinate these functions and integrated marketing communications (IMC) is the key.

Integrated marketing communications is the strategic development and coordination of messages and media used by an organization to influence value perception of the organization and its brands. In contrast to the traditional functional approach, Figure 9-2 shows the IMC process in which marketing communications objectives and strategies are collectively decided—ideally, not by the firm's own marketing communications specialists but by an outside communications agency that would be working with the firm.

Integration can occur on several levels. At the most basic level, it means all the messages say the same thing—such as Pepsi's "one voice, one look" youth generation advertising does—or they may say different things to different audiences but with a consistent theme, such as Coca-Cola's "Always" campaign does with its different images and styles for MTV viewers and their grandparents. At a higher level, IMC refers to the use of two-way communications to create a dialogue between marketers and their stakeholders that leads to a mutually beneficial relationship.

Figure 9-2
Functional and Integrated Marketing Communications Models

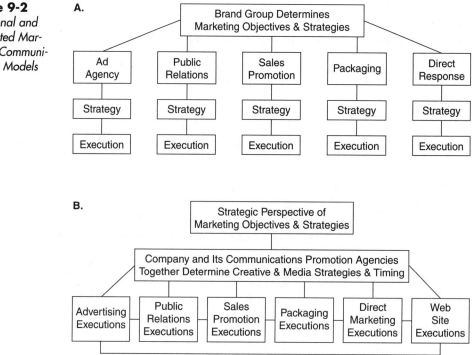

At the most sophisticated level, IMC means "mission marketing." The firm's mission and its sense of social responsibility are integrated into all facets of marketing communications. Companies practicing IMC at this level believe product satisfaction is not enough. They are determined to offer social and/or moral satisfaction as well to purchasers of their products. As technology enables companies to quickly match their competitors' offerings, product difference will be minimized. Therefore, customers will base their brand selections on things other than product differences.

ADVERTISING

Advertising is paid for, non-personal communications in measured media. This includes television, radio, print, outdoor, cinema, and the Internet. The advertising plan is usually prepared by an advertising agency and presented to you, the client, for approval. For greater details on the use of, selection of, and compensation for an advertising agency, it is best to consult an advertising text.

Preparing the Advertising Plan

For many years, people believed that advertising worked in a simple way, with the advertiser sending a message and the target receiving it and understanding it. Research, however, has shown that in an over-communicated society, the process is more complex. Figure 9-3 gives some indication of the process involved. Advertising, then, is not the straightforward activity that many people believe it to be.

Perhaps the greatest misconception of all about advertising is that objectives for advertising for the purpose of measuring effectiveness should be set in terms of sales increases. Naturally, we hope that advertising will have an important influence on sales levels, but in most circumstances advertising is only one of a whole host of important determinants of sales levels such as product quality, prices, customer service levels, and the competence of the sales force. In general, it is inappropriate to set sales increases as a direct objective for advertising. So, what communication objectives should be set for advertising? Start by agreeing that we need to *set* objectives for advertising, for the following reasons:

- To determine whom our target audience is.
- To determine the content of advertisements.

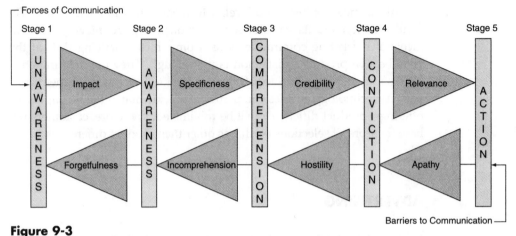

Figure 9-3
*Brand Loyalty
Ladder: The
Five Stages of
Communication*

- To decide on what media to use.
- To decide on the frequency of advertising.
- To decide how to measure the effectiveness of our advertising.
- To set the budget for advertising.

These decisions can be summarized under the following ten categories:

1. *Why* (objectives)
2. *Who* (target)
3. *What* (copy platform)
4. *Where* (media)
5. *How* (creative platform)
6. *When* (timing)
7. *How much* (budget)
8. *Schedule*
9. *Response*
10. *Evaluation*

Advertising Objectives

Research has shown that many companies set objectives for advertising that advertising cannot achieve on its own. For example, it is unreasonable to set as an objective "to convince our target market that our product is

---

What Can Advertising Do?
- Convey information
- Alter perceptions/attitudes/image/position
- Create desires
- Establish connections (e.g., powdered cream/coffee)
- Direct actions
- Provide reassurance
- Remind
- Give reasons for buying
- Demonstrate
- Generate inquiries

---

best" if it is perfectly clear to the whole world that someone else's product is better. You cannot blame your advertising agency if this objective is not achieved!

The first step, then, is to decide on reasonable objectives for advertising. The question that must be asked is: "Is it possible to achieve the objective through advertising alone?" If the answer is *yes*, it is an objective for advertising. If the answer is *no*, it is not an objective for advertising.

Setting reasonable, achievable objectives, then, is the first and most important step in the advertising plan. Advertising is not directed only at consumers. It can be directed at channel decision makers, shareholders, media, employees, suppliers, and government, all of whom have an important influence on a firm's success. All the other steps in the process of putting together the advertising plan flow naturally from this and are summarized briefly below.

Who . . . is (are) the target audience(s)?

What are their demographics? Psychographics?

What do they already know, feel, believe about us and our product/service?

What do they know, feel, believe about the competition?

What sort of people are they? How do we describe/identify them?

What . . . response do we wish to evoke from the target audience(s)?

. . . are the specific communications *objectives*?

. . . do we want to "say," make them "feel," "believe," "understand," "know" about buying/using our product/service?

. . . are we offering?

... do we *not* want to convey?

... are the priorities of importance of our objectives?

... are the objectives that are *written* down and *agreed* upon by the company and advertising agency?

How ... are our objectives to be embodied in an appealing form?

What is our creative strategy/platform?

What evidence do we have that this is acceptable and appropriate to our audience(s)?

Where ... is the most cost-effective medium(s) to expose our communications (in cost terms *vis-à-vis* our audience)?

... is the most beneficial place(s) for our communications (in expected response terms vis-à-vis the "quality" of the channels available)?

When ... are our communications to be displayed/conveyed to our audience?

What is the reasoning for our scheduling of advertisements/communications over time?

What constraints limit our freedom of choice?

Do we have to fit in with other promotional activity on our products/services supplied by our company?

Other products/services supplied by our company?

Competitors' products?

Seasonal trends?

Special events in the market?

Result What results do we expect?

How will we measure results?

Do we intend to measure results and, if so, do we need to do anything *beforehand*?

If we cannot say how we would measure precise results, then maybe our *objectives* are not sufficiently specific or are not communications objectives?

How are we going to judge the relative success of our communications activities (good, bad, indifferent)?

Should we have action standards?

Budget How much money do the intended activities need?

How much money is going to be made available?

How are we going to *control* expenditure?

Schedule: Who is to do what and when?

              What is being spent on what, where, and when?

The role of advertising changes during the life cycle of a product. For example, the process of persuasion itself cannot usually start until there is some level of awareness about a product or service in the marketplace. Creating awareness is, therefore, usually one of the most important objectives early on in a life cycle. If awareness has been created, interest in learning more will usually follow.

Attitude development now begins in earnest. This might involve reinforcing an existing attitude, or changing previously held attitudes, in order to create interest in the product. This role obviously tends to become more important later in the product life cycle, when competitive products are each trying to establish their own "niche" in the market. The aim is to get the prospect to consider trying the product and then becoming a repeat purchaser of the product.

We know, for example, that the *general* characteristics of opinion leaders are that they are venturesome, socially integrated, cosmopolitan, socially mobile, and privileged. So we need to ask ourselves what are the *specific* characteristics of these customers in our particular industry. We can then tailor our advertising message specifically for them.

SALES PROMOTION

Sales promotion is a specific activity, which can be defined as the making of a featured offer to defined customers within a specific time limit. The objective of sales promotion is to influence:

- Salespeople to sell
- Distributors to stock
- Customers to buy more
- Customers to use earlier
- Users to buy faster

Different Kinds of Sales Promotion

The many and varied types of sales promotions are listed in Table 9-2. Each of these different types is appropriate for different circumstances, and each has advantages and disadvantages. For example, with a trade promotion that consists of a free case bonus, it is possible to measure pre-

TABLE 9-2 Types of Sales Promotions

Target market	Money Direct	Money Indirect	Goods Direct	Goods Indirect	Services Direct	Services Indirect
Consumer	Price reduction	Coupons Money equivalent Sweepstakes Rebates	Free goods Premium offers Gifts Trade-in offers	Coupons Money equivalent Sweepstakes	Guarantees Special exhibitions and displays Sponsorships	Cooperative advertising Coupons Vouchers for services Events admission Sweepstakes
Trade	Loyalty programs Incentives Full-range buying	Extended credit Delayed invoicing Sale or return Coupons Money equivalent	Gifts Trial offers Trade-in offers	Coupons Money equivalent Sweepstakes	Guarantees Free services Risk reduction programs Sponsorships Training Special exhibitions Displays Demonstrations Reciprocal trading programs	Coupons Vouchers for services Sweepstakes
Sales force	Bonus Commission	Coupons Points systems Money equivalent Sweepstakes	Gifts	Coupons Points systems Money equivalent	Free services Sponsorships	Coupons Points systems for services Event admission Sweepstakes

cisely both the cost of the extra cases and the additional volume resulting from the offer. It is fast and flexible; it is effective where the customer is profit conscious; it can be made to last as long as required; and it is simple to set up, administer, and sell. On the other hand, it has no cumulative value to the customer, is unimaginative, and can often be seen as a prelude to a permanent price reduction. Great care is necessary, therefore, in selecting a scheme appropriate to the objective sought.

The Strategic Role of Sales Promotion

Sales promotion is an important part of marketing strategy, but it is one of the most mismanaged of all marketing functions. Because sales promotion is essentially used as a tactical device, it often amounts to little more than a series of spasmodic gimmicks lacking in any coherence. Yet, the same management that organizes sales promotion usually believes that advertising should conform to some overall strategy. Perhaps this is because advertising has always been based on a philosophy of building long-term brand franchise in a consistent manner, whereas the basic rationale of sales promotion is to help the company retain a tactical initiative.

Even so, there is no reason why there should not be a strategy for sales promotion, so that each promotion increases the effectiveness of the next. In this way, a bond between seller and buyer is built up, so that the tactical objectives are linked in with some overall plan, and so that there is generally a better application of resources.

There is widespread acknowledgment that sales promotion is one of the most mismanaged of all marketing functions. Companies can no longer afford not to set objectives, or to evaluate results after the event, or to fail to have some company guidelines. For example, a one case allowance on a product with a contribution rate of three per case has to increase sales by 50 percent just to maintain the same level of contribution.

The objectives for each promotion should be clearly stated, such as trial, repeat purchase, distribution, display, a shift in buying peaks, combating competition, and so on. Thereafter, the following process should apply:

- Select the appropriate technique
- Pre-test
- Mount the promotion
- Evaluate

Spending must be analyzed and categorized by type of activity (e.g., special packaging, special point-of-sale material, loss of revenue through price reductions, and so on).

As for the sales promotional plan itself, the objectives, strategy, and brief details of timing and costs should be included. It is important that too much detail should *not* appear in the sales promotional plan. Detailed promotional instructions will follow as the marketing plan unfurls. For example, the following checklist outlines the kind of detail that should eventually be circulated. However, only an outline of this should appear in the marketing plan itself.

Checklist for Promotional Instruction

	Heading	Content
1	Introduction	Briefly summarize content—What? Where? When?
2	Objectives	Marketing and promotional objectives for new product launch.
3	Background	Market data. Justification for technique. Other relevant matters.
4	Promotional offer	Detail the offer: special pricing structure; describe premium; etc. Be brief, precise, and unambiguous.
5	Eligibility	Who? Where?
6	Timing	When is the offer available? Call, delivery, or invoice dates?
7	Date plan	Assign dates and responsibilities for all aspects of plan prior to start date.
8	Support	Special advertising, point of sale, presenters' leaflets, public relations, samples, etc.
9	Administration	Invoicing activity. Free goods invoice lines. Depot stocks. Premium (re)ordering procedure. Cash drawing procedures.
10	Sales plan	Targets. Incentives. Effect on routing. Briefing meetings. Telephone sales.
11	Sales presentation	Points to be covered in call.
12	Sales reporting	Procedure for collection of required data not otherwise available.
13	Assessment	How will the promotion be evaluated?

Additional Needs

The following additional needs for sales promotion are usually designed to be carried by salespeople as an aid to selling the promotion:

- Summary of presentation points
- Price structures/profit margins
- Summary of offer
- Schedules of qualifying orders
- Blank order forms for suggested orders
- Copies of leaflets

QUESTIONS SUCESSFUL COMPANIES ASK

1. Who is the target audience? What do we know about them? What sort of people are they?
2. What response do we want to achieve? What do we want to say, convey, make them feel, believe, or understand?

3. How are we going to proceed? What is our creative platform? Can we be sure this is appropriate?
4. Where is the best place to put our communications? Will it be cost-effective? Does it generate the right image?
5. When will our communications be displayed? Is this the best time? Does it mesh in with other activities?
6. Result—What do we expect to achieve? How will we measure this?
7. Budget—How much is needed? How much is going to be available? How will it be controlled?

10 The Communication Plan: Sales

Chapter 10 discusses the importance and role of personal selling in the marketing mix and goes on to outline a method for determining the number of salespeople required. Quantitative and qualitative sales force objectives are defined and a method for improving sales force productivity is given. Sales force management is briefly discussed. Finally, the reader is shown how to prepare the sales plan. For a discussion of how the Internet is affecting personal selling, see Chapter 8.

Personal selling has an important strategic role to play in communicating between a company and its customers. To have a chance of success, management must be able to answer the following kinds of questions:

- How important is personal selling?
- What is the role of personal selling in the marketing mix?
- How many salespeople do we need?
- What do we want them to do?
- How should they be managed?

These and other questions will be considered in this chapter as important determinants of the sales plan.

HOW IMPORTANT IS PERSONAL SELLING?

Most organizations had an organized sales force long before they introduced a formal marketing activity of the kind described in this book. In spite of this fact, sales force management has traditionally been a neglected area of marketing management. There are several possible reasons. One is that not all marketing and product managers have had experience in a personal selling or sales management role; consequently, these managers often underestimate the importance of efficient personal selling.

Another reason for neglect of sales force management is that sales personnel themselves sometimes encourage an unhelpful distinction between sales and marketing by depicting themselves as "the infantry." After all, is there not something slightly daring about dealing with real live customers as opposed to sitting in an office surrounded by marketing surveys, charts, and plans? Such reasoning is obviously misleading. Unless a good deal of careful marketing planning has taken place before the salesperson makes his or her effort to persuade the customer to place an order, the probability of a successful sale is much reduced.

The suggested distinction between marketing "theory" and sales "practices" is further invalidated when we consider that profitable sales depend not just on individual customers and individual products but also on groups of customers (that is, market segments) and on the supportive relationship of products to each other (that is, a carefully planned product portfolio). Another factor to be taken into account in this context is the constant need for the organization to think in terms of where future sales will be coming from, rather than to concentrate solely on present products, customers, and problems.

In our experience, many companies lack planning and professionalism in their sales forces. Salespeople frequently have little idea of which products and which groups of customers to concentrate on, have too little knowledge about competitive activity, do not plan presentations well, rarely talk to customers in terms of *benefits*, make too little effort to close the sale, and make many calls without any clear objectives. Even worse, marketing management is rarely aware that this important and expensive element of the marketing mix is not being managed effectively.

The fact that many organizations have separate departments and executives for the marketing and sales activities increases the likelihood of such failures of communication. Recent surveys show that more money is spent by many companies on their sales forces than on advertising and sales promotion combined. Personal selling, then, is a vital and expensive element in the marketing mix.

The solution to the problem of poor sales force management can only be found in the recognition that personal selling is a crucial part of the marketing process. It must be planned and considered as carefully as any other element. It is an excellent idea for any manager responsible for marketing to go out into a territory for at least one week each year and attempt to persuade customers to place orders. It is a good way of finding out what customers really think of the organization's marketing policies.

THE ROLE OF PERSONAL SELLING

Personal selling is part of the *communications mix.* (Other elements of the communications mix are advertising, sales promotion, public relations, direct mail, exhibitions, sponsorship, and the Internet.) Chapter 9 shows that organizations cannot leave the communications task only to the sales force. The same question remains, however, as with advertising: How is the organization to define the role of personal selling in its communications mix? The answer lies in a clear understanding of the buying process that operates in the company's markets.

The efficiency of any element of communication depends on achieving a match between information required and information given. To achieve this match, the marketer must be aware of the different requirements of different people at different stages of the buying process. This approach highlights the importance of ensuring that the company's communications reach *all* key points in the buying chain. No company can afford to assume that the actual sale is the only important event.

To determine the precise role of personal selling in its communications mix, the company must identify the customer and major influencers in each purchase decision and find out what information they are likely to need at different stages of the buying process.

Most institutional buying decisions consist of many separate phases, from the recognition of a problem through performance evaluation and feedback on the product or service purchased. Furthermore, the importance of each of these phases varies according to whether the buying situation is a first-time purchase or a routine re-purchase. Clearly, the information needs will differ in each case.

Once an order has been obtained from a customer and there is a high probability of a re-buy occurring, the salesperson's task changes from persuasion to reinforcement. All communications at this stage should contribute to underlining the wisdom of the purchase. The salesperson may also take the opportunity to encourage consideration of other products or services in the company's range.

Advantages of Personal Selling

1. Personal selling is a two-way form of communication. It gives the prospective purchaser the opportunity to ask questions of the salespeople about the product or service.
2. The sales message itself can be made more flexible and, therefore, can be more closely tailored to the needs of individual customers.
3. The salesperson can use in-depth product knowledge to relate his or her message to the perceived needs of the buyer and to deal with objections as they arise.
4. Most importantly, the salesperson can ask for an order and, perhaps, negotiate on price, delivery, or special requirements.

In different markets, different weighting is given to the various forms of communication available. In the grocery business, for example, advertising and sales promotion are extremely important elements in the communications process. However, the food manufacturer must maintain an active sales force that keeps in close contact with the retail buyers. This retail contact ensures vigorous promotional activity in the chain. In the wholesale hardware business, frequent and regular face-to-face contact with retail outlets through a sales force is a key determinant of success. In industries where there are few customers (such as capital goods and specialized process materials), an in-depth understanding of the customers' production processes has to be built up; here, again, personal contact is of paramount importance. In contrast, many fast-moving industrial goods are sold into fragmented markets for diverse uses; in this area, forms of communication other than personal selling take on added importance.

DETERMINING THE REQUISITE NUMBER OF SALESPEOPLE

The organization begins its consideration of how many salespeople it needs by finding out exactly how work is allocated at present. Start by listing all the things the current sales force actually does. These might include opening new accounts, servicing existing accounts, demonstrating new products, taking repeat orders, and collecting debts. This listing should be followed by an investigation of alternative ways of carrying out these responsibilities. For example, telephone selling has been shown to be an alternative to personal visits, particularly for repeat business. The sales force can thus be freed for missionary work (searching for new customers). Can debts be collected by mail or by telephone? Can products be demonstrated at exhibitions or showrooms? It is only by asking these kinds of questions that we can be certain we have not fallen into the common trap of committing the company to a decision and then seeking data and reasons to justify the decision. At this stage, the manager should concentrate on collecting relevant, quantified data and then use judgment and experience to help in making a decision.

All sales force activities can be categorized under three headings. A salesperson:

- Makes calls
- Travels
- Performs administrative functions

These tasks constitute what can be called the *workload*. If we first decide what constitutes a reasonable workload for a salesperson, in hours per month, then we can begin to measure how long their current activities take, hence the exact extent of their current workload. This measurement can be performed either by some independent third party or, preferably, by the salespeople themselves. All they have to do for one simple method of measurement is to record distance traveled, time in and out of calls, and the outlet type. This data can then be analyzed to indicate the average duration of a call by outlet type, the average distance traveled in a month, and the average speed according to the nature of the territory (that is, city, suburbs, or country). With the aid of a map, existing customers can be allocated on a trial-and-error basis, together with the concomitant time values for clerical activities and travel. In this way, equitable workloads can be calculated for the sales force, building in, if necessary, spare capacity for sometimes investigating potential new sales outlets. There are, of course, other ways of measuring workloads. These results are summarized in Table 10-1.

Table 10-1 shows the company how a salesperson's time was spent and approximately how much of their time was actually available for selling. One immediate action taken by the company was to initiate a training program that enabled more time to be spent on selling as a result of better planning. Another was to improve the quality of the sales performance while face-to-face with the customers. Armed with this kind of quantitative data, it becomes easier to determine how many salespeople are needed and how territories can be equitably allocated.

TABLE 10-1 Breakdown of a Salesperson's Total Daily Activity

		Percent of Day		Minutes per Day	
Outside call time	Drive to and from route	15.9		81	
	Drive on route	16.1		83	
	Walk	4.6		24	
	Rest and breaks	6.3		32	
	Pre-call administration	1.4		7	
	Post-call administration	5.3		27	
			49.6		254
Inside call time	Business talks	11.5		60	
	Sell	5.9		30	
	Conversation	3.4		17	
	Receipts	1.2		6	
	Miscellaneous	1.1		6	
	Drink	1.7		8	
	Waiting	7.1		36	
			31.9		163
Evening work	Office work	9.8		50	
	Recording sales	3.9		20	
	Plan route	4.8		25	
			18.5		95
			100.0		8 hr 32 min.

DETERMINING THE ROLE OF THE SALESPEOPLE

Whatever the method used to organize the salesperson's day, there is always comparatively little time available for selling. In these circumstances, it is vital that a company should know as precisely as possible what it wants its sales force to do. Sales force objectives can be either *quantitative* or *qualitative*.

Quantitative Objectives

Principal quantitative objectives are concerned with the following measures:

- How much to sell (the value of unit sales volume)
- What to sell (the mix of product lines to sell)
- Where to sell (the markets and individual customers that will take the company toward its marketing objectives)
- Desired profit contribution (where relevant and where the company is organized to compute this)
- Selling costs (in compensation, expenses, supervision, and so on)

The first three types of objectives are derived directly from the marketing objectives (see Chapter 9), which constitute the principal components of the sales plan.

There are, of course, many other kinds of quantitative objectives that can be set for the sales force, including the following:

- Number of point-of-sale displays organized
- Number of letters written to prospects
- Number of telephone calls to prospects
- Number of reports turned or not turned in
- Number of trade meetings held
- Use of sales aids in presentations
- Number of service calls made
- Number of customer complaints
- Safety record
- Collections made
- Training meetings conducted
- Competitive activity reports
- General market condition reports

Salespeople may also be required to fulfill a coordinating role between a team of specialists and the client organization. A company selling mining machinery, for example, employs a number of "general salespeople" who establish contacts and identify which ones are likely to lead to sales. Before entering into negotiations with any client organization, the company selling the machinery may feel that it needs to call in a team of highly specialized engineers and financial experts for consultation and advice. The salesperson in this company needs to identify where specialist help is required and co-ordinate the people who become involved in the negotiation. Most objectives are subservient to the major objectives outlined above, which are associated directly with what is sold and to whom.

Qualitative Objectives

Qualitative objectives can be a potential source of problems if sales managers try to assess the performance of the sales force along dimensions that include abstract terms such as "loyalty," "enthusiasm," "co-operation," and so on. Such terms are difficult to measure objectively. In seeking qualitative measurements of performance, managers often resort to highly subjective interpretations, which cause resentment and frustration among those being assessed.

However, managers can set and measure qualitative objectives that actually relate to the performance of the sales force on the job. It is possible, for example, to assess the skill with which a person applies their product knowledge on the job, or the skill with which they plan their work, or the skill with which they overcome objections during a sale presentation. While still qualitative in nature, these measures relate to standards of performance understood and accepted by the sales force.

Given such standards, it is not too difficult for a competent field sales manager to identify deficiencies, to get agreement on them, to coach in skills and techniques, to build attitudes of professionalism, to show how to self-train, to determine which training requirements cannot be tackled in the field, and to evaluate improvements in performance and the effect of any past training.

One consumer goods company with thirty field sales managers discovered that most of them were spending much of the day in their offices engaged in administrative work, most of it self-made. The company proceeded to take the offices away and insisted that the sales managers spend most of their time in the field training their salespeople. To assist them in this task, they trained them in how to appraise and improve salespeople's performance in the field. There was a dramatic increase in sales and, consequently, in the sales managers' own earnings. They rapidly overcame their resentment at losing their offices.

IMPROVING SALES FORCE PRODUCTIVITY

Many salespeople might secretly confess to a proclivity to call more frequently on those large customers who give them a friendly reception and less frequently on those who put business in their way. If we classify customers according to their friendliness, as well as their size, it is easy to see how a simple matrix can be developed to help us decide where our major effort should be directed. From Figure 10-1, it can be seen that the boxes that offer the greatest potential for increased sales productivity are boxes 4 and 5, with boxes 1 and 2 receiving a "maintenance" call rate. Boxes 7 and 8 should receive an "alternative strategy" approach to establish whether hostility can be overcome. If these alternative approaches fail, a lower call rate may be appropriate. Box 9 is the "Do not bother" box, while boxes 3 and 6 will receive the minimum attention consistent with our goals.

None of this is meant to indicate definitive rules about call frequencies, which will always remain a matter of management judgment. Its sole purpose is to question our assumptions about call frequencies on existing

Figure 10-1
*Improving
Sales Force
Productivity*

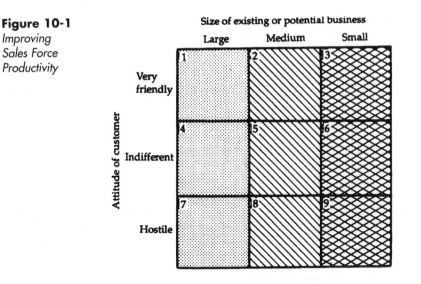

Size of existing or potential business

and potential accounts to check that we are not using valuable time that could be more productively used in other directions.

PREPARING THE SALES PLAN

No two sales plans will contain precisely the same headings. However, some general guidelines can be given. Table 10-2 is an example of setting objectives for an individual salesperson. Clearly, these objectives will be the logical result of breaking down the marketing objectives into actual sales targets.

All companies set themselves overall objectives, which lead to the development of specific marketing objectives and which in turn lead to establishing specific sales objectives for sales force members. In this chapter, we have discussed personal selling in the context of the overall marketing activity. This approach leads us to the following hierarchy of objectives: *corporate objectives—marketing objectives—sales objectives*, as outlined in Figure 10-2.

The benefits to sales force management of following this approach can be summarized as follows:

1. Coordination of corporate and marketing objectives with actual sales effort. (Note that a company may make the sales force objective 10 percent higher than the marketing objective as a cushion to assure that the marketing number will be met.)

TABLE 10-2 Objectives for the Individual Salesperson

Task	The Standard	How to Set the Standard	How to Measure Performance	What to Look For
1. To achieve a personal sales target	–Sales target per period of time for individual groups or products	–Analysis of • territory potential • individual customers' potential –Discussion and agreement between salesperson and manager	–Comparison of individual salesperson's product sales against targets	–Significant shortfall between target and achievement over a meaningful period
2. To sell the required range and quantity to individual customers	–Achievement of specified range and quantity of sales to a particular customer or group of customers within an agreed time period	–Analysis of individual customer records of • potential and • present sales –Discussion and agreement between manager and salesperson	–Scrutiny of individual customer records observation of selling in the field	–Failure to achieve agreed objectives –Complacency with range of sales made to individual customers
3. To plan travel and call frequencies to achieve minimum practicable selling cost	–To achieve appropriate call frequency on individual customers –Number of live customer calls during a given time period	–Analysis of individual customers' potential –Analysis of order/call ratios –Discussion and agreement between manager and salesperson	–Scrutiny of individual customer records –Analysis of order/call ratio –Examination of call reports	–High ratio of calls to an individual customer relative to that customer's yield –Shortfall on agreed total number of calls made over an agreed time period
4. To acquire new customers	–Number of prospect calls during time period –Selling new products to existing customers	–Identify total number of potential and actual customers who could produce results –Identify opportunity areas for prospecting	–Examination of call reports records of new accounts opened ratio of existing to potential customers	–Shortfall in number of prospect calls from agreed standard –Low ratio of existing to potential customers
5. To make a sales approach of the required quality	–To exercise the necessary skills and techniques required to achieve the identified objective of each element of the sales approach –Continuous use of sales material	–Standard to be agreed in discussion between manager and salesperson related to company standards –Regular observations of field selling using a systematic analysis of performance in each stage of the sales approach	Regular observations of field selling using a systematic analysis of performance in each stage of the sales approach	–Failure to • identify objective of each stage of sales approach • develop specific areas of skill, correct weakness • use of support material

(Based on the original work of Stephen P. Morse while at Urwick Orr and Partners.)

Figure 10-2
*Objectives for
the Individual
Salesperson*

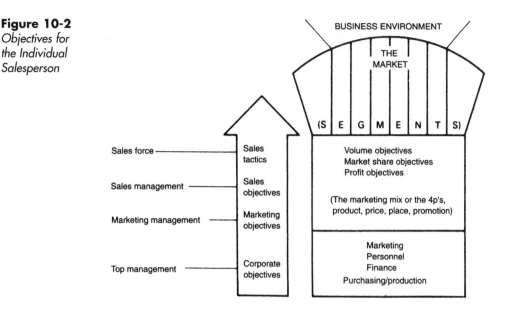

2. Establishment of a circular relationship between corporate objectives and customer wants.
3. Improvement of sales effectiveness through an understanding of the corporate and marketing implications of sales decisions.

The following example illustrates the main point: that a sales force cannot be managed in isolation from broad corporate and marketing objectives. The sales force of a company manufacturing stainless steel containers was selling almost any kind of container to almost anybody who could buy. This caused severe production planning and distribution problems throughout the business, down to the purchase of raw materials. Eventually, the company's profitability was seriously affected. The sales force was finally instructed to concentrate on certain kinds of products and on certain kinds of user industries. This decision led to economies of scale throughout the whole organization.

To summarize, the sales force is a vital but very expensive element of the marketing mix and as much care should be devoted to its management as to any other area of marketing management. This is most likely to be achieved if intuitive sense, which is associated with experience, can be combined with the kind of logical framework of thinking outlined here (see Figure 10-3).

Figure 10-3
Effective Sales
Management:
Thinking + Data
+ Intuition

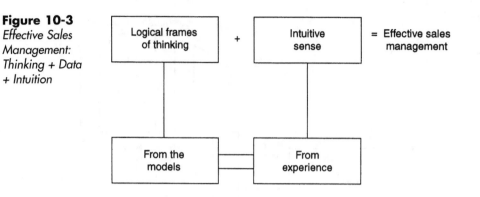

QUESTIONS SUCCESSFUL COMPANIES ASK

1. What are the key functions of salespeople in your organization? How is their work coordinated?
2. How is the sales force deployed: by geographical territory, by product range, by type of customer? Is this deployment optimal? What other patterns of deployment should be considered by your organization?
3. Who is responsible for the sales force in your organization? What is the relationship between this post of responsibility and other marketing responsibilities in the organization? Does this cause any problems? Where problems arise, how could they be solved?
4. Can you make a case to justify the present size and type of sales force used? Could you defend your position if you were requested to cut back the sales force by 30 percent? How would you make your case? What do you believe the consequences of a 30 percent cutback would be?
5. How can we maximize sale performance? Incentives can be rewards consistent with performance, giving praise and recognition when it is due, minimal boredom and monotony, freedom from fear or worry, a feeling of belonging, and a sense of doing a useful job.
6. How is the Internet affecting the role of the salesperson? What changes should we make to take advantage of the Internet in our communications effort?

11 The Pricing Plan

Chapter 11 addresses the pricing decision in the marketing plan in the context of portfolio management, product life cycle analysis, and product positioning. Costs are explored as an input for pricing policy, as is pricing for distribution channels. There is a section on pricing for competitive advantage through value-in-use pricing. Finally, the reader is shown how to prepare a pricing plan.

Pricing is a critical element of the marketing plan. The first thing to say about pricing is that there are two boundaries that must always be kept in mind: the upper boundary of competition and the lower boundary of cost. In general, the price offer cannot be greater than a comparable offer from the competition nor can it be, in the long term, less than cost. That having been said, it still remains to be established what is a comparable offer from the competition, and what are costs. As you will see, neither is easy or simple to determine.

The pricing decision is important for two main reasons: price not only affects the margin through its impact on revenue, but also affects the quantity sold through its influence on demand. In short, price has an interactive effect on the other elements of the marketing mix, so it is essential that it is part of a conscious marketing plan, with objectives that have been clearly defined. Although in some areas of the economy, pricing may be determined by forces that are largely outside the control of corporate decision makers, prices in the marketplace are normally the result of decisions made by the company management. What should the decision be, when on the one hand accounting wants to increase the price of a product in order to increase margins, while the marketer wants to hold or even reduce the net selling price in order to increase market share? The answer would appear to be simple. Get the calculator out and see which proposal results in the biggest "profit."

OBJECTIVES AND THE PRODUCT PORTFOLIO

Unfortunately, many arguments within firms about pricing take place in the sort of vacuum that is created when no one has bothered to specify the *objectives* to which pricing is supposed to be contributing.

We know now that it is important for a company to have a well-defined hierarchy of objectives to which all its activities and actions, including pricing, can be related. For example, corporate objectives may well dictate that the generation of short-term profits is a requirement. This may well be due to a particular business unit's position in a matrix vis-à-vis other units in the same corporation. For example, a group decision may have been made to invest heavily in one business unit's growth and to fund this growth from one of their "cash cow" units elsewhere in their portfolio.

Corporate objectives have an important influence on *marketing* objectives. In the same way, a company's marketing objectives for a particular product may dictate a short-term emphasis on profitability rather than on market share, which will influence the pricing strategy. This will be a function of that product's position vis-à-vis other products in the portfolio. For example, it may be that a product is one of many "question marks," and the company has chosen others, rather than this particular one, to invest in. This would naturally result in a wish to make the biggest possible contribution to profits from the product, and the pricing strategy would seek to achieve this.

The setting of marketing objectives for any particular product is the starting point in any consideration of pricing.

Product Positioning

Price is one of the clearest signals a customer has as to the value of the offer that a company is making him, and there has to be a sensible relationship between the two. For example, several years ago, Smirnoff was a popular vodka brand not clearly positioned as a premium vodka. To change the positioning of Smirnoff, the price was increased by $1.00 a bottle, 50 cents of which was invested in advertising. The remaining 50 cents per bottle was dropped to the bottom line. The pricing change, combined with the new advertising campaign, successfully "repositioned" Smirnoff into the luxury vodka category and sales and profits increased. Product positioning, then, is another major consideration in the pricing decision.

Competition and Potential Competition

All products have competitors, and *potential* competitors, and they must be carefully considered in the pricing decision. Some firms launch new products at high prices to recover their investment costs, only to find that they have created a price "umbrella" for competitors, who then launch similar products at much lower prices. Their lower prices enable them to take market share and move down the experience curve quicker, giving them a cost advantage over their competitors. A lower launch price, with possibly a quicker rate of diffusion and hence a greater rate of experience, may make it more difficult for a potential competitor to enter the market profitably.

Some products are perceived as being generic, with little distinctiveness so consumers can easily switch brands. In this case, a few pennies difference in the selling price generally causes the consumer to switch to the lower-priced brand. Brands with high awareness and esteem allow a company to charge a higher price. Without the little alligator on an Izod shirt, it is a generic product. By attaching the alligator, a symbol of quality and style, consumers are willing to pay a higher price so the price of the shirt goes up.

Costs

Another key factor for consideration is costs—not just our own costs. The conventional profit-maximizing model of economists tends to indicate that a price should be set at the point where marginal cost equals marginal revenue (i.e., where the additional cost of producing and marketing an additional unit is equivalent to the additional revenue earned from its sale). The theory is indisputable, but in practice this procedure is difficult, if not impossible, to apply. This is largely because the economists' model assumes that price is the only determinant of demand, whereas in reality this is not always so.

In practice, the costs of manufacturing (or provision of a service) provide the basis for most pricing decisions (i.e., a "cost-plus" method). The trouble with most such "cost-oriented" pricing approaches is that they make little attempt to reconcile what the customer is prepared to pay with what it costs the company to be in business and make a fair return on its investment of resources. An example of the "cost-oriented" approach is

Figure 11-1
Break-even
Analysis

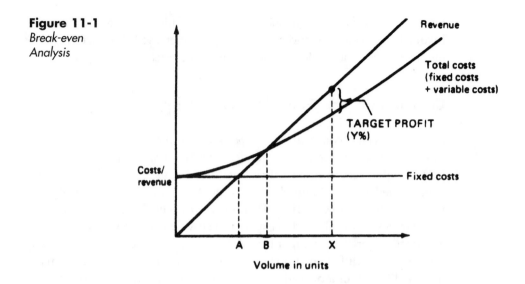

when a company targets for a certain return on costs (i.e., the company will set itself a target level of profits at a certain projected level of sales volume). In fact, this type of approach uses a simple form of "break-even" analysis as depicted in Figure 11-1.

In the diagram, fixed costs are shown as a straight line and all other costs are allocated on a cost-per-unit basis to produce an ascending curve. At point A, revenue covers only fixed costs. At point B, all costs are covered and any additional sales will produce net profit. At point X, Y percent target profit is being achieved. The problem with this approach to pricing is that it assumes that at a given price, a given number of products will be sold, whereas in reality the quantity sold is dependent on the price charged. Also, this model assumes a break-even *point*, whereas in most companies the best that can be said is that there is a break-even *area* at a given level of production. It is, however, quite useful for helping us to understand the relationship between different kinds of costs.

By far the most common way of setting price is to use the cost-plus approach, arriving at a price that yields margins commensurate with declared profit objectives. When making a pricing decision, it is wise to consider a number of different costing options, for any one can be misleading on its own, particularly those that allocate fixed costs to all products in the portfolio. Often the basis of allocation is debatable, and an unthinking marketer may well accept the costs as given and easily make the wrong pricing decision.

Consider the following scenario: In difficult economic times, when cost savings are sought, unprofitable products are eliminated from the range.

Unprofitable products are identified by the gross or net margins in the last complete fiscal year, and also by estimates of these margins against estimated future sales. However, because conventional cost accounting allocates the highest costs to high-volume products, they show lower margins, so sometimes these are sacrificed. But product elimination often saves only small amounts of direct costs, so the remaining products have to absorb higher costs, and the next profitability crisis appears. Product elimination also reduces the scale of operations, as well as reducing the product mix, so there is less incentive to invest and the company is less competitive.

This is not intended to be an attack on any kind of the total average costing method. Our intention here is merely to advise caution and a broader perspective when using any kind of costing system as a basis for pricing decisions.

Channels of Distribution

Channel intermediaries perform a number of functions. In return for their services, these intermediaries need to be rewarded; this reward is in effect the "margin" between the price of the goods from the factory, and the price the consumer pays. However, the total channel margin may have to be shared between several intermediaries and still reach the consumer at a competitive price. Intermediaries, therefore, live or die on the economics of their respective operations. The ideal reward structure in the marketing channel is to ensure that an acceptable rate of return on investment is earned at each level. This situation is often not achieved because of the imbalances of bargaining power present.

A number of devices are available for rewarding channel intermediaries, most of which take the form of discounts against a nominal price list. These are:

Trade discount   This is the discount given against the price list for services made available by the intermediary (e.g., holding inventory, buying in bulk, redistribution, etc.).

Quantity discount   A quantity discount is offered to intermediaries who order in large lots.

Promotional discount   This is the discount given to distributors to encourage them to share jointly in the promotion of the product(s) involved.

Cash discount   In order to encourage prompt payments of accounts, a cash discount of around 2.5 percent for payment within ten days is often offered.

Figure 11-2
*Marketing
Objectives and
Channel Margins*

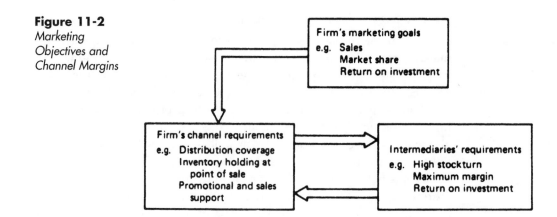

In a dynamic marketing channel, there is constant pressure upon suppliers to improve margins. Because of these pressures, the question of margins should be seen at a strategic as well as at a tactical level. This whole area of margin management can be viewed as a series of trade-off decisions that determine how the total channel margin should be split. The concept of the total channel margin is simple. It is the difference between the level of price at which we wish to position our product in the ultimate marketplace and the cost of our product from the factory. Who takes what proportion of this difference as shown in Figure 11-2, is what margin management is about.

The firm's channel requirements will only be achieved if it either carries them out itself or if it goes some way toward meeting the requirements of an intermediary who can perform those functions on its behalf. The objective of the firm in this respect could therefore be expressed in terms of willingness to trade off margin in order to achieve its marketing goals. Such a trade-off need not lead to a loss of profitability; indeed as Figure 11.3 suggests, the margin is only one element in the determination of profitability, profitability being defined as the rate of return on net worth (net worth being stockholders equity and capital reserves plus retained earnings).

By improving the utilization of capital assets (capital management) as well as by using greater leverage, it is possible to operate successfully on lower margins if this means that marketing goals can be achieved more effectively.

PREPARING THE PRICING PLAN

We have so far considered some of the main issues relevant to the pricing decision. We can now try to pull all of these issues together. However, let

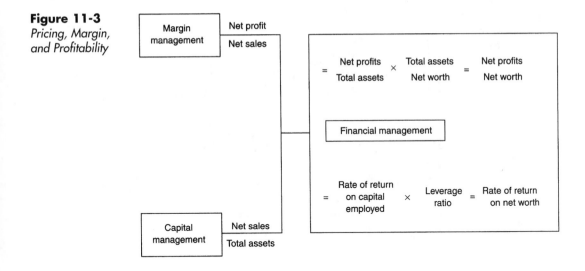

Figure 11-3
*Pricing, Margin,
and Profitability*

us first recapitulate on one of the basic findings that underpin the work of
the Boston Consulting Group.

Generally, real costs decline with accumulated experience. Figure 11-4
describes this effect. One of the implications of this is that unless a firm
accumulates experience at the same or at a greater rate than the market as
a whole, eventually its costs will become noncompetitive. Figure 11-5 illustrates this point.

A skimming policy is a high initial price, moving down the experience
curve at a slower rate, while a penetration policy is a low initial price, with
a much faster rate of product adoption, hence a steeper experience curve.
Both policies are summarized in Figure 11-6.

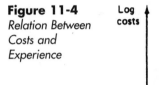

Figure 11-4
*Relation Between
Costs and
Experience*

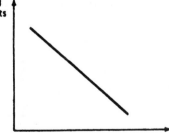

Figure 11-5
*Experience, Cost,
and Competitive
Position*

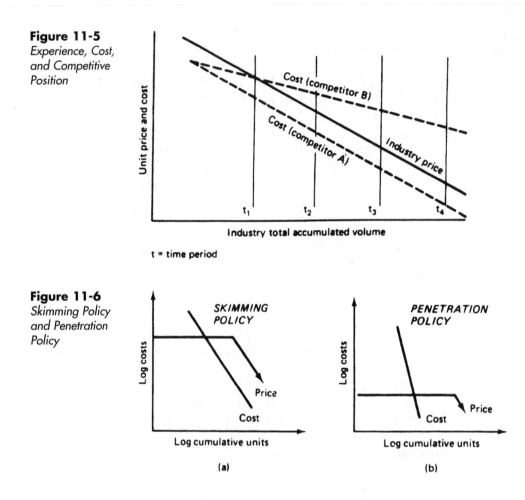

Figure 11-6
*Skimming Policy
and Penetration
Policy*

The circumstances favoring a skimming policy are:

1. Demand is likely to be price inelastic.
2. There are likely to be different price-market segments, thereby appealing first to those buyers who have a higher range of acceptable prices.
3. Little is known about the costs of producing and marketing the product.

The circumstances favoring a penetration policy are:

1. Demand is likely to be price elastic.
2. Competitors are likely to enter the market quickly.
3. There are no distinct and separate price-market segments.
4. There is the possibility of large savings in production and marketing costs if a large sales volume can be generated (the experience factor).

Figure 11-7
Pricing Policy

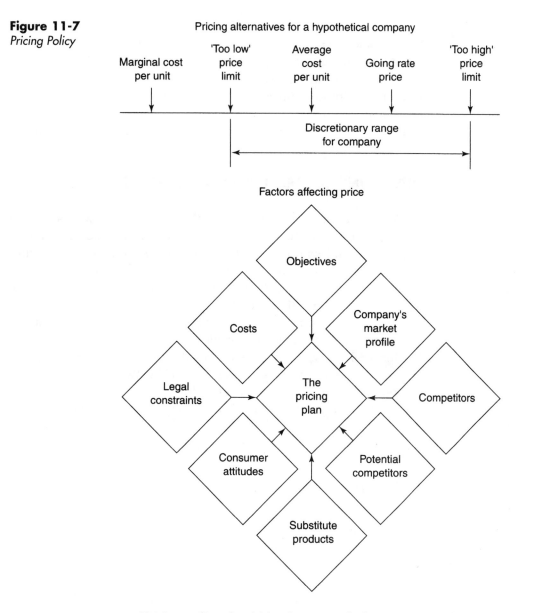

Pricing alternatives for a hypothetical company

Factors affecting price

Pricing policy should be determined after an account has been taken of all factors that impinge on the pricing decision. These are summarized in Figure 11-7. The first shows the discretionary pricing range for a company. The second shows those factors we should take account of in reaching a pricing decision. The price offer is influenced by:

- Marketing objectives
- The cost structure

- Legal constraints
- Consumer attitudes and values
- Competition (direct)
- Competition (substitutes)
- Company/product image
- Economic situation
- Product positioning (e.g., luxury products vs. standard or economy)

QUESTIONS SUCCESSFUL COMPANIES ASK

1. When you last introduced a new product or service, how was the price established? Was the pricing decision correct? What additional information could you have used to help you with the pricing decision? What would you do differently given the same circumstances?
2. Describe your pricing strategy for one of your major products. How does it compare with that of your major competitors?
3. Describe how you deal with pricing (a) in times of high inflation and (b) at each phase in the product life cycle.
4. During the past ten years, what trends have occurred in margins in your industry? Are these trends acceptable? What policy does your organization have toward these trends?
5. Are trade margins justified? What is your policy toward trade margins?

12 The Distribution Plan

Chapter 12 encourages readers to consider distribution in its widest sense as a critical aspect of marketing management rather than just "physical distribution management." It goes on to explore the various components of the distribution mix. Marketing channels are discussed and a method for their evaluation is provided. The essential components of customer service are listed and finally the reader is shown how to prepare a distribution plan.

At Coca-Cola, one of the world's most admired and successful companies, channels are the cornerstone of the company's success. Coca-Cola knows that the key to their global success is that "the product must be within an arms reach of desire." Coke's distribution around the world is a testament to that company's success in creating a worldwide association of business partners who have put Coke within an arms reach of desire around the world.

The topic of product distribution involves three main decision areas, each of which will be examined in turn:

1. How is the physical movement of our product organized?
2. Through what marketing channels do we reach our customers (or what channels do our customers utilize to acquire our products)?
3. What level of availability of our product does our customer require (and how well do we meet this requirement)?

PHYSICAL DISTRIBUTION

The physical distribution function of a firm provides the place and time dimensions, which constitute the third element of the marketing mix. This is depicted in Figure 12-1, which also shows its relationship to the other utility-producing elements. The figures on the diagram are illustrative only, although they are realistic for some industries. If a product is not available when and where the customer wants it, it will surely fail in the market.

THE DISTRIBUTION MIX

In a typical manufacturing company with a formal distribution structure, the responsibility for distribution-related matters is spread across the other functional departments. For example, production may control warehousing and transportation; marketing may control the channels through which the product moves, the levels of service provided to the customer, and inventory obsolescence; and the finance department may control com-

Figure 12-1
Physical Distribution

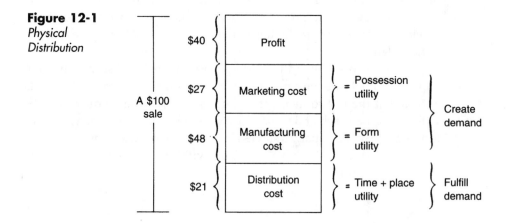

munications, data processing, and inventory costs. Such a compartmentalized arrangement leads to each department working to its own objectives, attempting to optimize its own particular activity, oblivious of others or of the good of the whole company.

Introducing a more formalized distribution arrangement into the corporate organizational structure, although not completely eliminating interdepartmental friction, does at least ensure that all distribution-related activities are organized under a more centralized control, thereby gaining focus. This, then, is the basis of the total distribution concept, because it now becomes possible to seek out potential trade-offs (i.e., consciously to incur costs in one area in order to achieve an even larger benefit in another). For example, should a series of field warehouses be maintained, or would one suffice, supplemented by an improved trucking operation? Of course, these types of potential "trade-off" situations place a heavy burden on the cost-reporting systems of a company.

The professional distribution manager, therefore, has several variables to contend with in the search for trade-offs; taken together, these constitute the *distribution mix*.

Each of these is examined briefly.

Facilities

Decisions in this area are concerned with the problem of how many warehouses and plants should be established and where they should be located. Obviously, for the majority of companies it is necessary to take the location of existing plants and warehouses as given in the short term, but the question does arise in the longer term or, indeed, when new plants or warehouses are being considered. The principal marketing task here is to forecast the nature, size, and geographical spread of demand.

Increasing the number of field locations will result in an increase in trucking costs and a reduction in retail distribution costs. So, another marketing task is to determine the customer service levels that are likely to be required in order to be able to make a decision about this particular trade-off.

Inventory

A major element in any company's total distribution costs is the cost of inventory, which is often as high as 30 percent of its value per annum. This is because of items such as interest charges, deterioration, shrinkage, insurance, administration, and so on. Thus, decisions about how much inventory to hold, where to hold it, in what quantities to order, and so on are vital issues. Inventory levels are also instrumental in determining the level of service that the company offers the customer.

Logistics

Logistics is the branch of military operations that deals with the procurement, distribution, maintenance, and replacement of material. In business, the task of logistics is to minimize cost and maximize the value to customers of the place utility of a company's product or service. Transportation issues include the mode of transportation to use, whether to own vehicles or lease them, how to schedule deliveries, how often to deliver, and the like.

The transportation industry has integrated air, rail, and road transport with information technology in ways that allow for previously impossible degrees of control and performance. Dell, for example, realized several years ago that it did not need to ship monitors and computers from the same location. Dell can schedule the coordinated same day delivery of computers and monitors from different assembly/factory locations to customers. The savings in this for Dell is significant, and the customer gets the order as if it had been shipped from a single location.

Communications

Distribution not only involves the flow of materials through the distribution channel, but also the flow of information. Here, we are talking about the order processing system, the invoicing system, the demand forecasting system, and so on. Without effective communications support, the distribution system will never be capable of providing satisfactory customer service at an acceptable cost.

Unitization

The way in which goods are packaged and then subsequently accumulated into larger unit sizes (e.g., a pallet-load) can have a major bearing upon distribution economics. For example, the ability to stack goods on a pallet, which then becomes the unit load for movement and storage, can lead to considerable cost savings in terms of handling and warehousing. Similarly, the use of containers as the basic unit of movement has revolutionized international transport and, to a certain extent, domestic transport as well. Mobile racking systems and front-end pricing by means of scanners are other unitization innovations that have had a dramatic effect upon the way goods are marketed.

MARKETING CHANNELS

The fundamental role of a company's distribution function is to ensure that the "right product is available at the right time and in the right place." This implies some organization of resources into channels through which the product moves to customers. A marketing channel is the route taken in the transfer of the title of a product or service from its original source of supply to its ultimate consumption. It is necessary to consider both the route of exchange and the physical movement route of the product—they may well be different.

Many companies use multiple marketing channels to reach their customers, often involving one or even several "intermediaries." The role of an intermediary is to provide the means of achieving the widest possible market coverage at a lower unit cost. Many intermediaries hold stock and thereby share some of the financial risk with the principal (or supplier). Figure 12-2 shows that using an intermediary carries benefits for the manufacturer, but it

Figure 12-2
Marketing Channels and Use of an Intermediary

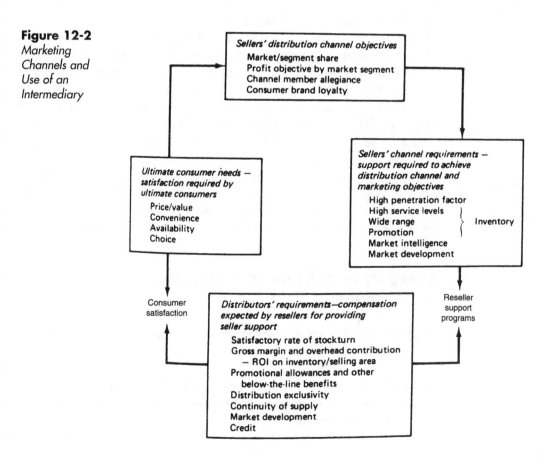

Figure 12-3
The Alternatives

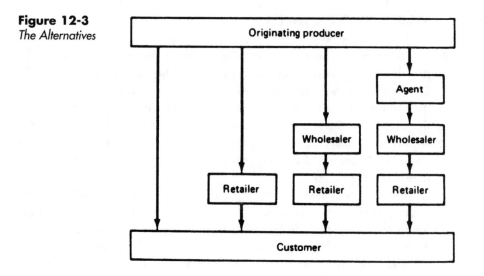

also involves significant "costs," the most important of which is the loss of control that accompanies such a channel strategy.

Often, too, considerable conflict exists between the respective objectives of suppliers and their distributors; this gives rise to conflict and suspicion in the relationship. Nevertheless, suppliers must evaluate the costs and benefits of each marketing channel potentially open to them and decide on a combination that best suits their type of business and the markets they are engaged in. The alternatives depicted in Figure 12-3 quite obviously have different cost/revenue profiles.

Any cost/benefit appraisal needs to be undertaken in the widest context possible. It needs to consider questions of market strategy, the appropriateness of the channel to the product, and customer requirements, as well as the question of the comparative costs of selling and distribution.

EVALUATION CRITERIA FOR CHANNEL INTERMEDIARIES

Regardless of the type of intermediary to be used, there are a number of basic evaluation criteria, for example:

- Do they now, or will they, sell to our target market segment?
- Is their sales force large enough and trained well enough to achieve our regional sales forecasts?

- Is their regional location adequate in respect of the retail (and other) outlets serviced?
- Are their promotional policies and budgets adequate?
- Do they satisfy customer after-sales requirements?
- Are their product policies consistent with our own?
- Do they carry competitive lines?
- What are their inventory policies regarding width, depth, and cover?
- Are they credit worthy?
- Is distributor management receptive, aggressive, and flexible?

All the above factors, and others, have to be considered when making specific decisions on choice of intermediaries, which in turn is part of the overall channel selection issue.

CUSTOMER SERVICE

The provision of customer service in all its various forms is likely to involve the firm in large financial commitments. (Note: Customer service applies to serving the channel intermediaries while consumer service applies to the ultimate consumer.) Figure 12-4 (A) shows the typical relationship between the level of availability and the cost of providing it. As

Figure 12-4A
Level of Availability and Cost

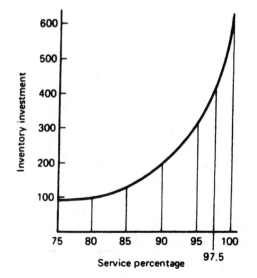

shown, the cost of increasing the service level by a small amount, say from 95 percent to 97.5 percent, results in a sharp increase in inventory costs. Figure 12-4 (B) shows how valuable it is to retain existing customers.

Many companies appear to be unaware of the level of service they are offering (i.e., there is *no* customer service policy as such). Even where such a policy does exist, the levels are quite often arbitrarily set and are not the result of a careful market analysis.

The question, then, arises: What level of availability *should* be offered? This question is relatively simple to answer in theory, but very difficult to quantify and achieve in practice, since different product groups in different market segments could well demand different levels of customer service.

In theory, at least, it is possible to say that service levels can continue to be improved as long as the marketing advantage that results continues to outrun the additional costs incurred. Conceptually, it is possible to draw an S-shaped curve (see Figure 12-5), which suggests that with very high

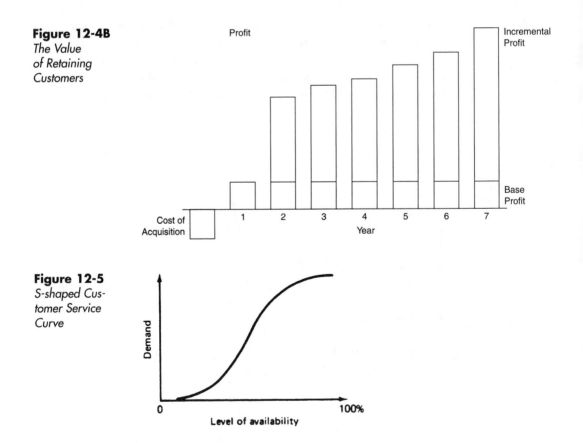

Figure 12-4B
The Value of Retaining Customers

Figure 12-5
S-shaped Customer Service Curve

levels of customer service, customers are unable to distinguish between small changes in the service offered. When a company is operating in this region, it is quite possibly incurring more costs than are necessary for the level of sales being achieved.

For example, marketing and sales managers who insist on offering maximum service to all customers, no matter what the profitability and location of those customers, are quite probably doing their company a disservice (remember the Pareto effect!). Somewhere between the costs and benefits involved in customer service, a balance has to be found. It is at that point where the additional revenue returns for each increment of service are equal to the extra cost involved in providing that increment. To attempt to ascertain this point of balance, certain information is required.

Developing a Customer Service Package

Service encompasses every aspect of the relationship between manufacturers and their distributors/customers. Under this definition, price, sales representation, after-sales service, product range offering, product availability, etc., are all dimensions of customer service (i.e., the total activity of

Questions to Determine Balance Between Costs and Benefits

1. How profitable is the product? What contribution to fixed costs and profits does this product make and what is its sales turnover?
2. What is the nature of the product? Is it a critical item as far as the customer is concerned, where stock-outs at the point of supply would result in a loss of sales? Does the product have characteristics that result in high stockholding costs?
3. What is the nature of the market? Does the company operate in a sellers' or a buyers' market? How frequently is the product purchased? Are there ready substitutes? What are the stockholding practices of the purchasers? Which markets and customers are growing and which are declining?
4. How profitable are the customers constituting each segment?
5. What is the nature of the competition? How many companies are providing an alternative source of supply to our customers? What sort of service levels do they offer?
6. What is the nature of the channel of distribution through which the company sells? Does the company sell direct to the end-customer, or through intermediaries? To what extent does the company control the channel and the activities of its members, such as the stock levels and order policies?

servicing one's customer). It is fundamental for suppliers to derive their concept of customer service from a study of their customers' real needs.

Determining customer needs will almost certainly mean designing different customer service packages for different market groups. Six steps are involved in this process:

1. Define the important service elements (and sub-elements).
2. Determine customers' viewpoints on these.
3. Design a competitive package (and several variations, if necessary).
4. Develop a promotional campaign to "sell" the service package idea.
5. Pilot-test a particular package and the promotional campaign being used.
6. Establish controls to monitor performance of the various service packages.

DEVELOPING THE DISTRIBUTION PLAN

Figure 12-6 shows the relationship between the marketing and distribution plans. Organizationally, it makes a lot of sense to make marketing responsible for distribution, since it is probably in the best position to make the difficult trade-off between very high levels of customer service and the high inventory-carrying costs associated with such levels.

Components of Customer Service to Be Researched

- Frequency of delivery
- Time from order to delivery
- Reliability of delivery
- Emergency deliveries when required
- Stock availability and continuity of supply
- Orders filled completely
- Advice on non-availability
- Technical support
- Convenience of placing order
- Acknowledgment of order
- Accuracy of invoices
- Quality of sales representation

- Regular calls by sales representatives
- Manufacturer monitoring of retail inventory levels
- Credit terms offered
- Customer question handling
- Quality of outer packaging
- Quality of inner package for in-store handling and display
- Consults on new product/package development
- Reviews product range regularly
- Coordination between production, distribution, and marketing

Figure 12-6
*Relation Between
Marketing and
Distribution Plans*

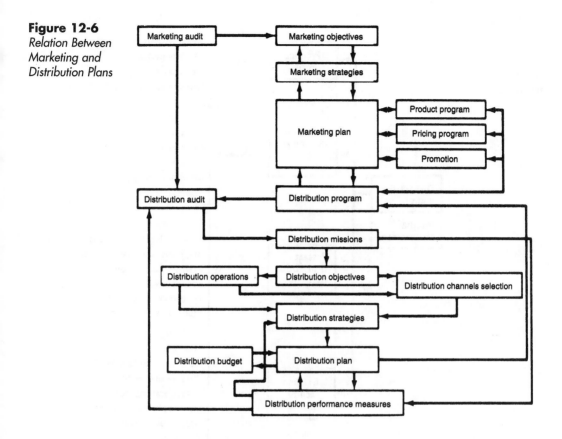

What Is Integrated Distribution Management?

Integrated distribution management is an approach to the distribution mission of the firm whereby two or more of the functions involved in moving goods from source to user are integrated and viewed as an inter-related system or sub-system for purposes of managerial planning, implementation, and control.

The Starting Point

Like the more general marketing audit referred to in Chapter 3, the distribution audit has two major parts: *internal* and *external*. Figures 12-7 and 12-8 illustrate the major components of the distribution audit.

Physical distribution ensures that products get to the right place, at the right time, and in the right condition. In some businesses, distribution

Figure 12-7
Elements of the
Distribution
Audit: Internal
Environment

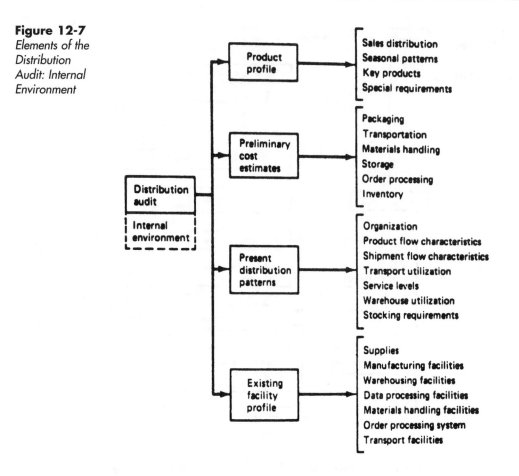

costs can amount to 20 percent or more of the selling price. From a range of possible distribution channels, choices should be made for the best competitive advantage.

Distribution objectives can be many and varied, but the following are considered basic for marketing purposes:

- Outlet penetration by type of distribution
- Inventory range and levels to be held
- Distributor sales and sales promotion activities
- Other specific customer development programs, such as incentives for distributors

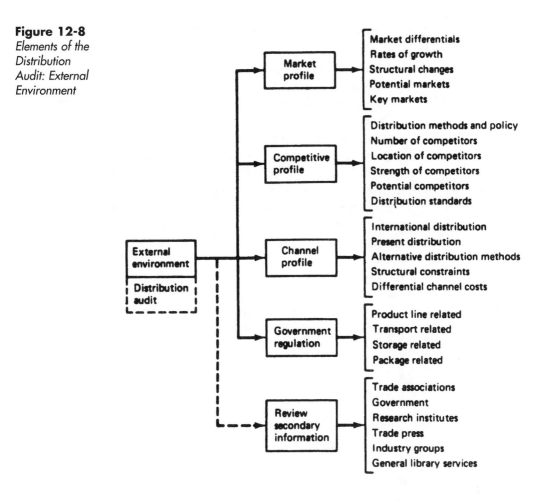

Figure 12-8
Elements of the Distribution Audit: External Environment

The following list illustrates a simple iterative approach to distribution planning that should help tighten what is often a neglected area of marketing management:

1. Determine marketing objectives.
2. Evaluate changing conditions in distribution at all levels.
3. Determine distribution task within overall marketing strategy.
4. Determine distribution policy in terms of type, number, and level of outlets to be used.
5. Set performance standards for the distribution organization.
6. Obtain performance information.
7. Compare actual with anticipated performance.
8. Adjustment where necessary.

QUESTIONS SUCCESSFUL COMPANIES ASK

1. What are the advantages and disadvantages of the channels currently used by your company?
2. Are there any cases where the channels used may not be the most appropriate?
3. If your company were new to the market, what channels would you use? How would your recommendations differ from existing arrangements? What prevents you from making these changes?
4. Are logistics adequately represented at board or senior management level in your organization? How could improvements be made?
5. What coordination takes place between physical distribution management and marketing management? How can any problems be minimized?
6. How are decisions currently made concerning customer service levels? How does it compare with competitors?
7. Can you see any way of making savings in your distribution system without reducing customer service?

13 Implementation Issues in Marketing Planning

Chapter 13 opens by discussing the implications of size and diversity of operations on marketing planning. This is followed by a summary of the main elements of the marketing planning process. There is a discussion of the role of the chief executive, followed by some thoughts on the marketing planning cycle and planning horizons. Finally, some insights are provided into how the marketing planning process works.

Some indication of the potential complexity of marketing planning can be seen in Figure 13-1. Even in a generalized model such as this, it can be seen that, in a large diversified company operating in global markets, a complex combination of product, market, and functional plans is possible. For example, what is required at regional level will be different from what is required at headquarters level, while it is clear that the total corporate plan has to be built from the individual building blocks. Furthermore, the function of marketing itself may be further functionalized for the purpose of planning, such as marketing research, advertising, selling, distribution, promotion, and so forth, while different customer groups may need to have separate plans drawn up.

Second, unnecessary planning, or overplanning, could easily result from an inadequate or indiscriminate consideration of the real planning needs at the different levels in the hierarchical chain. Third, as size and

In Chapter 3, we explained some of the many myths that surround marketing planning and listed the conditions that must be satisfied if any company is to have an effective marketing planning system. These are:

1. Any closed-loop marketing planning system (but especially one that is essentially a.forecasting and budgeting system) will lead to entropy of marketing and creativity. Therefore, there has to be some mechanism for preventing inertia from setting in through the over-bureaucratization of the system.

2. Marketing planning undertaken at the functional level of marketing, in the absence of a means of integration with other functional areas of the business at general management level, will be largely ineffective.

3. The separation of responsibility for operational and strategic marketing planning will lead to a divergence of the short-term thrust of a business at the operational level from the long-term objectives of the enterprise as a whole. This will encourage a preoccupation with short-term results at the operational level, which normally makes the firm less effective in the long term.

4. Unless the chief executive understands and takes an active role in marketing planning, it will never be an effective system.

5. A period of up to three years is necessary (especially in large firms) for the successful introduction of an effective marketing planning system.

Figure 13-1
Potential Complexity of Marketing Planning

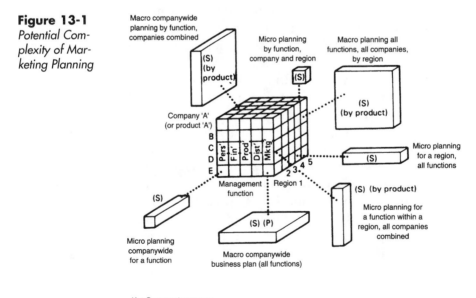

Figure 13-2
*Degree of
Formalization
of the Marketing
Planning Pro-
cess: Size and
Diversity*

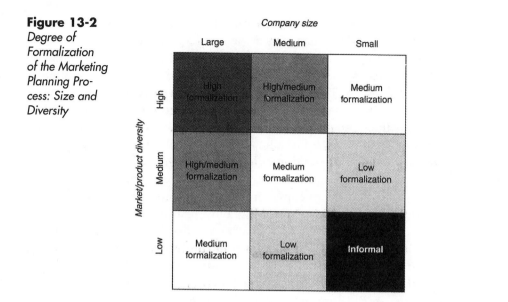

diversity grow, so the degree of formalization of the marketing planning process must also increase. This can be simplified in the form of a matrix (Figure 13-2). The degree of formalization must increase with the evolving size and diversity of operations. However, while the degree of formalization will change, the need for a complete marketing planning system does not.

Central to the success of any enterprise is the objective-setting process. Connected with this is the question of the design of the planning system and, in particular, the question of who should be involved in what, and how. For example, who should carry out the situation review, state the assumptions, set marketing objectives and strategies, and carry out the scheduling and costing-out program, and at what level? These complex issues revolve essentially around two dimensions—the size of the company and the degree of business diversity.

SIZE

Size of operations is, without a doubt, the biggest determinant of the type of marketing planning system used. In small companies, there is rarely much diversity of products or markets, and top management has an in-depth knowledge of the key determinants of success and failure. There is usually a high level of knowledge of both the technology and the market.

While in such companies the central control mechanism is the sales forecast and budget, top managers are able to explain the rationale lying behind the numbers, have a very clear view of their comparative strengths and weaknesses, and are able to explain the company's marketing strategy without difficulty. This understanding and familiarity with the strategy is shared with key operating subordinates by means of personal, face-to-face dialogue throughout the year. Subordinates are operating within a logical framework of ideas, which they understand. There is a shared understanding between top and middle management of the industry and prevailing business conditions. Such companies are, therefore, operating according to a set of structured procedures, and complete the several steps in the marketing planning process but in a relatively informal manner.

On the other hand, many small companies that have a poor understanding of the marketing concept, and in which the top manager leaves his strategy implicit, suffer many serious operational problems. These operational problems become progressively worse as the size of company increases. As the numbers and levels of management increase, it becomes progressively more difficult for top management to enjoy an in-depth knowledge of industry and business conditions by informal, face-to-face means. In the absence of written procedures and a structured framework, the different levels of operating management become increasingly less able to react in a rational way to pressures.

DIVERSITY OF OPERATIONS

From the point of view of management control, the least complex environment in which to work is an undiversified company (i.e., companies with limited product lines or homogeneous customer groups). For example, hydraulic hoses could be sold to many diverse markets, or a diverse range of products could be sold into only one market such as, say, the automotive industry. Both could be classified as "undiversified."

In undiversified companies, the need for institutionalized marketing planning systems increases with the size of the operation, and there is a strong relationship between size and the complexity of the management task, irrespective of any apparent diversity. For example, an oil company will operate in many diverse markets around the world, through many different kinds of marketing systems, and with varying levels of market growth and market share. In most respects, therefore, the control function for headquarters management is just as difficult and complex as that in a major, diversified conglomerate. The major difference is the greater level of in-depth knowledge that top management has about the key determinants of success and failure underlying the product or market worldwide, because of its homogeneity. Because of this homogeneity of product or market, it is usually possible for headquarters to impose worldwide policies on operating units in respect of things such as certain aspects of advertising, public relations, packaging, pricing, trademarks, product development, and so on, whereas in the headquarters of a diversified conglomerate, overall policies in areas like these are impracticable. To summarize, the smaller the company, the more informal and personal are the procedures for marketing planning. As company size and diversity increases, the need for more formalized procedures increases.

Companies that conform to the framework outlined here have systems which, through a hierarchy of bottom up/top down negotiating procedures, reach a nice balance between the need for detailed control at the lowest level of operations and centralized control. The main role of headquarters is to harness the company's strengths on a worldwide basis and to ensure that lower-level decisions do not cause problems in other areas and lead to wasteful duplication.

Figure 13.3 explores four key outcomes that marketing planning can evoke. Systems II, III, and IV, in which individuals are totally subordinate to a formalized system, individuals are allowed to do what they want

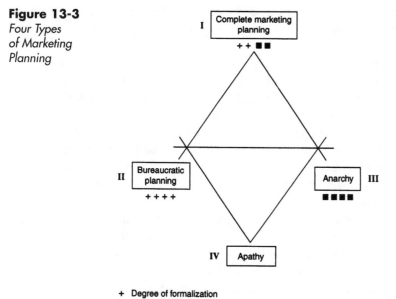

Figure 13-3
*Four Types
of Marketing
Planning*

I — Complete marketing planning
+ + ■ ■

II — Bureaucratic planning
+ + + +

III — Anarchy
■ ■ ■ ■

IV — Apathy

+ Degree of formalization
■ Degree of openness

without any system, or there is neither system, nor creativity, are less successful than system I, in which the individual is allowed to be entrepreneurial within a total system. System I, then, will be an effective marketing planning system, but one in which the degree of formalization will be a function of company size and diversity.

Creativity cannot flourish in a closed-loop formalized system. There would be little disagreement that in today's abrasive, turbulent, and highly competitive environment, it is those firms that succeed in extracting entrepreneurial ideas and creative marketing programs from systems that are necessarily yet acceptably formalized, that will succeed in the long run. Much innovative flair can so easily get stifled by systems.

There is ample evidence of international companies with highly formalized systems that produce stale and repetitive plans, with little changed from year to year and that fail to point up the really key strategic issues as a result. The waste this implies is largely due to a *lack of personal intervention by key managers during the early stages of the planning cycle*. There is clearly a need, therefore, to find a way of perpetually renewing the planning life cycle each time around. Inertia must never set in. Without some valve or means of opening up the loop, inertia quickly produces decay. The critical intervention of senior managers, from the chief executive down through the hierarchical chain, comes at the audit stage. Such a valve has to be inserted early in the planning cycle during the audit, or situation review stage. Essentially, what takes place is a personalized presentation of audit findings, together with proposed marketing objectives and strategies and outline budgets for the strategic planning period. These are discussed, amended where necessary, and agreed on in various synthesized formats at the hierarchical levels in the organization *before* any detailed operational planning takes place. It is at such meetings that managers are called upon to justify their views, which tends to force them to be more bold and creative than they would have been had they been allowed merely to send in their proposals. Obviously, however, even here much depends on the degree to which managers take a critical stance, which is much greater when the chief executive takes an active part in the process. *Every hour of time devoted at this stage by the chief executive has a multiplier effect throughout the remainder of the process.*

Until recently, it was believed that there may well be fundamental differences in marketing planning approaches, depending on factors such as the types of products and markets involved, company size, the degree of dependence on overseas sales, and the methods used to market goods abroad. In particular, the much-debated role of headquarters management in the marketing planning process is frequently put forward as being a potential cause of great difficulty. One of the most encouraging findings to emerge from our research is that the theory of marketing planning is universally applicable, and that such issues are largely irrelevant.

Although planning tasks are less complicated in small undiversified companies, and there is less need for formalized procedures than in large diversified companies, the fact is that exactly the same framework should be used in all circumstances, and that this approach brings similar benefits to all.

In a global company headquarters, management can assess major trends in products and markets around the world, and is able to develop strategies on a global basis. Subsidiary management is involved in this process by reporting on market and competitive developments in their territory. In addition to participating in the global strategy development process, subsidiary management is responsible for implementing the global strategy in its territory. This is achieved by means of synthesized information flows from the bottom upward, which facilitates useful comparison of performance around the world, and the diffusion of valuable information, skills, experiences, and systems from the top downward. The benefits that accrue to companies using such systems can be classified under the major headings of the marketing mix elements as follows:

- *Marketing information.* There is a transfer of knowledge, a sharing of expertise, and an optimization of effort around the world.
- *Product.* Control is exercised over the product range. Maximum effectiveness is gained by concentrating on certain products in certain markets, based on experience gained throughout the world.
- *Price.* Pricing policies are sufficiently flexible to enable local management to compete effectively, without creating a "gray market" for the company's products.
- *Place.* Substantial gains are made by rationalization of the logistics function.
- *Promotion.* Duplication of effort and a multitude of different platforms/company images are ameliorated. Efforts in one part of the world reinforce those in another.

The procedures that facilitate the provision of such information and knowledge transfers also encourage operational management to think strategically about their own areas of responsibility, instead of managing only for the short term.

BUDGETS

Detailed budgets (sometimes referred to as "appropriation budgets") should appear only in the detailed one-year operational marketing plan. In the three-year strategic marketing plan, all that is required are the financial implications (budget) of the agreed strategies. In a detailed one-year marketing plan, specific sub-objectives for products and segments are supported by more detailed strategy and action statements, such as what, where, when, and costs. They also include *budgets* and *forecasts* and, of course, a *consolidated budget*. The preparation of budgets and sales forecasts *must* reflect the marketing objectives. In turn, the objectives, strategies, and programs *must* reflect the agreed budgets and sales forecasts.

Forecasts (in lieu of objectives) are nothing more than an extrapolation of past experience. The marketing plan should take a "zero-based" view of the current and possible future environments in order to arrive at a viable set of objectives. Unit forecasts then follow. This is necessary in order to identify possible "discontinuities" in our future environment; simple extrapolation of historical data ignores the possibility that discontinuities can (and do) occur.

A deeper perception of the marketplace is needed in order to review and reveal viable marketing objectives and strategies, which are consistent with the company's distinctive competence. Individual budget items must clearly be retraceable to issues identified in the original SWOT. When measuring performance, at all times seek to relate to the outside market as well as to your internal budget.

THE WRITTEN MARKETING PLAN

A written marketing plan (or plans) is the outcome of the marketing planning process. It is effectively a business proposition containing proposed courses of action that in turn have resource implications. Written marketing plans verbalize (and formalize) our intuitive model of the market environment within which we operate. Written marketing plans help to make things happen. The acid test of any marketing plan presentation is to ask yourself, "Would I put my own life's savings into the plan as presented?" If the answer is *no*, then further work is needed to refine your ideas.

Good discipline in preparing "internally consistent" marketing plans is to use the following summary format:

SWOT issues ⇒ Objectives ⇒ Strategy ⇒ Specific actions and timing

ROLE OF THE CHIEF EXECUTIVE

Our research reveals that many chief executives do not have a clear understanding of:

- Purposes and methods of planning
- Proper assignments of planning responsibilities throughout the organization
- The talent and skills required in effective planning

The role of the CEO in marketing planning is critical: it is nothing less than to act as a catalyst for the entrepreneurial creativity that is inherent in every organization. Jack Welch, Chairman and CEO of General Electric and a model of the CEO as catalyst, calls this "delayering."

Welch describes delayering at General Electric

While we were restructuring the businesses, we also changed the management hardware at GE. We delayered. We removed "Sectors," "Groups," "Strategic Business Units," and much of the extensive command structure and staff apparatus we used to run the Company.

We cleared out stifling bureaucracy, along with the strategic planning apparatus, corporate staff empires, rituals, endless studies and briefings, and all the classic machinery that makes big-company operations smooth and pre-dictable—but often glacially slow. As the underbrush of bureaucracy was cleared away we began to see and talk to each other more clearly and more directly.[1]

Source: Annual Report, General Electric Company, 1995, pg. 2

THE MARKETING PLANNING CYCLE

The schedule should call for work on the plan for the next year to begin early enough in the current year to permit adequate time for market research and analysis of key data and market trends. In addition, the plan should provide for the early development of a strategic plan that can be approved or altered in principle.

A key factor in determining the planning cycle is the degree to which it is practicable to extrapolate from sales and market data, but, generally speaking, successful planning companies start the planning cycle formally somewhere between nine and six months before the beginning of the next fiscal year.

PLANNING HORIZONS

One- and five-year planning periods have been by far the most common, although three years has now become the most common period for the strategic plan, largely because of the dramatically increasing rate of environmental change. Lead time for the initiation of major new product innovations, the length of time necessary to recover capital investment costs, the continuing availability of customers and raw materials, and the size and usefulness of existing plant and buildings are the most frequently mentioned reasons for having a five-year planning horizon. Increasingly, however, these five-year plans are taking the form more of "scenarios" than the detailed strategic plan outlined in this book.

Many companies, however, do not give sufficient thought to the planning horizon for their particular circumstances. A five-year time span is clearly too long for some companies, particularly those operating in volatile fashion-conscious markets or in industries with rapidly changing technical constraints and possibilities. On the other hand, for companies in industries that require long-term capital commitments, five years may be far too short a horizon. Each company must select the appropriate planning horizon.

HOW THE PROCESS WORKS

There is one other major aspect to be considered. It concerns the location of the marketing planning activity in a company. The answer is simple. Marketing planning should take place as close to the marketplace as possible. Since, in anything but the smallest of undiversified companies, it is not possible for top management to set detailed objectives for operating units, it is suggested that at this stage in the planning process, strategic guidelines should be issued. One way of doing this is in the form of a *strategic planning letter*. Another is by means of a personal briefing by the chief executive at "kick-off" meetings (Table 13.1).

The interdependence between the top-down/bottom-up process is illustrated in Figures 13.4 and 13.5, which show a similar hierarchy in respect of objective and strategy setting to that illustrated in respect of audits.

TABLE 13-1 Chief Executive's Strategic Planning Letter (Possible Areas for Which Objective and Strategies or Strategic Guidelines Will Be Set)

Financial	*Operations*
Remittances	Land
Dividends	Buildings
Royalties	Plant
Gross margin %	Modifications
Operating profit	Maintenance
Return on capital employed	Systems
Debtors	Raw materials
Creditors	Supplies
Bank loans	Purchasing
Investments	Distribution
Capital expenditure	Stock and control
Cash flow controls	Transportation
	Warehousing
Human resources and organization	*Marketing*
Management	Target markets
Training	Market segments
Industrial relations	Brands
Organization	Volumes
Remuneration and pensions	Market shares
	Pricing
	Image
	Promotion
	Market research
	Quality control
	Customer service

Figure 13-4
Top-Down and Bottom-Up

Top-down and bottom-up

Overall objectives and strategies (strategic guidelines)

Unit objectives and strategies

Having explained carefully the point about *requisite* marketing planning, these figures also illustrate the principles by which the marketing planning process should be implemented in any company, irrespective of whether it is a small company or a major multinational. In essence, these exhibits show a *hierarchy* of audits, SWOT analysis, objectives, strategies, and programs.

Figure 13.6 is another way of illustrating the total corporate strategic and planning process. This time, however, a time element is added, and

Figure 13-5
*Strategic and
Operational
Planning*

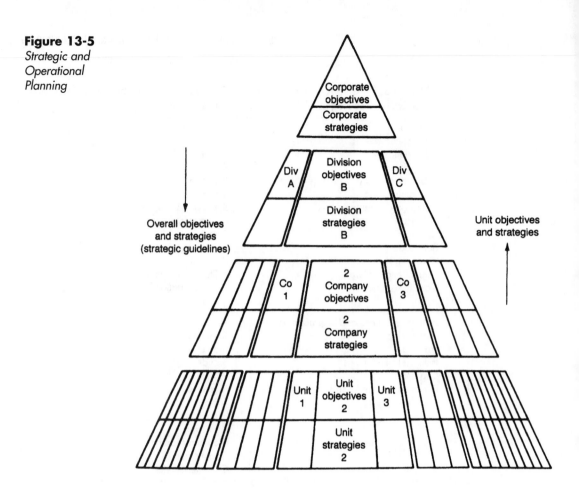

Figure 13-6
*Total Corporate
Strategic and
Planning Process*

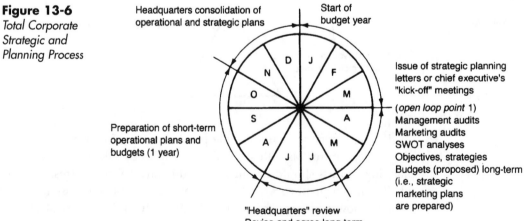

the relationship between strategic planning and short-term operational plans is clarified. It is important to note that there are two 'open loop' points on this last diagram. These are the key times in the planning process when a subordinate's views and findings should be subjected to the closest examination by a superior.

CONCLUSION

We must stress that there can be no such thing as a ready-made marketing planning system. Nonetheless, our research and experience indicate that marketing planning remains one of the great bastions of management ignorance, largely because of the complexity of the process and its organizational, political, and cultural implications.

It is for these reasons that we have added a final chapter that contains both a very brief summary of the main points described in the book and a simple, step-by-step system that can become the basis of your own planning procedures. The system provided has been used successfully in businesses ranging from big international industrial companies to small domestic service organizations.

Success comes from *experience*. Experience comes from making mistakes. You can minimize your mistakes if you combine *common sense* with the *models and conceptual frameworks* provided in this book. If you read this book carefully and use the models creatively, marketing planning becomes one of the most powerful tools available to a business today.

QUESTIONS SUCCESSFUL COMPANIES ASK

1. Does the principle of hierarchies of audits, SWOTs, objectives, strategies, and programs apply in your company? If not, describe how they are handled.
2. If it does, describe in what ways it differs from the principles outlined here.
3. Design a simple system for your company, or describe in what ways your existing system could be improved.

14 Marketing Planning in Review

Chapter 14 is a review of the strategic marketing planning process. It starts by re-emphasizing the need for a written plan and iterating basic principles key to the success of the process. The chapter then summarizes the components of the plan and its physical structure.

Figure 14-1 is a summary of what appears in a strategic marketing plan and a list of the principal marketing tools/techniques/structures/ frameworks that apply to each step. Marketing planning has never been just the simple step-by-step approach described so enthusiastically in most prescriptive texts and courses. The moment an organization embarks on the marketing planning path, it can expect to encounter a number of complex organizational, attitudinal, process, and cognitive problems, which are likely to block progress. By being forewarned about these barriers, there is a good chance of successfully using the step-by-step marketing planning system described in this chapter to arrive at excellent marketing planning that will bring all the claimed benefits, including a significant impact on the bottom line through the creation of competitive advantage.

THE STRATEGIC MARKETING PLAN

The first priority in the strategic marketing planning process is to have a strategy and a plan and then communicate it to the entire organization. If the people who are executing a marketing strategy and plan do not understand the plan, it does not exist, even if is written and bound in a handsome leather volume. So, first things first, and the first thing is the strategy and the plan. The second priority is to put the strategy and the plan into writing. The written plan is an invaluable tool because it is a record of the key facts, assumptions, and rationale of the marketing strategy. It can be shared and reviewed by people within and outside the organization. If things are going well, it is important to know why; if the underlying reasons for success change, you will also need to change your marketing plan. If things are not going well, it is also important to know why in order to recognize what must be done to reverse a decline.

An illustration of what can happen without a written marketing strategy and plan is the case of General Motors. The company announced in late 2000 that it was going to shut down its oldest unit, the Oldsmobile Division. The division and the company have been losing market share worldwide and in the United States for over thirty years. It has been clear to the author that a core problem and source of GM's difficulty has been the fragmentation and waste that is associated with the company's fifteen plus automobile divisions and marques (seven of which operate in the U.S. auto market).

All of GM's competitors, with the exception of Ford Motor Company, operate in the same global market with, at most, two brand marques. Toyota, for example, has the Toyota and Lexus marques. BMW has only the BMW marque. GM, in contrast, has Chevrolet, Pontiac, Oldsmobile, Buick,

Figure 14-1 *Marketing Planning and Theory*

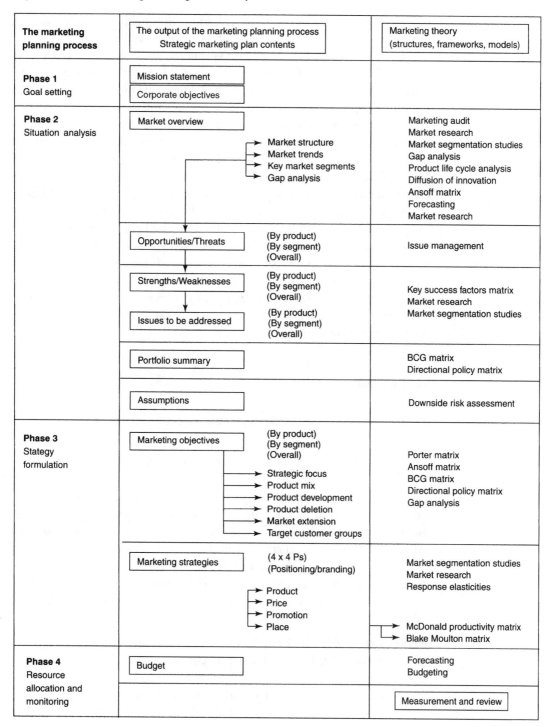

Cadillac, Saturn, GMC, Opel, EV1, Holden, Hummer, Saab, and Vauxhall as well as GM Network marques Fiat, Fuji, Isuzu, and Suzuki.

The competition is focused and GM is fragmented. This is obvious to anyone who looks at GM objectively, but it has not been clear to GM, which wasted billions of dollars on the Oldsmobile marque right up until the day the company announced that it was shutting down the division. Does GM have a strategic marketing strategy and plan? In the author's view, the company has a marketing plan and strategy that is well designed for the market that existed in the period from 1915 to about 1970. In other words, GM has a historical document, a blast from their past, but not a contemporary marketing strategy and plan that addresses the realities of consumers and competitors in today's automobile market.

Is the GM marketing strategy written down? I don't know the answer to this question, but if it is, it would not get a passing grade in my strategic marketing planning class. And this is the advantage of a written marketing plan. If it is down in writing, you can or should be able to look at it objectively, or if you cannot muster up the consciousness to look at it objectively, you can at least give it to someone who can be objective and then listen to that person's critique.

THE PRINCIPLES

The basic principles of marketing planning are listed below.

Principle 1. Strategic Plan Before Tactical Plan

Develop the strategic marketing plan first. This entails greater emphasis on scanning the external environment, the early identification of forces emanating from it, and developing appropriate strategic responses, involving all levels of management in the process. A strategic plan should cover a period of between one and five years, and only when this has been developed and agreed upon should the one-year tactical marketing plan be developed. Never write the one-year plan first and extrapolate from it.

Principle 2. Marketing Is the Responsibility of Everyone in the Organization

Everyone in the organization should be a potential contributor to the marketing planning process. Where practicable, have both marketing and sales report to the same person, who should not normally be the chief executive officer.

Principle 3. Shared Values About Marketing

Marketing is a management process whereby the resources of the whole organization are utilized to satisfy the needs of selected customer groups in order to achieve the objectives of both parties. Marketing is an attitude rather than a series of functional activities.

Principle 4: Structure Around Markets

Organize company activities around customer groups, if possible, rather than around functional activities, and conduct marketing planning in these strategic business units. Without excellent marketing planning in strategic business units, corporate marketing planning and brand management is of limited effectiveness.

Principle 5. Scan the Environment Thoroughly

An effective scan of the environment must include both external and internal information. This, in turn, will lead to a marketing audit that is specific and valuable to the planning efforts. The marketing audit, a prerequisite to any consideration of future strategies, should not consist of vague generalities like "poor economic conditions" and should incorporate such tools and models as product life cycles and portfolios.

Principle 6. Summarize Information in SWOT Analyses

Information is the foundation on which a marketing plan is built. From information (internal and external) comes intelligence. A SWOT analysis does the following:

- Focuses on each specific segment of crucial importance to the organization.
- Is a summary emanating from the marketing audit.
- Is brief, interesting, and concise.
- Focuses on *key* factors only.

- Lists *differential* strengths and weaknesses in relation to competitors, focusing on competitive advantage.
- Lists *key* external opportunities and threats only.
- Identifies the *real* issues. It should not be a list of unrelated points.
- Is clear enough for a reader to grasp instantly the main thrust of the business, even to the point of being able to write marketing objectives.
- Answers the implied question "which means that . . ." to get the real implications.

Principle 7. Skills and Knowledge

Ensure that all those responsible for marketing in the SBUs have the necessary marketing knowledge and skills for the job. In particular, ensure that they understand and know how to use the more important tools of marketing, such as:

- Information scanning/probing
- Positioning
- Market segmentation
- Targeting
- Product life cycle
- Gap analysis
- BCG matrix
- Portfolio management
- 4 Ps of marketing—product, price, place, and promotion

Principle 8. Systematize the Process

It is essential to have a set of written procedures and a well-argued common format for marketing planning. The purposes of such a system are:

- To ensure that all key issues are systematically considered.
- To pull together the essential elements of the strategic plan in a consistent manner.
- To help corporate management, in a multi-business enterprise, to compare diverse businesses and to understand the overall condition of, and prospects for, the organization.

Note: For readers who would like to take advantage of marketing planning software designed to guide planners in systematic marketing planning, see the author's note at the end of the book.

Principle 9. Sequence Objectives

Ensure that all objectives are prioritized according to their impact on the organization and the urgency with which they need to be achieved. Make sure that resources are allocated accordingly.

Principle 10. Style and Culture

Marketing planning is not effective without the active support and participation of top management. But, even with this support, the type of marketing planning has to be appropriate for the phase of the organizational life cycle. This phase should be measured before attempting to introduce marketing planning.

THE MARKETING PLANNING PROCESS

There are four steps in the planning process:

1. *Analysis.* The business must analyze both its marketplace and its own position within it, relative to the competition.
2. *Objectives.* The analysis must be used to construct a realistic set of quantitative marketing and financial objectives, consistent with those set by the organization.
3. *Strategy.* The business must determine the broad strategy that will accomplish these objectives, conforming to the organization's corporate strategy.
4. *Tactics.* The business must draw together the results of the analysis, the objectives, and the strategy, and use them as the foundation for detailed tactical action plans that are capable of implementing the strategy and achieving the agreed objectives.

This process is formally expressed in two marketing plans, the strategic marketing plan and the tactical marketing plan. The strategic marketing plan, the focus of this book, is designed for business units to be able to take a long-term, logical, and constructive approach to planning for success, whereas the tactical marketing plan focuses on short-term objectives and translation of strategic objectives into tactical issues.

For an action-focused strategic marketing plan, a considerable amount of background information and data needs to be collected, collated, and analyzed. An analytical framework to guide this analysis is provided in Figure 14-1. However, the commentary given in the strategic marketing plan should provide the main findings of the analysis rather than a mass of raw data. It should compel concentration upon only that which is essential. The analysis section should, therefore, provide only a short background.

Timing of the marketing planning process is linked to the fiscal year. To do a thorough job, the strategic plan may take several months to complete, while the tactical plan based on the strategic marketing plan may take an additional several months. Of course, plans for new products will take longer to complete than for products with existing plans that may only need revision. For the sake of simplicity, it has been assumed that the organization's year runs from January to December. Figure 14-2 outlines the timing of the marketing planning process.

1. Executive Summary

Over and over, you've heard how important a resume is to a job applicant. If the resume does not press the reviewer's buttons, it is discarded. An executive summary is just as important to a business or marketing plan as a good resume is to a job opportunity. If the executive summary is not well written, the rest of the plan will not be read. If a business or marketing plan is not read, the plan is dead as a tool for communicating and motivating no matter how good the plan is.

The executive summary is your chance to grab your reader's attention and generate an interest and motivation to read your plan. Busy executives will conclude, with justification, that a poorly written, hard to understand, uninformative, unconvincing executive summary is a good clue about the plan that it purports to describe. A busy executive will act rationally and not waste his or her time reading the plan that follows.

What is an executive summary? It is a short, one- to two-page summary of the key facts, assumptions, and rationale of the plan. In the written plan, it should appear as the first section of the plan in the table of contents. It should be the first and the last section of the plan to be written because it is a summary of the contents of the entire plan. You should prepare a draft executive summary before you write your plan, and you should revise that draft after you have completed your plan. In short, the executive summary is the alpha and the omega of the plan preparation process.

The name "executive summary" is derived from the fact that it is intended for executives who are extremely busy and may not care to read the contents unless the plan contains something of importance at the level of

Figure 14-2
*Strategic Plan-
ning Time Frame*

This is the marketing planning
process. It must not be confused
with what appears in the plan itself,
which is described on the right.

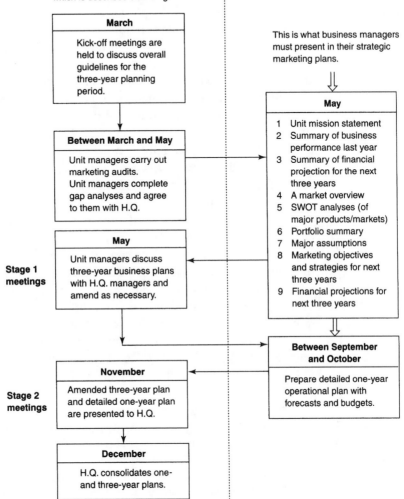

March
Kick-off meetings are held to discuss overall guidelines for the three-year planning period.

This is what business managers
must present in their strategic
marketing plans.

May
1   Unit mission statement 2   Summary of business performance last year 3   Summary of financial projection for the next three years 4   A market overview 5   SWOT analyses (of major products/markets) 6   Portfolio summary 7   Major assumptions 8   Marketing objectives and strategies for next three years 9   Financial projections for next three years

Between March and May
Unit managers carry out marketing audits. Unit managers complete gap analyses and agree to them with H.Q.

Stage 1 meetings

May
Unit managers discuss three-year business plans with H.Q. managers and amend as necessary.

Between September and October
Prepare detailed one-year operational plan with forecasts and budgets.

Stage 2 meetings

November
Amended three-year plan and detailed one-year plan are presented to H.Q.

December
H.Q. consolidates one- and three-year plans.

the executive and above. Therefore, it is short, concise, and contains only the most important facts and assumptions.

Remember that your reader is a busy executive or investor, and has no shortage of things to read. Does this surprise you? The document that you spent so much time in preparing must be seen from the reader's eyes. Your plan may be competing with numerous other plans he/she has to read. If it is a venture capital firm reviewing requests for funds, there are literally hundreds of plans to read. If your plan is going to an executive in an organization where it will be read regardless of the quality of the executive summary, a poor summary throws away an opportunity to really grab your reader and drive home the essential and fundamental essence of your strategy.

The executive summary should be concise (i.e., short) because its purpose is to save executives time by filtering out good proposals just like a bad resume filters out candidates who do not appear to be good prospects. If the resume is good, the candidate will then be called in for an interview to provide additional information. If the executive summary is good, the reader will probably proceed to read the rest of the document. If the executive summary is not good, the plan will either be rejected as in the case of a business plan, or be read under duress if it is an internal marketing plan.

An executive summary is not a verbal table of contents. It should not read, "This plan will discuss details of XYZ Company and how it will succeed in business. It consists of an analysis of the business and recommendations." No, no, no, a thousand times no! These are not key facts that the executive can use to make better, important decisions.

Furthermore, the executive summary is not a history lesson. Does it matter to the executive reading it that "the XYZ Company was founded in 1948 by Mr. Ding and Mr. Dong." No. The only exception to this guideline may be in a business plan where the information about the founding fathers/mothers is critical to the credibility of the proposal.

What should the executive summary contain? One to two sentences on the WHO, WHAT, WHY, WHERE, WHEN, HOW, and AT WHAT COST.

The example below illustrates the outline of an executive summary:

The XYZ Company plans to open a 25,000-square-foot retail facility in Anywhere, USA, selling widgets to its primary target market of women, ages 19–49, with individual incomes over $35,000 per year. The start-up expenses are estimated to be $1,000,000. Sales for the year 200x are estimated to be $500,000. Consecutive years sales are projected to be $750,000 in 200x + 1, $1,000,000 in 200x + 2, and $1,500,000 in 200x + 3. These represent increases of 50%, 33%, and 50% respectively.

These sales will be achieved by offering (list product categories). The company will position itself as (what it is, what it is not) and will offer a unique value to consumers in the form of (explain the unique value). The basic strategy of the company will be (describe the position you will create and defend, or the unique resources you will assemble, or the simple rules you will follow).

It will be supported by an integrated marketing communications program with a budget of $xx. Advertising and marketing PR will be handled by

ABC and XYZ agencies. Sales promotion will be handled in-house. Web programs will include xx, etc.

Although there is an expected loss of $ in 200x, the break-even is expected at the year 200x + 1 with profits of $ in 200x + 2 and $ in 200x + 3.

In summary, here are some guidelines to help write an effective executive summary:

1. Prepare the draft summary before you begin writing your plan.
2. Include only the most important facts that are key to decision making.
3. List your key assumptions, and underline that they are assumptions.
4. Describe the estimated sales and profit levels for the time period under consideration along with the percent change from previous years.
5. Describe your market position and share for the time period of the plan.
6. Describe your strategy. Explain how your plan will lead to a unique value for customers and marketing success.
7. Keep it short! Remember, brevity is the essence of life.

Write the final version of the executive summary after you have completed the entire plan.

2. Mission Statement

The purpose of the mission statement is to ensure that the raison d'être of the business is clearly stated. It is discussed in greater detail in Chapter 3, The Marketing Planning Process.

A mission statement should cover the following points:

- *Role or Contribution of the Unit.* For example, profit generator, service department, opportunity seeker.
- *Definition of Business.* For example, the needs you satisfy or the benefits you provide. Do not be too specific (e.g., "we sell milking machinery") or too general (e.g., "we are in the engineering business").
- *Distinctive Competence.* This should be a brief statement that applies only to your business. A statement that could equally apply to any competitor is unsatisfactory.
- *Indications for Future Direction.* A brief statement of the principal things you would give serious consideration to (e.g., move into a new segment).

A statement about what you *will* consider, *might* consider, and *will never* consider can be quite useful.

3. Summary of Financial Objectives and Projections

The purpose of the summary of financial projections is to enable the person reading the plan to see the financial implications over the full planning period. It should be presented as a simple chart along the lines shown in Table 14-1. This should be accompanied by a brief commentary. For example: "This three-year business plan shows a 28.6 percent increase in revenue from $700 million to $900 million and an increase in profit from $100,000 to $400,000 for an increase of 300.0 percent."

4. Marketing Audit

The marketing audit (situational analysis or business review may also be used) is a formal, systematic review of the marketplace and the results of the currently executed strategic and tactical marketing plans. The audit is introduced in Chapter 2. Chapters 6 and 7 deal with customers and markets, and products, respectively.

The marketing audit will inevitably require considerably more data preparation than is required to be reproduced in the marketing plan itself. Therefore, all managers should keep a *running reference file* for their area of responsibility during the year, which can also be used as a continual reference source and for verbal presentation of proposals.

This summary is designed to give a bird's-eye view of total marketing activities. In addition to a quantitative summary of performance, as shown

TABLE 14-1 Summary of Financial Projections

	t-1*	t-2	t-3	t-4	t-5
Sales					
Gross margin					
Research and development					
Selling, general, and administrative					
Operating expenses					
Interest and other income (expense)					
Net Income					

*t = time period (i.e., year or quarter)

in Table 14-1, managers should give a summary of reasons for good or bad performance.

The marketing audit is intended to provide a picture of the market before descending to the particular details of individual market segments. This system is based upon the *segmentation* of markets, dividing these into homogeneous groups of customers, each having characteristics that can be exploited in marketing terms. *This approach is taken because it is the one that is often the most useful for managers to be able to develop their markets.* The alternative, product-oriented approach is rarely appropriate, given the variation between different customer groups in the markets in which most organizations compete.

It should be possible (following completion of the marketing audit) to present a market overview that summarizes what managers consider to be the key characteristics of their markets. In completing this section, managers should consider the following:

1. What are the major products and markets (or segments) that are likely to be able to provide the kind of business opportunities suitable for the organization?
2. How are these changing? That is, which are growing and which are declining?

This section should be brief and there should be some commentary by management about what seems to be happening in their market. It is very helpful if managers can present as much of this information as possible visually (e.g., bar charts or pie charts, product life cycles, etc.). A market "map" can be extremely useful for clarifying how the market works. (For further details of this technique, see Chapter 3.)

5. SWOT Analyses

There are three major parts to doing an effective SWOT analysis: compiling the information, completing it, and applying it.

Compiling the SWOT Analyses

To decide on future marketing objectives and strategy, it is first necessary to summarize your *present* position in its market(s). This was done in the previous section. The marketing audit must now be summarized in the form of a *SWOT analysis* for each of the major products/markets (segments) highlighted in the previous section. The acronym SWOT derives from the initial letters of the words *strengths, weaknesses, opportunities,* and *threats.* It is discussed in greater detail in Chapter 13.

In simple terms, the SWOT asks these questions:

- What are the unit's differential strengths and weaknesses vis-à-vis competitors? In other words, why should potential customers in the target markets prefer to deal with your organization rather than with your competitors? These are internal factors that the company has direct control over.
- What are the positive trends in the marketplace –(i.e., opportunities)? What are the negative trends (i.e., threats) in the marketplace? These are external factors that the company cannot control.
- What are the future strengths, weaknesses, opportunities, and threats to the business in each of the segments that have been identified as being of importance?

Completing the SWOT Analysis

Based on findings from the SWOT analysis, you can identify what you consider to be the key product/market (segments) on which you intend to focus. For presentation purposes, it is helpful if you can present a brief SWOT for each of these key product/market segments.

Section I concerns *strengths* and *weaknesses.* Section II is intended to indicate how the *opportunities* and *threats* section of the SWOT should be completed. Section III summarizes *key issues to be addressed.* Section IV describes the setting of assumptions, marketing objectives, and strategies for each product/market segment. Section V summarizes the position of competitors.

I. Strengths and Weaknesses—Important factors for success in this business (critical success factors). Factors such as product performance, breadth of services, speed of service, and low costs are often the most important factors for success. You should now make a brief statement about your organization's *strengths and weaknesses* in relation to these most important factors for success that you have identified. To do this, consider competitors in the same segment in order to identify why you believe your product and organization can succeed and what weaknesses must be addressed in the three-year planning period.

These factors are called critical success factors (CSFs). A layout such as that shown in Figure 14-3 is useful. You should then weight each factor out of 100 (e.g., CSF 1 = 60; CSF 2 = 25; CSF 3 = 10; CSF 4 = 5). It is suggested that you score yourself and each competitor out of 10 on each of the CSFs. Then, multiply each score by the weight. This will give you an accurate

Figure 14-3
Critical Success
Factors

Critical success factors \ Competitors	Weighting factor	Your organization	Competitor A	Competitor B	Competitor C
CSF 1					
CSF 2					
CSF 3					
CSF 4					
Total weighted score	100				

reading of your position in each segment vis-à-vis your competitors. It will also highlight which are the key issues that should be addressed in the three-year planning period.

Great caution is necessary to ensure that you are not guilty of self-delusion. Obviously, it is desirable to have independent evidence from market research in order to be able to complete this section accurately. Also, it is quite useful if you can get a number of customers to complete this independently, as sometimes it reveals a lot about what they believe to be the factors for success.

II. Opportunities and Threats—Summary of outside influences and their implications. This summary includes a brief statement about how important environmental influences such as technology, government policies and regulations, and the economy have affected this segment. There will obviously be some opportunities or positive trends and some threats or negative trends. They should be listed in descending order of importance.

III. Key issues to be addressed. Based on your findings in Sections I and II, you should select a number of key issues to be addressed in the rest of your plan. This selection is critical, as many businesspeople love to develop a laundry list of SWOT instead of concentrating on the most important factors and how to address them. The contents of the plan should be balanced between analysis and future action.

IV. Assumptions, marketing objectives, and marketing strategies. Assumptions can now be made and objectives and strategies set. It should be stressed at this point that such assumptions, objectives, and strategies relate only to each particular product/market segment under consideration. These will guide your thinking when setting overall assumptions, marketing objectives, and strategies later on.

V. Competitor analysis. For each major or potentially major competitor, you should indicate their sales within the particular product/market segment under consideration, their market share now and in the past three years, *and their expected share three years from now.* The greater a competitor's influence over others, the greater their ability to implement their own independent strategies, hence the more successful they are. It is suggested that you should also classify each of your main competitors according to one of the classifications in the guide to competitive position classifications in Table 14-2 below (i.e., leadership, strong, favorable, tenable, weak). List the competitors' principal products or services and their business direction and current strategy. Next, list their major strengths and weakness. The format shown in Figure 14-4 is useful.

Applying Conclusions from the SWOT

All that remains is to summarize (remember, emphasize only the most important) each of these SWOTs in a format that makes it easy to see at a glance the overall position and relative importance of each of these segments to the organization. This can be done by drawing a diagram in the form of a four-box matrix, which will show each of the important product/market segments described earlier. A matrix is shown as Figure 14-5.

TABLE 14-2 Guide to Competitive Position Classifications

Leadership	• Has a major influence on the performance or behavior of others
Strong	• Has a wide choice of strategies • Is able to adopt an independent strategy without endangering their short-term position • Has low vulnerability to competitors' actions
Favorable	• Exploits specific competitive strengths, often in a product-market niche • Has more than average opportunity to improve their position; has several strategies available
Tenable	• Their performance justifies continuation in business
Weak	• Currently has an unsatisfactory performance and significant competitive weakness • They must improve or withdraw

Figure 14-4
Competitor Analysis

Competitors					
Main competitor	Products/ markets	Business direction and current objectives and strategies	Strengths	Weaknesses	Competitive position

Figure 14-5
Portfolio Matrix

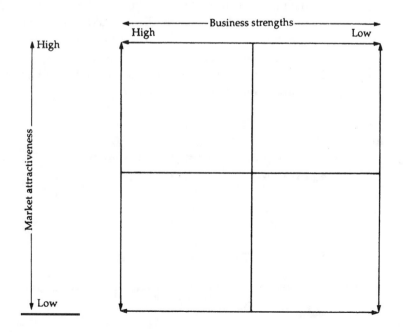

Some easy-to-follow instructions follow on how to complete such a matrix. More detailed instructions are provided in Chapter 4.

The *portfolio matrix* (referred to as the directional policy matrix in Chapter 4) enables you to assess which products or services, or which groups of customers/segments, will offer the best chance for commercial success. It will also aid decision making about which products or services (or market segments) merit investment, both in terms of finance and managerial effort.

1. List your market segments and decide which ones are the most attractive. (Note that these "segments" can be countries, divisions, markets, distributors, customers, etc.) To arrive at these decisions, you will need to take many factors into account, including:
   • The size and rate of growth of the markets
   • Market needs
   • Pricing conditions and trends
   • The competition: quantity and quality
   • The business environment
   • Macro trends and developments; technology, economic conditions, regulations, etc.

   Imagine that you have a measuring instrument, something like a thermometer, but one which measures not temperature but industry attractiveness. The higher the reading, the more attractive the market. The instrument is shown in Figure 14-6. Estimate the position on the scale that *each* of your markets would record (should such an instrument exist) and make a note of it as shown by the example above. You should use the methodology outlined in Chapter 6.

2. Transpose this information onto the matrix in Figure 14-5, writing the markets on the left of the matrix.

Figure 14-6
Industry
Attractiveness

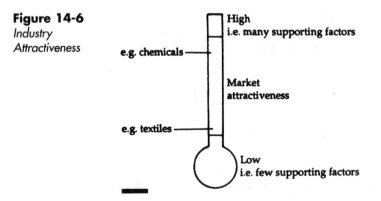

High
i.e. many supporting factors

e.g. chemicals —

Market
attractiveness

e.g. textiles —

Low
i.e. few supporting factors

Figure 14-7
Market
Attractiveness

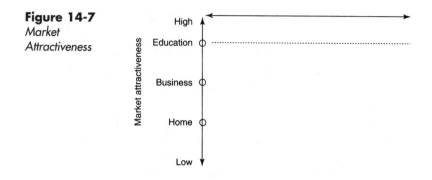

3. Still using the matrix, draw a dotted line horizontally across from the top left-hand market as shown in Figure 14-7.
4. Ask yourself how well your business is equipped to deal with this most attractive market. A whole series of questions needs to be asked to establish the company's business strengths, for example:
   - Do we have the right products?
   - How well are we known in this market?
   - What image do we have?
   - Do we have the right technical skills?
   - How close are we to this market?
   - How do we compare with competitors?

   The outcome of such an analysis will enable you to arrive at a conclusion about the "fitness" of your unit and you will be able to choose a point on the horizontal scale of the matrix to represent this. The left of the scale represents many unit strengths, the right few unit strengths. The analysis completed in the previous section (Section 4 on SWOT analyses) should be used, since you have already completed the necessary quantification. Draw a vertical line from this point on the scale as shown in Figure 14-8, so that it intersects with the horizontal

Figure 14-8
Market
Attractiveness
and Business
Strengths

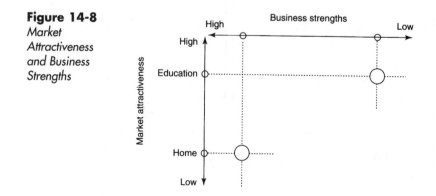

line. (Be certain, however, to use the quantitative method outlined in Chapter 7.)

5. *Redraw* the circles, this time making the diameter of each circle proportional to that segment's share of your total sales turnover. (Please note that to be technically correct you should take the square root of the volume, or value.)

6. Indicate where these circles will be in three years' time (Figure 14-9) and their estimated size. The matrix may, therefore, have to show segments not currently served. There are two ways of doing this. First, in deciding on market or segment attractiveness, you can assume that you are at t0 (i.e., today) and that your forecast of attractiveness covers the next three years (i.e., t + 3).

If this is your chosen method, then it will be clear that *the circle can only move horizontally along the axis*, as all that will change is your business strength. The second way of doing it shows the current attractiveness position on the vertical axis, based on the past three years (i.e., t – 3 to t0) and then forecasts how that attractiveness position will change during the next three years (i.e., t0 to t + 3). In such a case, the circles can move both vertically and horizontally. This is the method used in the example provided (Figure 14-9), but it is entirely up to you which method you use. It is essential to be creative in your use of the matrix. Be prepared to change the name on each axis and to experiment with both products and markets.

Figure 14-9
Market Attractiveness and Business Strengths Analysis

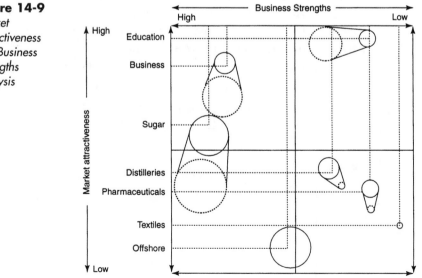

6. Assumptions

Each business must highlight the assumptions that are critical to the fulfillment of the planned marketing objectives and strategies. Key planning assumptions deal, in the main, with outside features and anticipated changes that would have a significant influence on the achievement of marketing objectives. These might include such things as market growth rate, your organization's costs, capital investment, and so on.

Assumptions should be few in number and relate only to key issues such as those identified in the SWOT analyses. If it is possible for a plan to be implemented irrespective of the assumptions made, then those assumptions are not necessary and should be removed. You should find that the more detailed lists of assumptions made for each of the principal product/market segments analyzed in the SWOT stage (Section 4) will be helpful in deciding what the macro assumptions should be.

7. Overall Marketing Objectives and Strategies

Following identification and statement of key strengths, weaknesses, opportunities and threats, and the explicit statement of assumptions about conditions affecting the business, the process of setting marketing objectives is made easier, since they will be a realistic statement of what the business desires to achieve as a result of market-centered analysis.

As in the case of objective setting for other functional areas of the business, this is the most important step in the whole process, as it is a commitment on a business-wide basis to a particular course of action, which will determine the scheduling and costing out of subsequent actions.

Marketing objectives and strategies were more fully discussed in Chapter 4. An *objective* is what the unit wants to achieve. A *strategy* is how it plans to achieve it. Thus, there are objectives and strategies at all levels in marketing. For example, there can be advertising objectives and strategies, pricing objectives and strategies, and so on. However, the important point about marketing objectives is that they should be about products and markets only, since it is only by selling something to someone that financial goals can be achieved. Advertising, pricing, and other elements of the marketing mix are the means (the strategies) by which the business can succeed in doing this. Thus, pricing objectives, sales promotion objectives, and advertising objectives should *not* be confused with marketing objectives.

If profits and cash flows are to be maximized, it is important to consider carefully how its current customer needs are changing and how products offered need to change accordingly. Since change is inevitable, it is necessary to consider the two main dimensions of growth: product development and market development.

Marketing objectives are concerned with the following:

- Selling existing products to existing segments or market penetration
- Developing new products for existing segments or product development
- Extending existing products to new segments or market development
- Developing new products for new segments or diversification

All marketing objectives should be *quantitative,* and should be expressed where possible in terms of *values, volumes,* and *market* shares. General directional terms such as "maximize," "minimize," and "penetrate" should be avoided unless quantification is included. The marketing objectives should cover the full three-year planning horizon and should be accompanied by broad strategies (discussed in the following section) and broad revenue and cost projections for the full three-year period.

Marketing strategies, on the other hand, should state in broad terms *how* the marketing objectives are to be achieved. The list below provides examples of selected marketing strategy alternatives:

- Consolidate product line.
- Withdraw from markets.
- Change and/or standardize product design, performance, quality, or features.
- Change service levels.
- Change unit price.
- Change and/or consolidate delivery or distribution.
- Improve marketing productivity.
- Change and/or integrate advertising, promotion, and sales force communication.
- Acquire markets, products, and facilities.

Guidelines for setting marketing objectives and strategies

Completing a portfolio matrix for each major product/market segment with each unit translates the characteristics of the business into visible and easily understood positions vis-à-vis each other. Additionally, each product/market segment's position on the matrix suggests broad goals which are usually appropriate for businesses in that position, although unit managers should also consider alternative goals in the light of the special circumstances prevailing at the time. The four categories on the matrix are:

1. Invest
2. Maintain Position
3. Harvest Cash
4. Selective Investment

Each of these is considered in turn.

Invest

Products in this category enjoy competitive positions in markets/segments, are characterized by high growth rates, and are good for continuing attractiveness. The obvious objective for such products is to maintain growth rates at least at the market growth rate, thus maintaining market share and market leadership, or to grow faster than the market, thus increasing market share.

Three principal factors should be considered:

1. Possible geographical expansion
2. Possible product line expansion
3. Possible product line differentiation

These could be achieved by means of internal development, acquisition, or joint ventures. The main point is that, in attractive marketing situations like this, *an aggressive marketing posture is required,* together with a very tight budgeting and control process to ensure that capital resources are efficiently utilized.

Maintain Position

Products in this category enjoy competitive positions in markets/segments that are not considered attractive in the long term. Here, the thrust should be toward maintaining a profitable position, with greater emphasis on present earnings rather than on aggressive growth. The most successful product lines should be maintained, while less successful ones should be considered for divesting. Marketing effort should be focused on differentiating products to maintain share of key segments of the market. Discretionary marketing expenditure should be limited, especially when unchallenged by competitors or when products have matured. Comparative prices should be stabilized, except when a temporary aggressive stance is necessary to maintain market share.

Harvest Cash

Products in this category have a poor position in unattractive markets. These products are "bad" only if objectives are not appropriate to the company's position in the market segment. Generally, where immediate divestment is not warranted, these products should be managed for cash. Product lines should be aggressively pruned, while all marketing expenditure should be minimized, with prices maintained or wherever possible raised. However, a distinction needs to be made between different types of products. The two principal categories are:

Those that are clearly uncompetitive in unattractive markets.

Those that are quite near to the dividing line.

Products in the first of these categories should generally be managed as outlined above. The others should generally be managed differently. For example, the reality of low growth should be acknowledged, and the temptation should be resisted to grow the product at its previous high rates of growth. It should not be viewed as a "marketing" problem, which will be likely to lead to high advertising, promotion, inventory costs, and lower profitability. Growth segments should be identified and exploited where possible. Product quality should be emphasized to avoid "commodity" competition.

Selective Investment

It is necessary to decide whether to invest for future market leadership in these attractive markets/segments or whether to manage for present earnings. Both objectives are feasible, but it must be remembered that managing these products for cash today is usually inconsistent with market share growth, and it is usually necessary to select the most promising markets and invest in them only.

Further Marketing and Other Functional Guidelines

We recommend that you consider three or more options before deciding on the "the best." Other marketing and functional guidelines that you should consider are outlined in Chapter 6.

Database and Summary of Marketing Objectives

The forms included in the database provide both an analytical framework and a summary of marketing objectives, which are relevant to all strategic business unit managers. This summary is essential information that underpins the marketing plan.

Forms included in database:

Market segment sales values, showing, across a three-year period, total market demand, the business unit's own sales, and the market share these represent for the various market segments.

Market segment gross profits, showing, across a three-year period, the business unit's sales value, gross profit, and gross margin for the various market segments.

Product group analysis, showing, across a three-year period, the business unit's sales value, gross profit, and gross margin for different product groups.

Summary of main marketing objectives and strategies.

8. Expected Results

Based on the decisions made so far in the planning process, final expected results may be developed for each product or strategic business unit. This document will now be used to develop the budget.

9. Alternative Plans and Mixes

This is the section of the plan known as the contingency plan. Because of the thorough and detailed research that has gone into developing the strategic marketing plan, most managers do not assume room for drastic change. Although detailed alternative plans are not necessary, some thought should be given to "what if . . ." scenarios. Periodically, even the best economic assumptions may change—would your company/product still be able to survive?

10. Budgets

Finally, marketing managers in conjunction with financial managers should provide financial projections for revenue and expenses for the planning period under all the principal standard revenue and cost headings. Normally, these projections are prepared quarterly for the first year of the plan, and annually for subsequent years.

THE WRITTEN MARKETING PLAN

The written plan should contain the following:

- Title page
- Executive summary
- Table of contents (Be sure to number the pages!)
- Mission statement
- Corporate financial assumptions
- Audit of current market and business, including SWOT, etc.
- Recommendations and strategies for coming year(s), including assumptions
- Expected sales and corresponding budget
- Alternative scenarios
- Appendices

FINISHING TOUCHES

After many long months of work, the strategic marketing plan is finally completed. Congratulations. What is next? First of all, the final physical document should be approved by top management. It should then be distributed widely in your own organization and to your strategic partners (e.g., your advertising and public relations agencies—the financial information may be removed or edited if you do not care to share this information) to insure that they understand the strategy and plan. Their understanding is essential for effective implementation and to insure that they can effectively participate in the ongoing process of planning. Remember, the marketing plan is not a plan for all time: if circumstances in the environment change, they may require a change in the marketing plan and planning is everyone's job.

Finally, good luck!

Authors' Note

Many readers of the first edition of this book expressed an interest in obtaining decision support software for marketing planning. To respond to this need, the authors have developed two marketing planning software tools.

DECISION SUPPORT SOFTWARE

A new software package, StratMarkPlus, designed specifically to assist readers of the second edition of *Marketing Plans That Work*, is in development. This package is designed to assist marketing planners in applying the concepts, tools, and techniques outlined in the book in a systematic way. Purchase information and availability of this new decision support tool will be available at www.wkainc.com.

In addition to the above application, EXMAR© is a fully developed decision software package that can be obtained from The Marketing Process Company. For information about this application, contact info@exmar.com or www.exmar.com.

If we can be of further assistance or if you have any comments regarding this book, please contact the authors at:

Warren Keegan Associates
210 Stuyvesant Avenue
Rye, New York 10580
e-mail: info@wkainc.com

Glossary

Advertising. All paid-for, non-personal communications in measured media. This includes television, radio, print, outdoor, transit, cinema, and the Internet.

Ansoff's Matrix. A framework of what is sold (the product) and to whom it is sold (the market). Ansoff identified four possible courses of action for the firm: selling existing products to existing markets, extending existing products to new markets, developing new products for existing markets, and developing new products for new markets.

Audit. A formal systematic review. *See* external audit, internal audit, management audit, and marketing audit.

Benefits. What the consumer is actually buying as opposed to the physical product.

Boston Consulting Group Grid (BCG). A matrix that classifies a firm's products according to cash flow and cash generation, where one axis is concerned with *relative market share* and the other with *market growth*.

Brand. An identity that distinguishes one offering from another by communicating a promise about the benefits of a product. Can consist of a name, logo, symbol, color, typeface, or package design.

Business. Defining what the company does in terms of the benefits it provides or the needs it satisfies, rather than what the company physically produces.

Communications Mix. The combination of varying amounts of advertising, sales promotion, public relations, direct mail, exhibitions, sponsorship, and the Internet.

Conceptual Mapping. The positions that the consumer holds regarding a product vis-à-vis competition.

Consumer Service. Applies to handling questions or problems of the ultimate consumer.

Corporate Plan. Contains long-range corporate objectives, strategies, plans, profit and loss accounts, and balance sheets.

Customer Service. Applies to serving the channel intermediaries.

Diffusion. The adoption of new products or services over time, by customers within social systems as encouraged by marketing.

Directional Policy Matrix (DPM). A four box matrix to plot businesses according to industry/market attractiveness and business/company strengths.

Distribution. The physical function a firm provides in the place and time dimensions of its products or services. It may consist of, but is not limited to, control of warehousing and transportation, the levels of customer service, inventory obsolescence, and cost and data processing associated with distribution.

E-commerce. A relatively new area of marketing that takes place on the Internet; has its own language and standards.

Executive Summary. A one-page summary of key findings of the strategic marketing plan. Similar to a resume but for a business rather than an individual.

External Audit. Concern with the uncontrollable variables affecting the company.

Gap Analysis. Studying whether corporate sales and financial objectives are greater than the corporate current long-range forecasts; if so, a gap exists that has to be filled.

Integrated Marketing Communications. Development and coordination of messages and media used by an organization to influence value perception.

Internal Audit. Concern with the controllable variables of the company.

Management Audit. A company-wide audit that includes an assessment of all internal resources against the external environment.

Market. An aggregation of customers who share similar needs and wants.

Market Attractiveness. A measure of the *potential* of the marketplace to yield growth in sales and profits.

Marketing Audit. A formal, systematic review of the executed marketing strategy and plan. The audit is a structured approach to the collection and analysis of information and data in the complex business environment and an essential prerequisite to problem solving.

Marketing Concept: Matching the capabilities of a company with the needs and wants of customers to achieve a mutually beneficial relationship. It is the consumer-oriented philosophy of business that emphasizes meeting consumer wants and needs.

Marketing Environment. The milieu in which the firm is operating.

Marketing Mix. The set of controllable variables in the marketing plan that are usually expressed as the four Ps—product, price, place, and promotion.

Marketing Plan. An outline of a design to accomplish an objective. The term *plan* often is synonymous in marketing literature with the terms *program* and *schedule*.

Marketing Planning Process. The application of marketing resources to achieve marketing objectives.

Marketing Research. The systematic gathering, recording, and analysis of data about problems and opportunities relating to the marketing of goods and services. *Reactive* or *primary* marketing research involves some form of proactive assessment in the marketplace. *Non-reactive* or *secondary* marketing research is based upon the interpretation of observed phenomena, or extant data.

Market Segmentation. The process that subdivides the market into distinct groups of buyers who might merit separate products and/or marketing mixes.

Market Map. A precursor to a more detailed examination of who buys what. A market map defines the value chain between the manufacturer and the final user, which takes into account the various buying mechanisms found in a market, including the part played by *influencers*.

Marketing Strategy. A set of integrated actions in pursuit of value for customers and competitive advantage for the firm.

Mission Statement. One of the most difficult aspects of marketing planning to master, largely because it is philosophical and qualitative in nature. It is a meaningful statement that is unique to the organization which defines its business and core competencies.

Objective. What the company wants to achieve.

Pareto Effect. A phenomenon commonly observed by most companies that a small proportion of their customers account for a large proportion of their business. This may also be referred to as the 80/20 rule, whereby about 20 percent of customers account for about 80 percent of business.

Personal Selling. Part of the communications mix. A face-to-face meeting between a salesperson and the customer.

Primary Market Research. Original research to answer a specific question.

Product (or Service). The total experience of the customer or consumer when dealing with an organization.

Product Life Cycle (PLC). The stages that a product category goes through from its introduction to the market until its decline.

Product Management. The process of having found out what customers want, after which the company develops products to satisfy those wants.

Product Portfolio. The idea for a company to meet its objectives by balancing sales growth, cash flow, and risk with different products.

Product Positioning. How product is viewed in the consumer's mind. *See* conceptual mapping.

Relationship Marketing. The aim of marketing is to create a mutually beneficial relationship with customers. The end result of marketing is a relationship that means long-term growth and profitability for the company and maximum satisfaction for the customer.

Sales Promotion. A specific activity, which can be defined as the making of a featured offer to defined customers within a specific time limit.

Secondary Research. "Off-the-Shelf" research gathered at an earlier time for another purpose by another organization. Also refers to public information.

Situation Analysis. The first part of a marketing plan. This section includes but is not limited to an analysis of strengths, weaknesses, opportunities, and threats (SWOT).

Strategic Business Units (SBUs) or Stock Keeping Units (SKUs). Share common segments and competitors for most of its products; is a competitor in an external market; is a discrete, separate and identifiable unit; and has a manager who has control over most of the areas critical to success.

Strategic Plan. A clear and simple summary of key market trends, key target segments, the value required by each segment, how the company intends to create superior value vis-à-vis competitors, with a clear prioritization of marketing objectives and strategies, together with financial consequences.

Strategy. Describes the direction a business will pursue and guides the allocation of resources and effort. It describes the business that the company is in and the business it desires to become. It also provides the logic that integrates the perspectives of functional departments and operating units and points them all in the same direction.

SWOT Analysis. Strengths, Weaknesses, Opportunities, and Threats analysis. It contains no more than four or five pages of commentary that focuses on *key factors* only. It highlights internal *differential* strengths and weaknesses in relation to competitors' *key* external opportunities and threats. A summary of reasons for good or bad performance is included.

Tactic. Short-term action taken to achieve the implementation of a broader strategy.

Three C's. Refer to the marketing planning strategy, which focuses on company, customers, and competitors.

Index